Ports into the next century

Proceedings of the conference *UK ports 2000* organized by the Institution of Civil Engineers and held in Hull on 17–18 October 1990

Thomas Telford, London

Conference organized by the Institution of Civil Engineers

Co-sponsored by Permanent International Association of Navigation Congresses (PIANC), UK section

Organizing Committee: C. R. Ford (Chairman), P. Lacey, A. D. M. Bellis, D. J. Palmer

British Library Cataloguing in Publication Data
Ports into the next century.
I. Ford, C. R.
387.1

ISBN 0 7277 1619 0

First published 1991

Published on behalf of the Institution of Civil Engineers by Thomas Telford Ltd, Thomas Telford House, 1 Heron Quay, London E14 4JD.

Printed and bound in Great Britain by Redwood Press Limited, Melksham, Wiltshire.

Contents

What of UK ports 2000?

E. LOEWY, BSc, FICE, Consulting Engineer

These Papers demonstrate clear, confident, co-operative and practical visions of the future of our industry in the near and medium term. We can no longer look to a government department, NPC or other planning supremo to provide a celestial vision of a national port plan, full of dubious assumptions, rigidity, bureaucracy and public service disdain for economic realities. The discipline of the market, be it in the personal, the corporate or the national sense, must prevail in the end. We probably face the most complicated challenge in the history of UK ports. The technological aspects -economical, rapid and efficient design, construction and operation—must take account of many other considerations. These include environmental, social and amenity considerations; financial and economic forecasts and justifications; co-operation, competition and marketing factors; EC, European Free Trade Association (EFTA) and East European impacts, as well as the familiar problems of changes in world trading patterns, in energy cost, and in ship and cargo-handling technologies. All these items must be embraced by the professional port engineers and managers of ports in the next century. It should then be possible to avoid some of the bureaucratic stupidities of commission and omission which created certain familiar white elephant investments and yet prevented the creation of a UK Europort, MIDA, because the selected areas were not in high-unemployment areas. We have the good fortune, now, to face our challenges within an enterprise culture which aims to encourage and reward success. The dependency culture of those earlier days tended rather to hamper success in a vain attempt to solve problems of a fundamental geographic and economic nature of the depressed areas by throwing money at them, money which often came from the same areas.

One of our difficulties, which, being largely self-imposed, will only be overcome by our own efforts, is the low public esteem and even lower public understanding of our industry's contribution to, and role in, the national economy. The deplorable lack of interest and information can be illustrated by my own difficulty in trying to quantify the situation for this address. Despite all my efforts and those of economists, I have been unable to ascertain, even roughly, the percentage of the GNP represented by all the trading activities of all ports. Analogous figures for assets and for global employment would also add some enlightenment. Even the published figures of the reduction in registered dock labour fail to tell the public about the resulting improvement in productivity. This is in contrast to the coal industry which has left the nation in no doubt that, since the coal strike, while total output has remained little changed, the number of mines and of miners have each been halved - a staggering productivity achievement.

An example of the harmful effects of this indifference to port and navigational interests is the current pursuit of esturial tidal barrage power projects. Despite the precarious economics of such projects (the French have not repeated their Rance project despite its technologic sucess) the pressure for renewable energy sources has produced a crop of proposals which pay scant or even no regard to the port and navigational problems they create. At best a navigation lock is sketched in at the edge of the barrage, to be paid for by the ports! Even if such matters as channel changes and dredging are ignored, the operational costs and restrictions could drastically affect a port's competitive position. In the face of such cavalier treatment it is up to our industry to analyse, in depth, the financial and economic consequences of such barrage projects upon the affected ports and ensure that they are properly incorporated in the overall feasibility assessments. The great diversity of interests, in our industry (those of employers, suppliers, agencies and associations) may help to explain but will hardly excuse the deplorable general disregard for public information, interest and involvement. To remedy the matter is part of our challenge. Recent full page press advertisements from THPA have helped to improve the public profile of ports. When I began drafting this Paper, I wrote to a large number of port administrations for any non-confidential information about future developments, short or long term which they could supply, together with any informal opinions, ideas, even dreams, about the future. To my delight, I received an overwhelming response in the form of brochures, plans, reports, letters and telephone calls. It would be impossible, invidious and wrong to attempt to summarize all that material; the important message was that nearly all authorities expressed confidence in the future. This applied even to the great west-coast ports, which face away from the European mainland but had had hopes of capturing more of the European trade through the Channel Tunnel. However studies have shown that the tunnel, alone, can not overcome geographical location. Of particular interest was the confidence shown by some of the smaller ports. All 'Scheme' ports referred to the enormous benefits that had come quickly, and were expected to increase, from the abolition of the National Dock Labour Scheme and from moves towards privatization and corporate structure.

In Britain, as in most Western countries, whose great ports were built solidly in Victorian days, the development of new port areas and the re-development, for other purposes, of older, redundant, dock areas must be seen together as aspects of ports in the next century. Conflict with planning authorities have occurred and may continue, perhaps due to the professionalism of some planners and the political stance adopted by some local authorities. London's docklands could have become one vast council housing estate if the Government had not intervened by establishing the London Docklands Development Corporation (LDDC). Architects may bemoan the dreary eclecticism of Canary Wharf architecture, but the developments have generated great increases in land values, employment and wealth without any cost to the tax payer. At the other extreme planning authorities could be hampering the development of small ports that seek to meet new market prospects in rural areas, due to mistaken ideas of rural sanctity. Where would Felixstowe be now if that had been the attitude thirty years ago? It is, in fact, the existence of alert, optimistic, entrepreneurial flexibility that has lain behind the most recent success stories and this will be even more essential in the future.

Fortunately, several remarkable redundant port-area redevelopment schemes are being worked out with the full co-operation of local authorities, planning authorities, and development corporations outside London. Examples which will transform the local urban environments are to be found in Cardiff, Southampton, Cleveland and several other areas. Beyond the necessity for long-term financial and economic viability of such schemes, it is interesting to find a great similarity in the basic philosophies in the UK and Japan of returning to the population, after improvement and modernization, all those parts of the urban waterfront which are not essential to the industrial port and port-related industries. These include shallow-water areas, passenger and ferry facilities and tug-boat berths (c.f. the Riva Schiavona in Venice). In Japan, where the problems are similar to the UK, the new approach 'aims to recover the social functions of the waterfront areas and to redevelop them to meet the needs of a maturing society and offer refreshing environments to the citizens'. Not only ports must reconcile themselves to this new public pressure, but also those other, increasing, coastal activities such as power generation, aggregate mining, waste disposal and fish-farming. Privatization and corporate structure are obvious advantages but a much deeper analysis of port constitutions is also needed for the next century. The Victorian concept of the public Trust Port, as established for many of the greatest ports in the world such as London, Bombay and Melbourne, was copied all over the world, where it was felt to have almost sovereign permanence and to dispense justice to all parties. It did not prevent the decline of the PLA or the bankruptcy of MDHB and was not adopted by Rotterdam, Antwerp, Hong Kong and other modern dynamic ports. Felixstowe (and a small part of Southampton) have gone beyond simple privatization into vertically-integrated corporations; Felixstowe owns and operates nearly all forms of surface transport facility. It is necessary to know to what extent this structure lies behind the success of those ports and hence, whether further such constitutional and financial integrations should be encouraged. The UK industry could usefully fund substantial research studies into the whole subject. These might conclude pragmatically that several constitutional structures are compatible with market sensitivity, efficient, competitive and profitable operations, high technical standards and environmental responsibility. Nevertheless, the Government could greatly help the industry by introducing an Enabling Bill to facilitate the conversion of Public Trust ports into private corporations without the need for each one to promote a Private Bill, an expensive process, which demands so much Parliamentary time that some would have to wait ten years. In the report of the Conservative Party Conference of 9 October 1990, the Secretary of State for the Department of Transport announced future legislation of this nature.

International lending agencies and the port industries and governments of developing countries, who used to assume, without question, that port ownership and operation had to be government monopolies now extol the virtues of privatization. Privatization and corporate structures need not inhibit co-operative enterprises in port-related industries as have been so successful in Europe (e.g. Rotterdam and Antwerp), in creating extensive regional industrial centres of initiative and development. Financial involvement of local government and private interests can be much freer and more flexible when central government is not expected to find subsidies.

British ports must accept that, neither in world nor in European terms can they necessarily remain in the top rank for size or throughput. If it can be shown that it is in the overall UK economic interest to trans-ship certain overseas cargoes via Rotterdam, Dunkirk, or the Channel Tunnel then we should welcome the benefits accruing rather than insist, in outdated mercantilism terms, that we must use our own ports at higher cost. Probably this hard lesson in economic nationalism has been learnt in the past ten years by our great ports so that I believe, London accepts that it is currently 'seeded' approximately twenty-fifth in the 'world port league'. This situation need be no barrier to the achievement of very high efficiency and productivity with low costs and absence of labour troubles. These are familiar challenges to port engineers and managers, where UK ports could provide world leadership. Here lies an opportunity and challenge for research, both operational and technological. Our industry should welcome this for the resulting benefits from the research and for the demonstration of its commitment to research, which is seriously lacking at the present time. When the NPC commissioned the MIDAS study, I tried, for example, in vain, to have the terms of reference extended to include research into the continuous, high-capacity, unloading of dry-bulk raw materials. The MIDAS industries would make heavy demands on such facilities whereas batch unloading had handling rates less than 20% of continuous out-loading rates. Only now, after twenty-five years, is such unloading becoming an effective option. Research is still needed in container operations, plant reliability, pavement design and maintenance, safety, retrieval operations, empties movements, lighter, cheaper plant for low utilization situations and automation in all fields. The industry will be the best identifying agency for research priority programmes but should not expect UK government (as opposed to EC) funding unless the national economic benefits can be shown to be large and too widely dispersed for industry funding. Some of the operational research should extend into the fields of operator training with the aim of establishing, in the ports, small groups of elite, highly qualified, skilled and motivated personnel which would give dock workers the status of skilled craftsmen rather than unskilled labourers. There are new opportunities for realization of such changes now that the removal of restrictive legislation has been achieved and welcomed by a large body of operatives despite some initial, ritual, condemnation from sections of the Trade Unions and the

PLP. The steel industry training activities now represent nearly £50 million (1% of its turnover).

UK ports have, in the past, had justification for complaints that they were denied certain hidden subsidies, which some continental ports obtained from sources such as central government funding of dredging. The issues were more complicated than they seemed at first sight. However, I believe we can obtain some longer-term reassurance that all such subsidies and obstacles to free competition, will progressively disappear as the EC competition policy begins to apply to the transport sector, notoriously absent in the Treaty of Rome originally. This will certainly take time and many private and public vested interests will have to be fought (e.g. the Dutch dominance of European road haulage arising from their exceptionally low track licence fees and higher pay load allowances). Although such established subsidy practices will disappear eventually, UK ports should not expect the Government or the EC to offer compensation for basic geographical and environmental disparities.

Some thirty years ago, when the then President Nkrumah of Ghana formally opened the new Port of Tema, he announced that it would be the 'Free Port of Africa'. Nobody dared ask him what he meant by that piece of bombast and no steps were ever taken by his or subsequent Ghanaian governments to implement it in any recognizable way. Nevertheless the terminology has been widely used for political effect even if the operational and economic benefits have often been slow to appear. Our government also, some years ago, made great play with the idea and there was much excitement about the selection, which included inland ports.

After some five years of comparative silence the Treasury has produced a report which states that of the six Free Zone locations originally chosen, three (Birmingham, Liverpool and Southampton) have made reasonable progress so that they will be offered a further ten years of designation with simpler procedures; proposals from new locations are to be invited. The 1992 Single Market arrangements may well reduce the attractiveness of the free zone concept, since, presumably for internal EC trade, all areas will gain the advantages. For the encouragement of activities, particularly manufacturing with good employment prospects, for export outside the EC (and we have to reckon that the EC area may eventually include the EFTA countries and East Europe) the free zone at UK ports may yet provide good long-term prospects.

By contrast the Channel Tunnel, which has a Paper of its own that will, no doubt, consider its two-way effect upon freight trans-shipment, will be only the first of several fixed links to be built in the next generation. The industrial groups which promoted bridges will, surely, not be abandoning their projects and it would not be surprising if one for road traffic were to be built within the first decade of the next century, not to capture port traffic but to absorb the overall trading increase.

The bulk trades, which have been in the forefront of mechanization, automation and labour reduction long before containerization appeared, first with liquid cargoes and then with increasing varieties of dry bulk commodities, will continue to benefit from further such developments in capacity, cost reduction and extension to new materials. The ingenuity of mechanical, electrical and electronic engineers is never exhausted as the new growth in continuous unloading of dry bulk materials is demonstrating, although handling rates are still below the continuous loading rates which can fill even the largest vessels in 24 hours. It is, however, these very trades, with their advanced technology, which bring forward the greatest environmental problems. Whereas the most spectacular oil spills have arisen from tankers at sea, in terms of numbers of incidents, oil terminals and their approaches have an unenviable record. Public opinion can scarcely be blamed for taking a jaundiced view of assurances from terminal operators about equipment and operations, which just do not seem to be effective enough. Resistance to further terminal developments will grow strongly unless this situation can be drastically improved. Dry bulk terminals do not normally provide opportunity for major disasters but they can be very objectionable from noise, dirt and dust pollution. Coal and ore terminals are among the most environmentally harmful facilities from their daily operation, rather than from the occasional failure. Each transfer point or change of mode generates extra noise and dust so that we must expect an insistence, even by legislation, upon expensive noise and dust control in the future, as is already to be found in the best installations in the USA. One of the most beautiful, and previously unspoilt, bays on the West coast of South Africa has been environmentally ruined by the construction and operation of a major ore export terminal without any such control measures. That would not be allowed today and UK terminals should be leaders in this field because, as a mature, developed, industrial country, we cannot claim that our economy is unable to afford environmental safeguards. These matters will no doubt be covered in the appropriate papers and discussions at this conference.

Although the engineering aspects of fishing ports and of the fishing industry are broadly similar to those of trading ports and shipping, the background market situation and economics are very different. Continuous improvement and automation of handling the products has been taking place in the main ports and it is a tribute to the enterprise of the NE Scottish ports that the Peterhead group is now the leading white fish port area in Europe. To remain so in a period when emphasis will increasingly be on conservation, quotas, regulation and competition with fish farming, will test the resolve of investors as well as of operators. The key word will probably be quality. Sceptics should visit the Tokyo fishmarkets any day at 5 a.m. and follow the products through to the shops and top restaurants. It is a revelation for a visitor from the UK, where fish used to be the cheap food for those too poor to eat meat, to see in Japan how price is related to quality. Although the efforts for quality begin on the vessels, most of the loss occurs in the ports. This problem applies also to the inshore industry, operating all round the UK coastline from small traditional fishing ports which for generations have determined the local culture-employment, architecture, leisure, language and tourism appeal. The small resources and smaller quotas will make quality the essential criterion and test the skill of local port engineers and managers.

The N.E. Scotland region of the UK, which demonstrated the flexibility of small ports to adapt to the new services demanded by the offshore petroleum industry, may expect a new expansion of that activity with the large, rapid increase in the petrol price, but should not assume that this will endure for long. Diversification and expansion also of non-oil trade facilities is the route being followed to prevent a repetition of the local slumps that resulted from the very low oil price in recent years. Certain ports in N.E. England are also involved in this offshore petroleum service as well as in conventional petrol refining and storage and these can also expect to benefit from the effects of higher oil prices with resulting increased offshore activity.

The road haulage industry, for all its value to the economy, does not have much public popularity in any developed country, least of all in the UK; nor is this unpopularity likely to change until that industry faces the need for exclusive heavy-haulage roads and really pays in taxes or user charges something close to the costs it imposes on the public purse by carriageway damage, congestion and accidents. A current example of road transport nonsense is the decision by the Bonn Transport Minister to retain the special subsidy for German trucks, which had been introduced to compensate them for the road toll that he had imposed for all trucks, German and non-German, using German autobahns, but which has been disallowed by the European Court of

Justice. The green outcry against such further encouragement of heavy road haulage is only a small example of the public resistance which, during the next generation, may require ports to modify some of their access and storage arrangements in favour of rail movements. Economics and free competition between transport modes will reinforce the public environmental concern. Nevertheless it was road haulage and not the ports or the shipping industries which brought about the two revolutions of containerization and roll-on/roll-off. Both modes still have a long way to go, particularly those who have done exceptionally well with the current modes such as the container-leasing firms? (One such UK firm, in little more than a decade, has expectations of £70 million profits). Such dynamic will surely make its mark on UK ports with the new ideas and technology discussed in these papers.

Many of the British PIANC members who attended the 1990 congress in Osaka (its first in Asia in its one hundred years' existence) will hardly have failed to be impressed by the stupendous scale and dynamic vigour of Japanese port and port-industrial development. Even those members who, like myself, have been working in and visiting Japan over more than thirty years and observing the projects will have been impressed by their continuous growth. The Kansai and the Tokyo areas dominate port development but there are many other areas which see port and related industrial expansion as keys to prosperity. Port development is accepted as an essential element in the national growth dynamic. We should not be too quick to dismiss this message as irrelevant to the UK scene, particularly during the current debate about a UK recession. Japan may have double our population and a more diligent and disciplined workforce, but it also suffers from serious handicaps which the UK does not suffer from. The Japanese islands are little bigger than the UK, have a tougher climate, less productive soil, more congestion, fewer natural resources, a poor road system (20 tons is still the maximum truck weight) and, in particular, no effective nearby mainland market and friendly, productive, countries such as the European Continent. On a crude comparison it could be argued that the UK has a far more favourable economic and political situation than Japan to justify confidence in port development so that we would be well advised to take a new look at the rationale behind those tremendous projects. Although we shall have need of more imaginative financing, of which we have more experience, success will depend upon the penetrating initiatives of our entrepreneurs, engineers and managers, resources which our industry does not lack.

Provided the endemic instabilities of the Middle East can be contained, we should be planning for economic miracles in the medium term in the Eastern European countries with an older industrial tradition and, in the longer term, for such a change also in the western parts of the Soviet Union. An enormous increase in trade, comparable to that produced by the earlier 'German Economic Miracle', would then slowly take place and transform the European transport situation.

Although it is a field of activity even more separate than fisheries from the main stream of activities of trading ports, sport and pleasure navigation should not go unmentioned. It is already the saving grace of many small, older, traditional ports and coastal areas and of many commercially redundant inland waterways. It has plenty of potential for the future. It may raise conflicts between conservation and development but, in imaginative hands, this need not happen and it can even provide the resources for conservation of living communities rather than fossilized museum exhibits. The strong seasonal climatic differences in the UK call for greater ingenuity to lengthen the season than is necessary in the Mediterranean but, here again we are not lacking in resources to meet the challenge.

Ferry ports deserve at least a brief mention since they have been among the UK ports' success stories over the last 20 years. Despite the effects, after 1993, of the Channel Tunnel, ferry ports more than, say, 50 miles from Dover and serving dispersed shipping routes may even increase their trades in the long term. Eastern European trade growth should further benefit ferry ports, such as Hull, on the east and north-east coasts. By the turn of the century, even Dover should have recovered its position, provided service and costs, especially on the passenger side, are more favourable. Quality may be the key, currently sadly lacking to my mind. Despite major developments, vehicle routing, traffic mix, pedestrian risks, appalling refreshment facilities and a maze of ugly bridges can give a negative, confusing and unwelcoming impression. The challenge to the engineers and managers of the newer, smaller, ferry ports still in the development stages will be to achieve higher standards.

It is to be expected, at a time of greatly increased confidence in our industry, that there will be a strong flow of new ideas about the future to match the enormous political and economic changes, vastly for the better, which have followed the initiatives in the Soviet Union, Eastern Europe and elsewhere. Even the problems in the Gulf cannot stem that tide. The very convening of this conference is testimony to these trends in UK ports.

1. Regulation versus deregulation in Europe

J. SHARPLES, British Ports Federation

Introduction

Since the inception of the Common Market following the signing of the Treaty of Rome in 1957, it has been a major objective of the member states of the European Economic Community to create a truly single European market to encompass more than 320 million people. To this end, in 1985 the heads of Government of the EEC members produced a White Paper "Completing the Internal Market" and committed themselves to completing the single market by the end of 1992. This commitment has how been included in a package of reforms to the Treaty of Rome. Called the Single European Act, it came into force in 1 July 1987, and aims at the complete abolition of existing barriers to the free circulation of goods, services, people and capital within the Community.

The Commission's main goals were ambitious but focused ones. By 1 January 1993, they hoped to:-

- eliminate controls as people, goods and capital cross national borders between member states of the Community

- standardise and harmonise national regulations and laws so that they no longer interfere with the free trade of goods and services within the Community

- open national public procurement in member states to all companies within the Community

- allow companies to be free to develop cooperative arrangements with companies in other member states

- to harmonise VAT and excise rates.

The whole Community should benefit from the elimination of unnecessary restrictions and constraints on production and consumption and from the new and competitive free market. It will provide the most dramatic stimulus to production and trade since the EEC began over thirty years ago.

The implications for transport systems in general and for ports in particular are enormous. The liberalising of transport services has an important place in the completion of the single market because of the economic importance of the transport industry itself and its vital role of facilitating the movement of goods and people between member states.

The Single Market will create a completely new environment for the transportation and distribution of goods throughout the EEC. The completion of the single market is also now likely to coincide with the opening of the Channel tunnel in 1993, leading to increased choice and competition in the vital cross-channel market for freight and passengers.

Ports should benefit from the increase in trade from the single market and from being freed from the burdens of unnecessary regulations. The decrease in bureaucracy, formalities and the resulting delays, should all be to the advantage of traders and travellers and hence, to the ports.

Deregulation

The removal of the **physical barriers** to trade by abolishing frontier controls between member states will be the most obvious and visible symbol of the single market and will be one of the main areas that will affect British ports in their position as frontier posts and hence, traditionally, as places for customs clearance. In the past, frontiers have been convenient points for customs posts where fiscal and preventive checks have been carried out. Ports, as frontiers in the UK, have also been convenient places for HM Customs to undertake agency functions for other bodies such as the Ministry of Defence, the Ministry of Agriculture, Fisheries and Food and the Department of Trade and Industry. Perhaps not all these restrictions and controls will be dismantled, although this must be the goal, but it is certain that procedures will be introduced to help speed goods through these barriers. From 1 January 1993, customs declarations will no longer be required for goods in free circulation arriving from, or destined for, other EC countries.

It has been estimated by HM Customs that 15% of the movements of goods between member states after 1992 will still have to use present Community Transit procedures. Goods travelling between member states which pass through an EFTA country will still be subject to customs procedures, as will goods subject to transitional rates of duty which are consigned from Spain or Portugal.

A major landmark in harmonising procedures and reducing the number of customs forms used throughout the Community was the adoption on 1 January 1988 of the Single Administrative Document by all member states. In addition to the obvious advantages in containing more than one type of customs declaration on a single form, general data requirements have been reduced. But even this document will not be needed after 1992 for intra-Community goods, although there is no agreement yet on what sort of documentation, if any, should accompany goods.

Another scheme that has already been introduced for faster customs clearance - on 1 August 1989 - is the Fast Lane Scheme, which, as its name suggests, aims to reduce to an absolute minimum the time taken by customs requirements on the movement of community goods. So far, the indications are that Fast Lane is working well although not all goods are eligible for the Scheme (such as those subject to health controls). The number of goods that do qualify is increasing, however, and it is important to ensure that preventive controls do not hold up Fast Lane traffic. This is of course a step in the right direction by Customs who are starting to implement the single market philosophy gradually, making things much easier for traders than an overnight change to a frontierless Europe. Also, a Simplified Period Entry Scheme (SPES), to be introduced later in 1990 and which should be available for the same category of goods as Fast Lane, will allow importers and agents to provide most of the information Customs require about these imports retrospectively by computer on a periodic basis.

A further system to facilitate the cross-border transit of goods is FLIC - Forwarders' Local Import Control which has introduced some non-port customs offices. It is being phased in from the Spring of 1990 till the end of 1991 and involves the freight forwarders completing the customs entries, thereby moving away from frontier controls to inland controls, so that goods can pass quickly through the ports. Customs are also modifying existing schemes of Local Import Control and Local Export Control to make it easier for traders to clear goods at their own premises.

West Germany, France, Belgium, Luxembourg and the Netherlands have recently signed the "Schengen Agreement", in which they agreed to scrap all border controls within the 5 countries. Although the Agreement is not due to come into force until the end of 1991, some of the arrangements will come into force sooner. This will also mean an end to passport controls at airports between Schengen states, and a greater degree of cooperation over crime across frontiers, such as allowing their police to pursue criminals into each others' territories. This is a major step towards the completion of a fully internal European market that will come into force well before the official beginning in 1993. It will be watched with interest by the rest of the Community as the success of this step will give a good indication of how the full single market will work.

No agreements have yet been made on "duty free" goods, nor on any border documents. The Commission has assumed that duty free facilities should be abolished for intra-EC travellers after 1992, but the UK Government recognises the economic significance of the UK duty free trade. Research is currently being carried out by the duty free industry into the effects of abolition.

Of course, immigration officials will still need to check passports to prevent illegal immigration so there will not be much change here, but as far as goods are concerned there will not be checks as at present, but only preventive checks done on intelligence to prevent smuggling and terrorism.

As well as physical frontiers, the European Commission has also presented the Council with details of proposals to eliminate fiscal frontiers in the field of indirect taxes. The essential feature of the Commission's proposals is the retention of the destination basis of VAT taxation for a 4 year transitional period ending 31 December 1996, and after that time adopting the origin system whereby EC goods are taxed before export at the rate of the exporting member state. Also the Commission propose that a reduced rate of VAT should apply to items of basic necessity such as food, heating and passenger transport.

As far as excises are concerned, the Commission has put forward proposals concerning the harmonisation of rates of taxation on cigarettes, other manufactured tobaccos, alcohol and mineral oils. There has as yet been no agreement on these proposals and there has instead been much criticism of them. Any compromise could still be some time off.

There is also a proposal for a Council Directive instituting a process of convergence of rates of VAT and excise duties. This aims to ensure that between now and 1992 member states come closer together on VAT and excise rates which are due for application from 31 December 1992.

Other measures adopted so far

With the advent of the single market drawing ever nearer, many of the measures necessary for its completion have already been put into place. Some businesses are sceptical about this and believe that not all the measures needed will be in effect by the end of 1992, and the programme of legislation will continue for several more years.

Originally 300 proposals for Directives for the 1992 programme were presented to the Council of Ministers in 1985 and by 1988 14 of them had been dropped as no longer appropriate. At the beginning of 1990 with three full years to completion date, the Commission has sent 142 measures to the Council of Ministers which have been adopted as proposals.

The list of Directives is quite diverse with a large number applying to specific industries, such as the food industry. A smaller number of Directives are not specific to any particular sector but affects all businesses. These general Directives lower the costs of moving goods, people and capital across borders, facilitate the process of standard setting, make technological cooperation easier and open up public procurement.

It is important to differentiate between the various types of legislation that the EEC can pass. These are: **Regulations** which are adopted by the Council and are binding in their entirety in all member states; **Directives**, which although also binding in all member states with regard to the results to be achieved, the method of achieving these results is left to the discretion of national authorities; **Decisions**, which are similar to regulations in that they must be adhered to but they need not apply to all member states but may apply only to one or more; **Recommendations**, which have no legal force at all and are merely advice given to Governments from the Commission.

Community legislation is the result of a complex and often lengthy process of consultation and negotiation. The process of legislation starts formally with adoption of proposals by the Commission. These are then submitted to the Council which, in turn, may, and in some cases must, consult either or both the European Parliament and the Economic and Social Committee before deciding to adopt the Proposals.

The main decisions adopted so far relate to technical harmonisation for example electro-magnetic compatibility, capital movements, the coordination of banking activities, the mutual recognition of diplomas, company law, telecommunications and the harmonisation of national trademark law. There are many environmental Directives already in force, ranging from measures to control the discharge of dangerous substances into rivers and seas to the protection of birds.

So far, few of the decisions adopted have had any real impact on ports, but ports are already feeling the effects of certain decisions such as those on public procurement and the abolition of frontier controls.

In the transport sector, the abolition of community and bilateral road haulage quotas was agreed upon as from 1993 and the right to engage in road haulage cabotage was acknowledged cautiously from 1 July 1990. Decisions have also been taken on the liberalisation of air transport, but measures still need to be adopted to ensure freedom to provide services for air, maritime and inland waterways throughout the EEC.

The Council of Ministers have also adopted four Regulations with regard to a European shipping policy. The principles behind Community action on shipping are those of a non-protectionist policy while applying the basic provisions of the Treaty of Rome relating to the freedom to provide services. The Regulations are concerned with unfair pricing practices in maritime transport, fair competition, coordinated action to safeguard free access to cargoes in ocean trades and ensuring that the competition principles can be effectively applied to protect the interests of transport users.

Harmonisation

Although the single market is partly being brought about through a system of deregulation to improve the business environment and cut out burdensome bureaucracy, conversely, in some spheres of activity, new regulations have had to be created in order to harmonise standards within the twelve member states.

An equally important aspect that should not be overlooked is the Social Action Programme for the EEC's Social Charter. This involves new legislation over the next few years with regard mainly to the living and working conditions of employees, and the Commission's plan is that it is adopted in parallel with the economic measures.

Much of the "re-regulation" will directly affect the ports industry and in some cases could add more red tape and work for port managements than there is at present. The proposed new Directives relevant to ports include:-

* Proposal for a Council Directive on the Procurement Procedures of Entities Operating in the Water, Energy, Transport and Telecommunications Sectors

* Proposal for a Directive concerning Strict Liability of Services Presenting a Safety Defect

* Proposal for a Regulation on the Establishment of an Alternative System for the Collection of Trade Statistics following the Abolition of all Remaining Internal Frontier Formalities and Controls

* Proposal for a Council Directive concerning Minimum Requirements for Vessels Entering or Leaving Community Ports Carrying Packages of Dangerous or Polluting Goods.

* Proposal on Fish Hygiene: Laying down the Health Conditions for the Productions and Placing on the Market of Fishery Products

Public Procurement - The regulation relating to public procurement is designed to prevent the practice of local or national governments offering their contracts for purchases only within their own region or country and not opening them more widely to competitive tender from companies within other member states. This will have an impact on the ports as they have been brought within the scope of the Directive if they undertake large investment projects over a certain threshold; ports will have to ensure that invitations to tender are extended throughout the whole European Community. The concern here is that when implemented, this rule could greatly increase the bureaucracy and paperwork for ports, the total opposite of what the Single Market is aiming to achieve.

Services with a Safety Defect - The draft Directive concerning strict liability for defective services could also have implications that would cause concern to ports. One of the problems is its very application to ports, as ports do provide services even though international transport is excluded from the Directive. The rules proposed for transport as they affect ports are unclear and unsatisfactory as international transport is governed already by international conventions which offer protection at least as high as that of the proposed Directive. The CBI believe that this Directive is not necessary to reduce obstacles to trade. It also attempts to treat all services alike, which is inappropriate and its very wide definition of services would impose unreasonable contingent liabilities on small and medium sized enterprises. But worse, in terms of deregulation, it could lead to a separate and different form of liability to that arising under the Product Liability Directive for the supply of instructions relating to the product. This could result in uncertainty and inconsistency.

Port Statistics - Present EC proposals aim to simplify methods of collecting statistics on intra-Community trade. As the proposal stands at present, the information required will be obtained from VAT forms by traders rather than at ports. The VAT forms will not give details of the mode of transport or the origin of the goods, so it is possible that ports will have to give more details than at present as there is a demand for detailed trade statistics from businesses as well as governments. The ports are concerned that a Port Statistics Directive will be issued which will mean more work for the ports through collecting more detailed statistical information than at present.

Also envisaged is that 20% of the biggest companies in the EEC, that is companies with an annual turnover over a certain amount, will have 7 extra boxes on their VAT forms to give detailed statistical information. This would apparently give 80% of all Community trade statistics in detail. There are still many problems and details to be worked out if this plan is to be put into force - not least is that Greece has no companies among the top 20% in the Community, so there would be no details on Greek trade!

Packaged Dangerous Goods - The Packaged Dangerous Goods proposal concerning the minimum requirements for vessels entering or leaving Community ports carrying packages of dangerous or polluting goods could have a considerable effect on UK ports, and BPF is closely following its progress.

If, as it appears at present, the proposed Directive is intended to restrict the trade in dangerous goods by sea, this would particularly concern the UK as an island, and severely impede UK trade in dangerous goods, putting it at a disadvantage compared to other EC states. Again, this restriction on trade is completely contrary to the aims of the Single Market, with its emphasis on the lifting of restrictions and the freeing of trade. BPF also feels that it would be more appropriate for this type of legislation to be implemented through the International Maritime Organisation, putting the regulations into a much wider international context, and to stop different standards applying in different parts of the world and different standards applying to ships flagged outside Europe within European waters. There are already international conventions in force which require that 24 hours notification be given of goods on board a vessel entering a port and the Commission has suggested that vessels will have to leave a list of dangerous substances being shipped with the authorities onshore before leaving the ports. The danger with this current proposal is that far from simplifying matters, further regulations would conflict with national legislation and international standards and result in confusion over procedures.

The proposal also puts forward the idea that ports should make the information relating to ships carrying dangerous goods available to ports workers' representatives and environmental protection organisations. If this had to be done in a port with a large number of sailings each day it would be a bureaucratic nightmare for ports with a huge increase in paperwork. This is hardly what was envisaged by a Single Market!

Fish Hygiene - The Fish Hygiene Directive is another one which could have major repercussions for UK fishing ports as well as other sectors of the fishing industry. It sets out conditions for the processing of fish and the placing of fish on the market. Although the aims behind the proposal are admirable, the first draft was very badly thought out. Even thought subsequent drafts have been improved, when brought into force, a large number of UK ports are going to find it necessary to invest considerable sums of money, time and effort in bringing their premises up to the standards dictated by the Regulations. It is not clear at present how certain aspects of the regulations will be interpreted.

There are two other proposals concerning the health conditions of products of animal origin and live bivalve molluscs, which could also effect ports in a similar way. Interpretation of certain Articles in the mollusc regulations could mean that port authorities who operate common user market facilities could have the added burden of being responsible for arranging laboratory examinations and record keeping. The Directive concerning products of animal origin, if it included fish markets where fish from fishing vessels are placed for auction immediately could well conflict with the specific fish hygiene regulations leading to confusion and more rather than less bureaucracy. Similarly, a Directive on the protection of animals during transport could cause ports a great deal of extra work if the certification is not in order and have major implications for lairage facilities at ports, that is, covered shelters for keeping livestock. With both general and specific new regulations proposed, there is a danger that there will be confusion due to conflicting rules.

What 1992 has not done for ports

So far then, the ports industry is not totally clear what 1992 will mean for it, or whether the advantages of more freedom and harmonisation will be outweighed by the disadvantages of additional regulation. What ports really want to know is whether the single market will address the main concerns and difficulties that face the ports industry in Britain today.

State Aids - One of the main concerns is that state aids to Community ports from their respective Governments are making it difficult for British ports to compete with their continental counterparts. The Treaty of Rome states that grants by member states to their industry which result in distortions to fair competition are against the principles of the Treaty. The BPF wants the EC to apply stricter criteria to the application of state aids which will allow ports to compete more fairly after 1992.

One of the problems is that of the different definitions used in the UK and other EEC Countries. Some EC Governments classify ports as part of their infrastructure while in Britain ports are regarded as commercial transport businesses. Therefore what some EC Governments regard as investment in infrastructure, Britain regards as unfair state aids.

Of course, on an individual basis the practice of supporting ports as a part of a country's infrastructure may have advantages nationally, but in the context of a single market it is a practice that results in distortions to competition.

British ports receive no state subsidies for port facilities from either national or local governments, whereas Belgium, France, West Germany and the Netherlands subsidise both the operating and investment costs of their major ports, resulting in them being able to keep their port charges at an artificially low level. British ports also fear that they may have to spend large amounts of money on environmental costs such as dredging and the provision of waste disposal facilities in ports and that this could be another area where continental ports will receive subsidies which will put them at a competitive advantage.

Transparency of Accounts - it has been impossible to determine the level of state aids to other EEC ports because at present many member states have not produced separate and detailed accounts for ports. In 1985, a Directive on the Transparency of Financial Relations between Member States and Public Undertakings was amended to apply to ports. This meant in theory that the Commission had the power to ask member states to provide information about the nature and level of state aids to ports, but in fact, they have not yet exercised this power.

Other EC members have argued that state aids do not seriously distort competition because port charges only make up about 5% of total transport costs. BPF and the British Government believe that a transport company's earnings depend on transit costs and they are naturally very sensitive to the charges they have to pay. Port charges are an important factor in deciding what port a company should choose.

Light Dues - Obviously, subsidised port charges in other European ports has lead to British ports being at a disadvantage. This is not helped by the additional burden of light dues. No other EEC member apart from Ireland and Greece charge light dues on ships. In the other countries the provision and maintenance of lighthouses, beacons and other navigational aids are paid for by the central Government. The fact that ships visiting British and Irish ports have to pay for their use of lights is a major trading disincentive to shipowners and shippers who might otherwise use British ports. A large tanker can incur costs of over £30,000 and a deep-sea container ship £13,000 for a single call at a UK port - and this is on top of other port charges! BPF has long been campaigning for the Government to bear the cost of light dues in line with the majority of other EC countries, and, until it does so, to limit the damage done to trade, by spreading the burden of payment more widely to ease the cost to commercial shipping. Of course, if the additional cost of light dues exceeds the revenue being earned the value of the port call becomes questionable and this encourages the practice of transhipment via north European ports.

What good is a single European market if British ports continue to struggle under the burdens of competitive disadvantage through no fault of their own?

The Social Charter

One of the Treaty of Rome's main objectives was that there should be improvements in living and working conditions within the EEC and to this end, on 30 November 1989 the Commission published its Action Programme for the implementation of the EC Social Charter which aims to enshrine fundamental social guarantees in the Community legal system. As well as all the proposals in the Single European Act, the Social Charter's Action Programme proposes 48 additional measures including up to 23 Directives which the Commission will bring forward over the next 3 years.

The social rights included in the Charter represent the main features which would give a social dimension to the completion of the internal market, especially with regard to the freedom of movement, living and working conditions, social protection and training. The proposals, if adopted, will have an effect on all UK businesses and employers - including ports - in relation to:

hours of work
rest periods
holidays
night and weekend work
overtime
minimum working age
obligation for employers to consult Trade Unions in advance when planning redundancies
site design and safety conditions
setting up training systems
minimum wage
child care methods
disabled persons
elderly persons

The strict regulations that the Commission is likely to propose, especially in relation to shift and night work, could be severely disruptive to UK ports. Other new measures proposed are the establishment of a safety, hygiene and health agency, a programme of equal opportunities for women, an annual report on "Employment in Europe" and a communication on supplementary social security schemes.

There is considerable support for the Social Charter, but there are misgivings among industries in member states on many aspects of the Social Action Programme.

The External Dimension of the Internal Market

With political changes in Eastern Europe taking place at a phenomenal speed, the EEC cannot afford to look inwards only. It has been accused of becoming a "fortress" after 1992, but this has been refuted by the Community. There are measures in the proposals, made within the framework of the White Paper, which cover the conditions of access by third countries to certain benefits arising from the Internal Market, especially in banking sectors and veterinary controls. An important place is also given to relations with EFTA (European Free Trade Association) and negotiations are currently underway to try to create a European Economic Area of 18 countries.

EFTA - The EFTA countries (Norway, Sweden, Finland, Iceland, Austria and Switzerland) met in June in Gothenburg to try to decide their future in the light of 1992. Austria has already decided that it has to have full membership of the EC if it is to have a direct say in shaping the new Europe and has applied to join. Norway appears to be about to make a similar decision, and debates on membership are going on in Sweden and Finland. The growing view in Brussels is that EFTA should be offered a limited agreement which involves no sharing of political power, and this would probably encourage countries like Norway to join the EEC.

Eastern Europe - The creation of the single market has of course been affected by the changes in

Eastern Europe, and the General Affairs Council have held a favourable discussion on an action plan proposed by the Commission to extend financial assistance to Bulgaria, East Germany, Czechoslovakia, Yugoslavia and Poland. Bulgaria and Czechoslovakia have signed cooperation agreements with the Community which will give them greater access to EC markets, and should encourage European investment in those countries. So far specific financial commitments have only applied to Poland and Hungary.

London is to be the headquarters for the new European bank for reconstruction and development for Eastern Europe. This new institution with a capital of almost 10 billion ecu will lend money at market rates to those countries in Eastern Europe committed to applying the principles of multi-party democracy and market economies.

With the imminent reunification of Germany meaning an added 17 million people in the European Community, the EC Commission recommended that to ensure the smooth integration of East Germany into the EC, West German legislation should be gradually applied on achievement of economic and monetary union. This was achieved on 1 July 1990, and political union is envisaged before the end of the year.

The EEC believes that to ensure satisfactory completion of the Single market, it will need to monitor carefully areas relating to the freedoms for goods, services, people and capital in East Germany. It will also have to ensure that East Germany receives no unfair state subsidies in the process of unification and that the opportunities for investment in the economy of the GDR are open to businesses in all member states of the Community.

Talks on trade are also going on with Japan and the United States - the Commission has recently issued a report which lists 50 tariff and non-tariff barriers which face EC exports to the USA.

2. Customs legislation in the 1990s

P. L. HIGGINS, HM Customs and Excise

For Europeans the decade ahead seems likely to be dominated by the process of democratization unfurling in the east, the completion of the single market in the west and the negotiations for the longer term future of the European Community. At the heart of these changes will be the liberalization of trade and travel not just within the EC but across the EFTA states and eastern Europe. During these changing times Customs will have a vital but difficult balancing act to perform in continuing to protect our society from menaces such as drugs, terrorism and disease while encouraging the economic growth that freer trade will bring.

It is a measure of the success of the Single Market publicity campaign which we and other Government departments have waged that the date "1992" has become firmly rooted in the public's conciousness. But there is a danger of this date being seen simply as a deadline, an end in itself, rather than the beginning - the beginning of the single market and the burgeoning of a whole series of new opportuntities for business and individuals. The momentum which carries the single market programme to success will not fizzle out but, reinvigorated, will prove the driving force behind the extension of single market ideals to a new and wider Europe.

Fundamentally the Single Market is about stimulating economic growth, providing the dynamic environment for wealth creation through increased competition and unrestricted trade. Three of the four freedoms of movement (goods, services and capital) are directly concerned with trade - eliminating protectionism, restrictions, reducing overheads, avoiding delays and uncertainties. The fourth freedom (free movement of people) is an inevitable concomitant. Of course, Customs has no small role in these. It is also on this basis that the UK negotiating principles for Single Market discussions are derived. Single Market arrangements must be deregulatory so as to encourage trade not deter it. They must be as simple and as close to domestic arrangements as possible if world traders are to manage separate EC/third country arrangements. However we need to be careful that the Single Market does not encourage fraud lest we undermine the revenue or expose legitimate business to unfair competition. But above all Single Market procedures must be capable of implementation by 1.1.93 so that traders are left free to concentrate on what they're supposed to be doing - trading.

In this heady atmosphere of liberalization some may be tempted to ask why do we need customs' services at all? However it is important to remember that one of the cornerstones of the European Community is the Customs Union, established by the Treaty of Rome to enforce the external frontier. Moreover at present Customs' are responsible for an array of tasks at the internal frontiers both at a Community and national level. Prominent amongst these tasks are the enforcement of a number of prohibitions and restrictions for the protection of society and for political, defence, health, cultural and conservation purposes. The most important of these affect the movement of drugs, firearms, strategic goods, national treasures, and pornography. Currently at the internal frontier we also collect VAT, excise duties, CAP charges and trade statistics.

Achievement of the single market objective of free movement of goods and people is therefore no simple matter and while UK Customs' commitment to this objective, demonstrated by a series of measures being undertaken to smooth transition to the single market, will mean radical changes to present procedures, we in Customs will be keeping up our guard to protect society from dangers such as drugs, terrorism and pornography. Few areas of the Commission programme designed to complete the single market have been the subject of as much ongoing debate as those concerned with the free movement of goods and people. So where do we stand on these issues now and how do we envisage our role changing?

Fiscal Frontiers

Abolition of fiscal frontiers, that is the arrangements for collecting indirect taxes, has been a particularly contentious area. The Commission's 1987 package of indirect tax measures proposed approximation of VAT rates into two bands; a clearing house mechanism to redistribute VAT collected; and harmonisation of excise duty rates according to an average prevailing in the member states. Several member states, including the UK, expressed serious reservations about the Commission's proposals, believing them to be over-bureaucratic and heavily prone to fraud.

It was clear that agreement on the Commission's proposals was simply not possible. The UK therefore tabled constructive counter-proposals and lobbied hard with the Commission and other member states to try and break the deadlock. In 1989 the Commission produced revised proposals which made important concessions; but they did not go far enough. EC Finance Ministers therefore asked an Ad Hoc Group of fiscal experts, in which Customs and Excise played a prominent part, to examine these proposals and alternatives put forward by member states. Their work came to fruition with the publication of the Commission's detailed technical proposals in June 1990. They are very much in line with the system we have been consistently advocating and working towards, and we have therefore given them a warm welcome. So what do the proposals say ?

VAT

For traders registered for VAT, goods exported from one member state to another would continue to be zero rated, but with the tax point being the acquisition or supply of the goods rather than their importation (as at present). The effect of this change in tax point is to remove the concepts of import and export from the tax treatment of intra-EC trade. So the great majority of transactions would continue to be handled on the present 'destination' principle; but with no fiscal intervention at the frontier. VAT payable on intra-Community transactions would be settled and paid periodically as for domestic transactions. Under these proposals intra-EC traders can look forward to an end to the multi-copy 54 box import entry document the "SAD" (Single Administrative Document) and to the need to finance Community transit guarantees and deferment guarantees for VAT.

This proposal broadly meets our requirement that Single Market procedures should be deregulatory while still effective against fraud and capable of implementation by 1.1.93. Nor does the proposal require new computer systems or any more than minimal use of novel procedures. However there are some unsatisfactory aspects such as the proposed automatic switch to an origin system on 1.1.97. We believe that any change should await experience of the transitional arrangements and proper evaluation before deciding upon a definitive system.

While we have welcomed the general thrust of the proposal some other member states are concerned that the fraud control system puts deregulation before enforcement. They hanker after the comfort of heavier controls such as mandatory listings of all exports. We believe that such a recapitulative list would be burdensome to business involving the non selective collection of data on a massive scale much of which would be entirely unnecessary (raw materials, capital goods, semi manufactures etc).Therefore we shall continue to argue strongly for the Commission's proposed audit based control system which has been well proven in UK domestic VAT controls (we have developed particularly sophisticated use of modern audit based methods, directed by risk analysis to make best use of resources - 1989-90 control visits yielded over £1 Billion in additional tax revenue).

Enhanced mutual assistance

To bolster these audit based controls against fraud the Commission have proposed an enhanced system of mutual assistance for VAT and, for the first time, excises after 1992. This would provide the means for a greater exchange of information between fiscal authorities to ensure that goods for which zero rating has been claimed have been duly shipped to the member state of destination and brought under fiscal control.

Statistics

The statistics proposal is also broadly on the right lines. It would link VAT and statistical systems in order to minimise the burdens on business. Only the largest traders in terms of value of intra EC imports and exports (around 20% of all traders) would be required to provide a specific statistical return. The remaining bulk (possibly some 80%) of traders would simply provide aggregate details of EC imports/exports as part of their normal VAT return. Our chief concern is that decisions are reached urgently. The new statistical systems will need new computer systems and long lead times are therefore involved. We have been urging the incumbent Italian Presidency to step up the pace in this area.

Excise Technical Proposals

Just over a week ago the Commission finally presented their proposals for controlling cross-border commercial consignments of excise goods after 1992 to the Council of EC Finance Ministers (ECOFIN). Excise duty will continue to be charged in the member state of consumption, with the majority of commercial movements travelling under a duty-suspension scheme between authorised warehousekeepers and traders.

Although the UK input during the creation of these proposals has clearly been influential we still have a number of concerns. These include the failure to properly address the arrangements for controlling movement of duty paid goods or to define commercial as opposed to private movement of goods. We also believe the proposed system of accompanying documentation for duty suspended goods moving between warehouses is cumbersome and bureaucratic. In the detailed discussion of the proposals due to begin shortly we will be pressing for arrangements which are deregulatory and reduce burdens on business by basing control upon the audit of traders' records, backed up by occasional physical checks on goods at traders' premises or during transit.

Tax Rates

Given the variations in the rates of VAT applied throughout the EC, early decisions on rates seem unlikely. The UK Government has made clear its commitment to its ability to retain permanently zero rates after 1992. The UK view is that retention of the destination system for the next few years effectively removes the need for centrally-determined tax rates and that providing scope for market forces, by gradually increasing travellers' allowances to allow greater cross-border shopping, will result in such convergence of rates as is necessary. As for excise duties the divergence in rates is even greater hence any agreement will be very difficult to reach.

Travellers' Allowances

In the run up to 1992 the Commission has proposed staged increases in the levels of travellers' allowances for goods bought duty/tax paid in other EC countries. These would quadruple the allowance for goods subject only to VAT and double the alcohol and tobacco limits. We support these proposals although others have serious reservations and so far even a modest Dutch compromise has failed to get agreement.

In principle after 1992, there should be no limits for tax paid private importations for personal consumption. However, we shall need to be able to distinguish between genuine private purchases for personal consumption and commercial quantities and to this end we shall press for some overriding limit for alcohol and tobacco.

As for duty-frees, these have yet to be discussed and no detailed proposals have been received. In pure Single Market terms there is no logical justification for continuing to grant what is effectively a tax allowance for crossing the very fiscal frontiers which we are all striving to remove. However the Government recognizes the economic significance to the UK of the duty-free trade and has undertaken to study all the arguments before any decisions are reached. We expect that duty and tax-free shopping will still be available to travellers departing directly for countries outside the Community.

CAP

Despite broad agreement that Monetary Compensatory Amounts (MCAs) are incompatible with the philosophy of the single market, there are important differences of view between member states and abolition is likely to be the subject of protracted negotiation.

Other Frontier Controls

Aside from fiscal responsibilities Customs operate a wide range of controls at the frontier to control legitimate trade (licensing arrangements etc) and to prevent illicit traffic in prohibited goods. The Commission wish to eliminate as many of these frontier control requirements as possible, relocating those which remain at trader's premises. Whilst totally committed to the abolition of routine fiscal frontiers the Government believes that a minimum level of frontier controls for other purposes will be required to protect our society.

Drugs are our major concern. In 1989, customs seizures by weight of cocaine increased by more than 44% over 1988 to 409 kilogrammes; seizures of heroin rose by over 46% to 337 kilogrammes and seizures of cannabis rose by 15% to well over 50 tonnes. And these drugs are not just reaching the UK from outside the EC: in 1989, 41% came from or via other member states. It is important not to overlook this.

Other EC countries have a comparable problem, both with overall seizures and with smuggling across the internal EC frontiers. Land frontiers are inherently more difficult to police than our natural water boundary, so to some extent it is more logical to relax controls at land frontiers and rely on internal checks. But in our view it is very difficult to compensate for the complete withdrawal of frontiers, particularly where existing checks are effective in intercepting major consignments of drugs coming into the UK in bulk before being broken down for distribution inland.

However, we recognise the need to make our checks at the internal EC borders less obtrusive than hitherto and to minimize their impact on legitimate Community trade and travellers. Following a radical review of our anti-smuggling strategy within Customs, we plan to achieve this by greater use of intelligence and targeting, so that our enforcement effort does not suffer. The first evidence of this more selective approach to checking cars and passengers is the Freeway system, introduced at all ferry ports this year. No longer is every car stopped so that a few questions can be asked of the driver. Instead, only selected cars are detained; the great majority now drive straight through. We have also been trialling a "red point experiment" here in Hull and at Terminal 2 Heathrow airport to help speed passenger flow.

Interim Customs Measures
Customs are already taking steps to facilitate trade with our EC partners well in advance of 1 January 1993. Amongst these measures are a Fast Lane for imports, and a Forwarders Local Import Control scheme (FLIC) under which eligible loads move rapidly through the ports direct to inland depots for Customs clearance. Taken together these will enable firms to simulate, to the greatest possible extent, the post 1992 situation.

Free Movement of People
Another key aspect of the single market programme is the free movement of people. Recognising this, in 1988, EC Heads of Government appointed a group of high level Co-ordinators to review and initiate action needed to make free movement of people a reality. The Co-ordinators identified various Community working groups to take action on measures such as enhancement of practical and legal cooperation between member states, strengthening external frontiers and greater convergence of enforcement standards. Customs have a major part to play in this process through the Mutual Assistance Group 1992 (MAG 92) which was set up specifically for this purpose.

The Way Ahead
Where does all this leave us? Much work remains to be done and both technical and some more fundamental questions remain. Answers are needed urgently if the changes to both your and our systems and operating arrangements are to be in place by 1993. However considerable and very encouraging progress has been made over the past 18 months and Customs will continue to maintain the momentum of discussion and press for the decisions necessary to keep 1992 on target.

Looking beyond 1992 it is already clear that the Community has become a point of reference for many countries. Turkey, Austria and Cyprus have all applied for membership and some east European countries are looking in this direction. In addition the Community has enlarged to incorporate the new unified Germany. The Community is also in the process of negotiating a new European Economic Area with the EFTA countries. Whether these negotiations result in a Customs Union or something more flexible remains to be seen but the principles of the Single Market, namely the four freedoms about which I spoke earlier, are its central objective. Both sides hope that the agreement can enter into force on 1.1.93. The countries of eastern Europe may well be brought within this Area or become the subject of similar association agreements.

Amidst what might be termed this "Europhoria" I have been struck during visits to countries on the periphery of Europe, such as Turkey, by the very real fear of a "Fortress Europe". We must guard against this and the increasing trend in recent months for discussions about the Single Market to focus on broader world issues affecting Europe is therefore very welcome. Not surprisingly given our role in the liberalization of trade and travel, Customs are thinking ahead so as to influence this debate. Accordingly we are about to undertake a major strategic look at Customs' role beyond 1992. Successive GATT rounds have cut the level of Customs duties, the last round reduced average CCT duties to 5.88% and the current Uruguay round has 3.44%

as its target. Compare that with the levels of VAT and excise duty we shall be controlling without frontiers in the Single Market and the arguments for greater facilitation of third country trade become irresistable.

Moreover, with our former Director Internal Taxes, Peter Wilmott, at the helm of DG XXI the Commission will be taking an increasingly progressive attitude to trade facilitation. It is likely that audit based controls for all Customs purposes will be seen as the ultimate goal. A study being conducted by the Institute of Maastricht into the future of EC customs services may well come to similar conclusions.

As all these developments occur the UK will continue to adopt the same approach: a pragmatic one, based on what can be achieved consistent both with the single market objectives, the need to protect society and the wider world climate. I believe this approach will serve both the UK and the new Europe well for the 1990s.

3. Ship legislation—a marine engineer's view

N. FINLAY, WNV (UK) and Partners

SYNOPSIS. Current legislation is fairly straightforward and comprehensive, covering all aspects of shipping from construction to safety, manning levels and navigational aids. It is enacted in all its various forms by Statutory Bodies, Classification Societies and in some instances by Port Authorities. Given the apparent rise in the number of marine " accidents " and environmental problems together with the corresponding rise in the number of " protesting " or " interested parties ", current and future legislation will reflect these issues to such an extent that Port Authorities may become involved as a matter of policy.

1. In the past Marine Engineers have had the reputation of being conservative, little liking change and generally living in a world which was full of bottom ends, boilers, condensers, winches etc. Indeed if one comes across a small gathering of such people, particularly the more middle aged or senior citizens then all conversation is lost save for the good old days when steam was king and a mans reputation was built on his ability to keep the daily consumption of coal or oil to a bare minimum, notwithstanding keeping the engines going as well.

2. However, although the apparent good old days are gone forever, nevertheless they did breed a type of engineer who has been the backbone of our Shipping Industry. These were the men who became the Superintendent Engineers, Consultants, Engine Builders etc and have fashioned today's complex machinery with all its attendant computerised controls etc.

3. They have also joined the Statutory and Independent Classification Societies who control our ships through enacting the various legislation laid down by Parliament or in the Classification Society Rules.

4. Very briefly this legislation covers all aspects of shipping from the moment a vessel is a gleam in an entrepreneur's eye, through the design and development stage, inspection during construction, testing and certification of materials and machinery, specifying the minimum fire fighting and safety equipment necessary, laying down heating and ventilation requirements, specifying navigation and radio aids etc. etc, so that vessels built are seaworthy, safe to operate, and comfortable to live on.

5. Despite the fact that generally within the Marine world and as a whole, this type of legislation is generally accepted as being the standards to which one must conform, I an still amazed that people adopt a cavalier attitude to this and believe that it can be ignored or got round. Some years ago was approached by a client to get a newly built vessel 'Classed'. After asking what I believed were all the right questions, I discovered that the Owners attitude was "well we have built it and they will have to Class it". Needless to say it was a very difficult proposition and those Statutory and Independent bodies approached, viewed it with some concern and requested a great deal of information and tests etc in order to ascertain the quality and standards of the vessel. Our client was quite aggrieved at their attitude and in the end accused us of being obstructive and in league with the Class Societies.

6. In the event we invited him in a polite manner to take his custom elsewhere and I understand that eventually he had it Registered by one of the more obscure Maritime Countries.

7. It is my opinion that the Owner should not have been able to find a loophole in the system but should have been made to comply with the rules and regulations of either a) the country where the ship was built or b) of the countries where it hoped to trade. Registration and Classification is there to benefit all parties, Owners, Insurers, Port Authorities, Crews and in today's world, environmentalists, although in the case of the latter I reserve my judgement since I believe that not all of what they say and do is beneficial.

8. As a Surveyor and past Chief Superintendent Engineer I also find it hard to understand that vessels are drydocked and the appropriate Class Surveyor not invited to attend, just in case he finds something wrong which could either cost money to repair or delay the vessel. I believe that if a

vessel needs to be repaired it should not put to sea before temporary or permanent repairs are carried out. In my experience most Class Surveyors are sympathetic towards Owners, particularly in today's financial climate and will be as helpful as possible. Quite often some minor doubling or strengthening in way of the damage will suffice until such times as the repairs can be carried out.

9. A positive attitude on behalf of the Owners representative is necessary, since in the event of any doubt about the course of action necessary, most surveyors, being human, will opt for that solution which is least likely to cause him problems. Inexperienced surveyors also fall into this category and unfortunately the rule book does not cover for all situations.

10. In discussing Legislation, it must be made clear that whilst sea going vessels are in the main subject to Class Requirements, various types of vessels which operate in harbours or estuarial waters do not need to be classed but usually are subject to local bye-laws or harbour regulations. Having seen over the years vessels which should not be floating, let alone working I wonder if Port Authorities are as vigilant in these matters as they might be. In today's climate where lawyers are looking for some one to blame and from whom to seek redress, I wonder what would be the situation if one of these vessels working within a port area but without a local sea-worthiness certificate were to be involved in an incident where loss of life was sustained. Could the Local Authority be held liable on the basis that they did not in effect enforce the local bye-law.

11. Over the years marine engineers in their various guises have contributed a great deal to the development of ships as we know them today. We have completely automated engine rooms, satellite navigation systems, automatic fire fighting installations, unbelievable radio technology and computer control systems which in my days at sea were only a figment of one's imagination. Even the much maligned dredger has control technology which belies the state of the vessels, but for all this we have to pay a price. The price, a severe drop in the standard of engineering skills. It has not been helped by the severe down turn in the number of British registered ships, in fact it can be said that because we have a shortage of engineering and

other seafaring skills we need to automate more to compensate, a chicken and egg situation. In 1970 I was talking to a very conservative Technical Director of a major shipping company who was being forced to accept at that time partial engine room automation. His comments were quite explicit but boiled down to the fact that be believed the financial benefits would be minimal and it would lead to a decrease in the standards of engineering. On the former I cannot really comment, but of the latter I am really certain, he was truly prophetic.

12. Whilst legislation governs the minimum number of crew a vessel should carry, it is unfortunate today that what are termed as 'flagged out' vessels carry crews of mixed nationality. It is my belief that standards are lower because of this and it also contributes to the number of accidents which take place on vessels.

13. Statistics show that most accidents are the result of man made errors and it is clear that lower standards are a prime cause.

14. A further problem arises because many mixed crews have two or possibly three nationalities and in an emergency situation it is my experience as both Owner and ship surveyor that this tends to cause confusion rather than rational behaviour. In an emergency, in a single crew situation despite chaos reigning everyone understands one another but in a multi lingual situation where at best understanding is poor the obvious tends to happen and orders are not understood. Years ago, when Britain had a very large fleet, ship's crews tended to be English, or English officers and Chinese or Lascar crews. Despite the difference in language the number of English officers was such that it didn't matter too much but in today's world where officers are at a bare minimum it makes a big difference. One worry that I personally have is of fire and I suspect others too share that worry for I can see a situation where a foreign ship with a multi language crew is in port and fire breaks out.

15. I understand that all ports have their own arrangements to combat this hazard but has anyone ever thought of having on hand a list of other nationals living locally who could be contacted in such an emergency to help with communications.

16. Legislation which has encouraged minimum manning levels had also brought in its wake a marked reduction in the standards of maintenance and

seamanship. Vessels particularly the smaller ones, tend to leave maintenance until repair periods and generally costs soar because as yet no one has disproved the proverb "a stitch in time saves nine". This has on occasions led to vessels not being in a sea worthy state and under the Port Safety Act have been stopped from sailing by the Department of Trade. In a large port this may not prove a problem but in a small port it could be disastrous if this stops the entry of other traffic.

17. Today, many and varied are the lobby groups which seek to protect us from all manner of things but it is my belief that not all of their efforts are to our advantage.

18. As a dredging engineer interested in what and where spoil can be dumped, I found the August edition of the Dredging and Port Construction magazine very interesting. An article gave details of the problems experienced by the port of Oakland, California, in their efforts to continue dredging and dumping the spoil, efforts thwarted by environmental groups. It seems to me that these pressure groups can tell us what we should not do and instantly at that, but fail to think the thing through and see the consequential problems. Failure to dredge could close some ports with the result that either new ports would be necessary or 24 hour working at other ports each of which have different environmental problems.

19. Recently I broached this subject with some representatives from Port Authorities and was surprised to be answered that " we will cross that bridge when we come to it. " Whether that is a general attitude or not I do not know but as times change so must we. Unless we give this matter some serious thought we may suddenly find ourselves subject to restraints which will be effected through European directives from Brussels.

20. One other current constraint is noise pollution and those of you who have experienced the clanking and screeching of the old bucket dredgers will know what I mean.

21. Although bucket dredgers are now not fashionable, for some jobs they are the only suitable tool. However it is possible to develop a " silent " bucket dredger, in fact one such dredger was in operation in 1979 and whilst working in hard material it was possible to get within 100 metres of the dredger and still not hear it. Unfortunately, in

order to achieve this very low noise level the bucket chain had to be designed simply as a mechanical chain using bearings with engineers tolerances and an individual greasing system. The cost of developing this system was substantial but despite this was extremely successful in terms of low noise levels. Unforeseen extra benefits came in the form of a 12.5% reduction in fuel consumption and an estimated 15 - 20% reduction in the wear of the top and bottom tumblers and ladder and bucket chain component parts.

22. Staying with dredging there has been talk of legislation to ensure that spoil is dumped in the correct designated areas and that a permanent record of dumping should be kept. This is not impossible. With the sophisticated trailer dredgers in operation today it should be possible using a combination of existing and new instrumentation but since the vast majority of vessels which dump spoil are by nature either dumb or of simple design the cost of fitting such equipment would be untenable.

23. What of the future, there is no doubt that both MARPOL and SOLAS will recommend further oil pollution and safety measures. There is currently under discussion methods of building oil tankers with double skins in order to stop oil spills if the vessel becomes damaged. Dumping at sea from ships of any and all types of waste materials will no doubt be legislated against and in this respect Port Authorities will have to find ways and means of accepting and disposing of this waste. Hopefully, stowage of toxic cargoes on decks will also be stopped since many of these cargoes particularly those stowed in drums can and have been washed overboard in bad weather.

24. My own hobbyhorse, I hope that future legislation will achieve the acceptance of each others standards within the European Community, it is most frustrating when transferring a vessel to the British Register for the Owner to find, as has happened in the past, that amongst many other things the number of holes in the shower head or the shower mixing valves are not to British standards and the Owner is faces with the bills for changing them. I appreciate that standards must be maintained but when a vessel is ten years old and given good and safe service under the supervision of a recognised Maritime Nation then as far as I am concerned it becomes expensive nit picking.

25. Also in the future, it is possible that the day may come when Ports do not need Pilots. Over the years the Pilot service has recruited qualified ship's officers to become Pilots but with the downturn in personnel the time will surely come when recruitment is a problem. Given the state of modern technology when we can talk down jumbo jets, set courses on vessels for world wide navigation, control vessel movements through radar, surely it is not beyond the wit of man to develop a suitable system for Port operation. Vessel manoeuvrability is or can be aided by bow and stern thrusters making it comparatively easy for Masters on board the vessel to control movements at the request of an on-shore "Pilot".

26. This is without doubt a very contentious subject but as I have said previously, "times change and we must change with them".

27. In conclusion, no matter what the "Legislation", unless we maintain high standards of Officers and Crews and proper manning levels we can never enact it, or be totally sure that Ports are safe from ships.

4. The Channel Tunnel — full-bore for 2000?

R. G. BAKER, MA, FICE, CDipFA, Consultant

SYNOPSIS. Examples of changes which have posed a challenge to U.K. Ports lead to the question 'How big a change is the Channel Tunnel?' Route costing shows that U.K. West Coast Ports cannot become the 'Gateway to Europe'. Trans-shipment cargo is shown to be minor, and unlikely to change. Whether road freight traffic is likely to transfer to Tunnel Shuttles will be governed only by price. An assessment is made of the possibilty of a freight transfer from road to rail, and comments are offered on what has to be done to make this happen. Foot passengers are likely to be lost to rail.

THE CHANNEL TUNNEL

1. From its announcement just before the last election, when it was heralded as evidence of Britain's wish to become an integral part of Europe, through to the financial, contractual, and managerial wrangles of early 1990, the Tunnel has featured in the media so often, that it is easy to understand why conflicting images have been created. Three misconceptions in regard to the Tunnel's engineering, finances, and trade opportunities are commonplace:

- By emphasising problems during construction, attention has been diverted from its great engineering merit. Linking the U.K. and the Continent with 50 Km. of twin rail tunnels, and a service tunnel is a magnificent project quite in keeping with the best Engineering traditions. First proposed by Napoleon, but only possible now with the latest 'cutting edge' technology.
- Reports of financial uncertainties have perhaps raised the question as to whether the Tunnel will ever be finished. This should be discounted at once. The Tunnel will be completed. What is in doubt is whether road and rail infrastructure on the U.K. side will be improved. In France the infrastructure is well in hand.
- Media reports have created the impression that the Tunnel is not only an unparallelled opportunity for U.K./E.E.C. trade, but that it is free! Or, at least, very much cheaper than existing transportation modes.

USER CHOICE OF ROUTE.

2. The Tunnel certainly is an opportunity. Just how big an opportunity is the subject of this paper. To do this, cross-channel traffic may be split into two groups, each of which has different reasons for choosing a particular route:

Private cars and foot passengers.

In the case of foot and car accompanying pasengers, there are several reasons. Cost, yes, but also emotional reasons, like sight-seeing along a particular route, convenience, concern about the weather, or even the novelty of travelling by shuttle.

Freight.

Only one thing determines a freight route.

Profit.

3. There is not a 'Grand Theory of Transport' which can be deduced from the existing pattern of traffic movements, and which could then be used to predict what changes the introduction of the Tunnel might produce. Present traffic flows are the result of hundreds of thousands of individual decisions, each of which takes into account the factors unique to that particular movement. In this Paper some aspects of route decisions, particularly those determined by cost, are examined.

CHANGE.

4. Many changes have occurred over the past decade:

- Containerised cargo needed fewer ports, but massive investment.
- Larger ships did the same.
- Creation of the E.E.C. switched trade from West Coast ports to South-East Coast ports.
- The Pipe Line Act altered coastal oil trade.
- The U.K. became self-sufficient in grain.

COPING WITH CHANGE.

12. These examples show that ports, in common with most industries over the last decade, have had to learn new skills, redirect their marketing, and invest in new facilities when faced with changes effecting their trade.

13. It is easy to assume, when a period of great change has been experienced, that somehow, change will stop. It won't. Change seems to have a momentum of its own.

14. No port is, or will be, immune from these changes. It is a common experience that a trade will move to save a few coppers a tonne, and abandon resources provided by port or third party investment. Even when the shipper has invested in port facilites, change may occur if the company is taken over, and the new owner applies different criteria to the operation.

THE TUNNEL - THE BIGGEST CHANGE YET?

15. The Channel Tunnel is no more, but certainly no less, than one of the changes which will occur. How might it effect U.K. ports trade?

- Will it be an opportunity for some?
- Will it take trade away from others, and if so, which, and by how much?

16. <u>What will the Tunnel provide for its customers?</u>

Pre-booking not required.
Frequent services.
Fast Immigration and Custom's controls.
Fast transit of the Channel.

Using:

- Rakes of shuttle wagons for freight vehicles.
- Through freight trains.
- Rakes of shuttle wagons for cars and tourist coaches.
- Scheduled inter-city trains.

17. <u>So what's new, compared with existing routes?</u> This, of course, is the basic question which this Paper tries to evaluate. To do so, and to justify the statement made in para. 2 that profit is the only factor which determines a freight route, unit costs for each transportation mode are used. As in all business negociations, a freight rate is fixed by market forces, and will depend on the Users clout, the Transporters level of business, and so on. It will be different for an owner-driver, compared with a large haulage company. It is also commercially confidential. The rates used in this paper, therefore, are only indicative of the level of charges, and cannot be regarded as correct for a particular movement. However, they have been slightly weighted to avoid bias in favour of any conclusion reached.

18. <u>The effect of the Tunnel on U.K. ports.</u> This will be considered under the headings:

Freight:

- Can the West coast U.K. ports become the Gateway to Europe?
- Will trans-shipment cargo change?
- Will road freight change from Ferries to Shuttles?
- Will freight change from road to rail?

Passengers:

- Will passengers with or without cars transfer to the Tunnel.

19. When comparing routes, the geography of North West Europe must be firmly in mind. Figure 1. is a map of this area.

FREIGHT.

CAN THE WEST COAST PORTS BECOME THE GATEWAY TO EUROPE?

20. <u>Landbridge Concept.</u> From time to time in the media, reference has been made to the great opportunity for ports on the West coast of the U.K. to discharge container ships and set up a landbridge to N.W. Europe, where the current

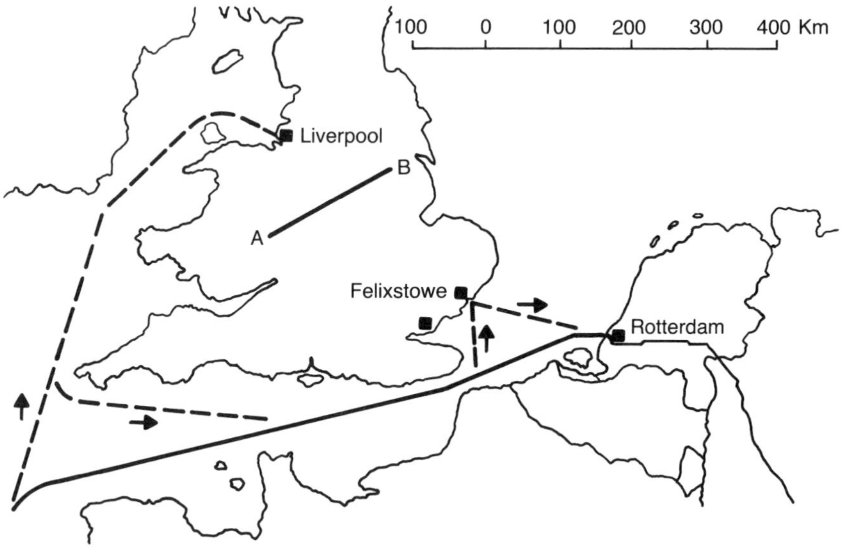

Figure 1 - Map of North West Europe.

container throughput is about 12.5 million TEU's. If this is a financially sound proposal, the question must be raised - Why is it not happening now? After all perfectly good road freight routes exist, though the Dover/Dunkirk train ferry, which is currently moving about 1m tonnes per year (about half its capacity) suffers gauge restrictions between London and Dover, and it is doubtful whether there are enough rail wagons to really make an impact on traffic. The answer must be - The Cost.

21. Before considering the cost of moving containers from the West Coast to Europe, two facts need to be noted:

- Most deep-sea container ships carry a cargo split U.K./Europe in about the ratio 25%/75%.
- Post-Pannamax ships cannot enter any West Coast port, and can only be handled at Felixstowe (shortly to be joined by the Isle of Grain).

22. Bristol as an entry port for Europe. Consider the costs of doing this. On Figure 1, 'A' is the point where a ship enters the Channel. 'B' is the same steaming distance towards Rotterdam from 'A' as is Bristol. Assume that the ship size is such that it can be handled at Bristol, that no further investment is needed, that the ultimate destination is Frankfurt, and that the container handling and port charges at Bristol and Rotterdam are the same. Then the comparison of costs is:

Discharge at Bristol.		£
By Road		
To Dover. 300 Km. at 30p.	=	90
Channel Crossing	=	100
To Frankfurt. 550 Km. at 30p.	=	165
Total		£355 per TEU
By rail - after the Tunnel is open.		
To Dover. 300 Km. at 20p.	=	60
Channel Crossing	=	100
To Frankfurt. 550 Km. at 20p.	=	110
Total		£270 per TEU

Discharge at Rotterdam.		£
Point 'B' to Rotterdam 340 km. at 7.5p.	=	25
Road to Frankfurt, 400 Km. at 30p.	=	120
Total		£145 per TEU.

It is difficult to believe that cross-Channel competition and/or a reduction in road or rail freight rates could alter the conclusion that it is very much cheaper to ship direct to Rotterdam.

23. Liverpool as an entry port for Europe. In early 1990, Liverpool was handling containers from four Lines. Typically, 800 TEU's out of 2700 TEU'S were discharged at Liverpool, leaving the remainder to be discharged on the Continent. In view of the diversion costs to Liverpool, it is interesting to find out why it is more profitable to divert to Liverpool rather than make the U.K port of call, a port on the South East corner of England. Liverpool doubtless offers an attractive service to their customers, but is there another advantage? In Figure 2 on the next page, the solid line shows the route of a ship sailing directly to Rotterdam. The two dotted lines are the diversion routes for either Liverpool or Felixstowe. The extra distance for each route is:

Liverpool - 650Km. Felixstowe - 100 Km.

24. Nevertheless, 150,000 TEU's per year are handled by Liverpool. It is understood that Liverpool's advantage lies partly in lower local road transport charges, but more importantly in its central position whereby a lorry can do a return trip in one day to London, Bristol, and Glasgow, whereas from Felixstowe a lorry driver would run out of hours for a return trip to the North of England, or beyond. It may not be the amount of the driver's overnight costs which is important, but the fact that the lorry cannot be used for another round trip using another driver, perhaps overnight. If the demand is there, it is obviously advantageous to do two trips per day to help offset the standing costs of a large artic of some £110 per day. It is easy to schedule a second trip from the same base, but well nigh impossible to do this from a point half-way through a return trip.

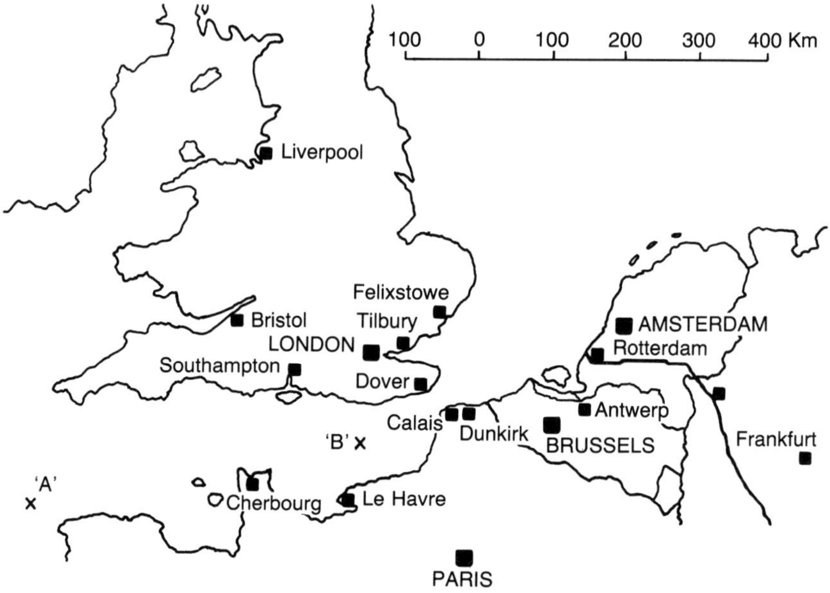

Figure 2 - Diversion Routes.

Also, if the ship diversion costs are balanced against road transport costs, then it is evident that the 'Destination Centre' of the boxes discharged at Liverpool must be North of the line A - B on Figure 2.

25. Having established why some ships discharge part-loads at Liverpool, is it economic to empty the ship, and send the containers overland to Europe? Using the same method of calculation as before:

Off-load at Liverpool

By road:	£	
To Dover. 440 Km. at 30p.	= 130	
Cross-channel to Calais	= 100	
To Frankfurt. 550 Km. at 30p.	= 165	
Total		£395 per TEU.
By rail after the Tunnel is open:	£	
To Dover. 440 Km. at 20p.	= 90	
Cross-channel to Calais	= 100	
To Frankfurt. 550 Km. at 20p.	= 110	
Total		£300 per TEU.

Discharge at Rotterdam

	£	
Liverpool/Rotterdam 1300 Km. at 7.5p.	= 100	
Road to Frankfurt, 400 Km. at 30p.	= 120	
Total		£220 per TEU.

For a ship-load of 2700 TEU's, split 800/1900 U.K./Europe, can one again escape the conclusion that competition on land and cross-Channel links cannot drop the overall cost sufficiently to the point where a landbridge is possible?

26. Cost of new facilities at a West Coast port. The extra costs of transporting containers from a West Coast port to the Continent effectively kill any proposal to build new facilities, but the argument is clinched by a consideration of the new-build costs below, geared to handle 0.5m. TEU's per year:

3 No: post-Pannamax cranes.	Buildings, paving, etc.
2 No: Gantries.	800 metres of quay.
50 No: Straddle Carriers.	

In round figures, say £75m, ignoring the costs for creating a new port. (None of the West coast ports can accept post-Pannamax ships, and it would hardly be prudent to build new facilities for anything smaller than current ships.).

CONCLUSION 1.

27. The extra transport costs of the landbridge concept preclude its introduction. If that were not so, the scale of investment required would do so.

WILL TRANS-SHIPMENT CARGOES CHANGE.

28. So far, it has been assumed that a 2700 TEU ship carries a cargo destined 800 to the U.K. and 1900 to Europe. If that balance changed dramatically in either direction, then, of course, the costs would be quite different. Suppose that such a ship arrived at Felixstowe with 2500 TEU for the U.K., and only 200 for Europe. Assume that the charges for taking off the ship and loading a lorry are the same in both Felixstowe and Rotterdam, then the extra cost of transporting the 200 TEU's to Zeebrugge by ferry would be about £20,000. This is about the daily operating cost of a medium container ship. These are only approximate costs. The split where it is cheaper to off-load 'X' containers, and trans-ship them will depend on the true charges made for:

Container discharge, and loading to tranport (road, rail, or feeder).
Water link.
Second port charges.

balanced against the operating cost of the container ship.

29. About 100,000 TEU'S are handled by Dover each year mainly from Rotterdam. The Tunnel will be a competitor for this traffic, either by road or rail. Whether this will increase, will depend on the U.K./Europe split changing radically, or a more dramatic change in the size of container ships. There was comment in mid-1990 on proposals to build even bigger ships, and facilities to match at Rotterdam. Discharge would be achieved in one day, with onward transmission, including the U.K., by whatever mode were cheapest. It will be interesting to observe the results of the switch of the CAST operation from Antwerp to Zeebrugge in late 1990. CAST run Feeder services to ports around the North Sea including Felixstowe, so if one-port discharge is cheapest, they have the facility to trans-ship. However, it

should be noted that Zeebrugge already has good rail facilities, as 75% of deep-sea (total 84K TEU p.a.) and 90% of short-sea (total 150K TEU p.a.) containers travel onward by rail to West Germany, Switzerland, and Italy. Looking at Figure 1, it is possible that the most direct route to a U.K. destination could be via Calais/Dover. The Tunnel would be a strong competitor for any such traffic.

CONCLUSION 2.

30. Although the Tunnel will be a competitor for trans-shipment cargo, the percentage of present ports throughput at risk is small, unless other major changes occur.

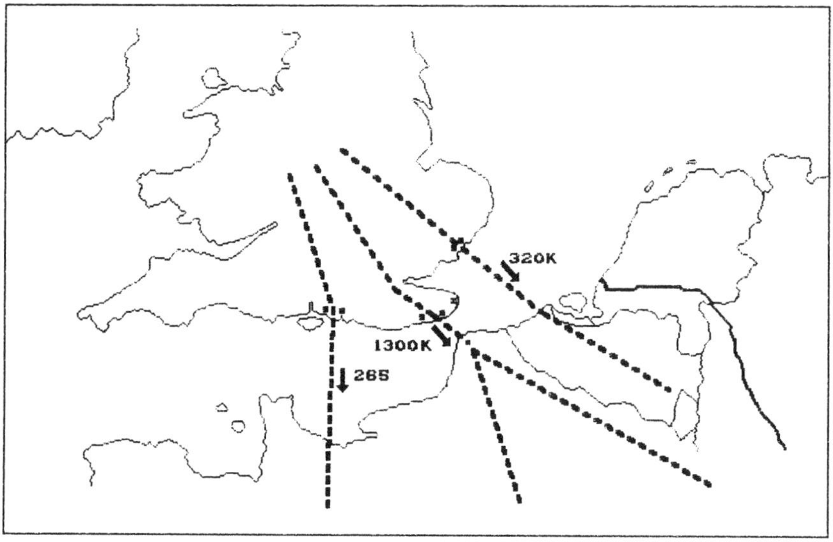

Figure 3 - Main Axes of Movements.

WILL ROAD FREIGHT CHANGE FROM FERRIES TO SHUTTLES?

31. So far, only cargo coming in to the E.E.C. as a whole has been considered. Most cross-channel traffic is generated inland, i.e. it moves from an inland source to an inland destination. As always, the route by which it travels will be the cheapest for that particular movement. Figure 3 shows the number of 'freight units' handled in 1989 on each of three axes.

32. Ports fairly remote from the Tunnel. In the case of Portsmouth and Poole, it seems very unlikely that traffic would divert to the Tunnel Shuttle service, thereby travelling an extra 350 Km. at a cost of £100. The argument is similar for Felixstowe and Harwich.

33. Ports close to the Tunnel route. Here freight can divert to the Tunnel without incurring extra land movement costs. The relevant freight statistics for for Dover alone

for 1989 are:

Freight units(a lorry + trailer is one unit)	1.1m.
Average weight(inc. empties)	13.3tonnes
Average value per tonne	£3,000

In the first two months of 1990, freight increased by 15%.

34. Factors which will govern any change. To assess whether road freight traffic might change to the Tunnel Shuttles, the following factors may be considered:

Competition.

Usually, changes have left port competing with port. In this case, the Ports plus the Ferry Operators are combining to compete against the Tunnel. Both are very bouyant.

Charges.

The Tunnel may undercut present ferry rates, but the Ferry operators are preparing for this by introducing larger ferries. There has been a sudden and large increase from the 350 car/1300 passenger ferries of the 80's to 700/2300 size ferries such as the 25,000 tonne 'Fantasia'. Crew costs are about the same.

No pre-booking for Tunnel.

The ferries are flexible now if space permits, but ferries are less frequent than shuttles, so there may be an advantage here.

Time to transit Immigration and Customs.

Dover is installing better failities to handle documentation now. Customs are also looking at ways to facilitate trade as well as collect duty. Dover's target is one hour for an outwards vehicle. Whether the Tunnel can better this, remains to be seen.

Immunity from bad weather.

Until bad weather occurs so often that significant, and therefore costly, delays occur, this is not thought to be important. The person who determines the route may be in a warm dry office, and may not care too much if the driver is storm-tossed on the Channel!

Security and Safety.

It remains to be seen whether anti-terrorist security will slow down overall transit times in the Tunnel, and no comment can be offered at this stage. In regard to safety of operation, the Tunnel will have a definite advantage as trains are not only seen as safe, but safer than ferries in view of recent incidents.

Drivers' Hours.

Drivers' hours do not run on a Ferry, nor will they on a Shuttle. This is not seen as a factor of prime importance

35. Some traffic is not sought by Eurotunnel. This is:

Non driver accompanied trailers.

In Jan/Feb 1990, about 12% of Dover's traffic was such. In May 1990, it was reported that Euro Tunnel stated that they would not handle unaccompanied trailers. The tractors would stay in the shuttles, or removal would double the loading time.

Large loads.

Tunnel shuttles cannot take out-of-size vehicles.

Some Dangerous Cargoes.

About 10% of cross-channel traffic is classed as such. It has been said that cargoes such as whiskey will not be permitted in the Tunnel. It has not (mid-1990) been decided whether cars and caravans with bottled gas aboard will be permitted on non-freight shuttles, or whether the containers will have to be removed, and stored in special compartments. Mundane, but indicative of the sort of problem faced by EuroTunnel.

CONCLUSION 3.

36. For road traffic, the Tunnel is just another competitor. It is possible that a price war could favour one mode or the other, but it seems unlikely that the Ferry Operators and Ports will be badly affected.

WILL FREIGHT CHANGE FROM ROAD TO RAIL?

37. This is the crunch point. If the Tunnel only offers an alternative to a Ferry, it is difficult to see why it is being built. Only if it is an essential link in the high-speed European rail network, and only if that service succeeds, will it be really justified.

38. One very great advantage which the Tunnel has is environmental pressure. The public perception of trains is that they are safe, reliable, and punctual, and do not damage the environment. In marked contrast to road transport which generates each year 54,000 deaths, 1.7m injuries, and millions of tonnes of air pollutant over the E.E.C. Restrictions on lorries at night, on weekends, and public holidays are variously in force in Austria and Switzerland. In early 1990, West Germany was considering the introduction of a DM6,000 tax on foreign lorries, though this may be no more than protection for their own industry. This 'Green' factor will increase in importance, and will change the attitudes of Governments because a Green policy will attract votes. Whether the pollution per passenger mile is less for a power station generating electricity to drive a train, than for other transport modes is immaterial, it is public perception than counts.

39. <u>Inter-modal Traffic.</u> This is the fastest changing transportation mode in Europe and indeed elsewhere. There are two types. Both are about 2.5m wide, just less than the E.E.C. maximum vehicle width:

- Bi-modal. A specially built semi-trailer on road wheels, but able to clip on to rail bogies at each end. Trains formed of these units then run between appropriate terminals. These trailers cost about 20% more than an ordinary road trailer. There is some doubt as to whether they can be run empty in mixed trains. Potential owners have expressed concern that their investment would be at risk thereby.

- Swop Bodies. These are containers rather lighter in construction than marine containers. Many sizes to maximise volume are either in use, or are proposed, just as there are in the case of marine containers.

40. Rail Structure Gauges. Historically, rail gauges were fixed, and then used to determine structural clearances and wagon sizes. An allowance for cant and overhang on bogie stock had, of course. to be made. The drive to maximise load cube and speed, has changed this. Railway Engineers nowadays speak of 'kinematic envelopes', and it is usual for a particular wagon to be cleared for a specified route, load, and speed. Refer to Figure 5 for a schematic illustration of some common gauges. The track between London and Dover is currently being upgraded to B.R. gauge W6.

41. Bi-modals. Structure gauge restrictions in the U.K. would limit road vehicles to an overall height of about 3.2m (10'-6") on B.R. W6 gauge, compared with a maximum vehicle height of 4.0m (13'-1") authorised now, but which may be increased to 4.2m. Only U.I.C. 'B+' has sufficient clearance to take a 4.0m road vehicle. It is possible, therefore, that bi-modals will cross the Channel on their road wheels, and on thus to their U.K. destination.

42. Swop Bodies. Because altering structure gauges is expensive, much thought has been given to developing rail wagons with small wheels. The downside is that increasing load cube and speed increases wheel and bearing wear. With the post-Tunnel U.K. market firmly in mind, S.N.C.F. were the first to bring into use a special wagon - the Multifret. This has 840mm wheels, and a load bed 940mm high. This is only 60mm less than a standard Freightliner wagon, but it does permit a 2.59m (8'-6") high Swop Body, or a 2.43m (8'-0") wide x 2.76m (8'-9") high load on B.R. W6. This is shown on Figure 4. However, there is a growing use of 2.9m (9'-6") high Swop Bodies, and unless an even smaller wheeled wagon is developed, these could not be carried in the U.K. unless the U.I.C. 'A' gauge were to be introduced. One such wagon has been developed by Powell Duffryn (others are being developed on mainland Europe). This is the 'Lowliner'. It has 520mm wheels, and a 700mm load bed height. As shown on Figure 5, it will carry the largest Swop Body on B.R. W6, and a 2.74m (9'-0") high container on the present London/Dover route. Swop Bodies are currently being moved by B.R. using 140 kph Multifrets leased from S.N.C.F., who are already using a 160 kph version. Whether small wheeled wagons can be safely and economically operated remains to be seen. S.N.C.F. are firmly against very small wheeled wagons at the moment.

43. Road versus Rail. There are two very great advantages enjoyed by road transport:

- The structure, i.e. roads, terminals, and vehicles exist.

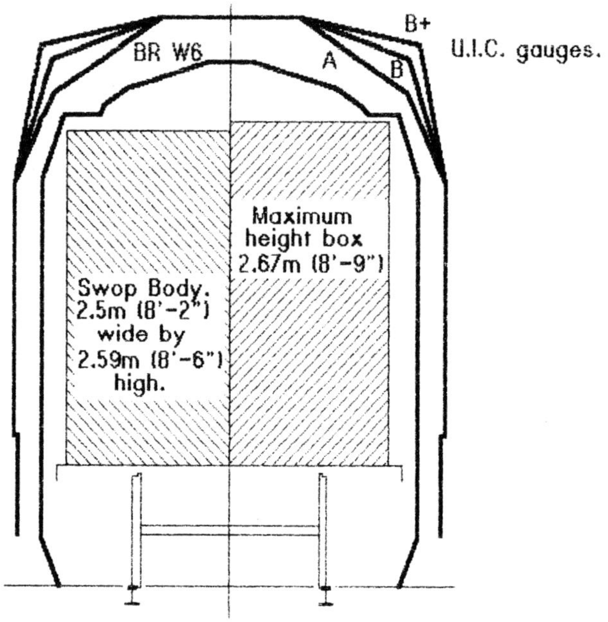

Figure 4 - Multifret Rail Wagon.

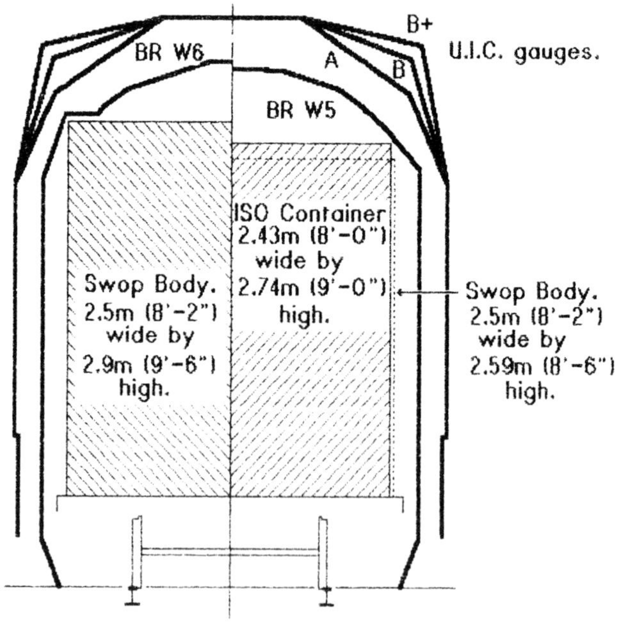

Figure 5 - Lowliner Rail Wagon.

- A vehicle is extremely efficient. It sets off as soon as it is loaded. It is under the personal charge of one man throughout its journey, whereas on a train, no one person is accountable for its transit. Despite Driver's hours limits, experience on mainland Europe is that it is not always true that rail is faster than road, because of time spent in Depots and at frontiers.

The biggest disadvantage for road transport is congestion. Unless investment in U.K. motorways keeps pace with with increased trade, congestion will increase, perhaps to the point where traffic is driven on to rail, because of the cost of delays.

Before rail can challenge road, many things have to happen:

- Terminals have to built, even on the Continent. There is virtually no spare capacity in West Germany, and little in France.
- Sizes and load capacities of Swop Bodies have to be fixed over the E.E.C. to maximise cube in both modes.
- Small wheeled wagons have to be developed for 160 kph.
- Investment in rolling stock, vehicles, and swop bodies, and a commitment to run scheduled trains is needed.
- At the very minimum, there has to be a 140 kph W6 track from Cheriton to London.
- To minimise overall journey time, one haulier has to control the transit from source to Depot, buy space on the trains, and control the transit from Depot to destination. It will not be easy to do this economically.

44. <u>Non containerised freight.</u> Bulk freights and new cars are in Railfreight Distribution's (B.R's. freight arm) marketing target. Cars can be easily carried by rail, though the costs of doing so may be higher than by sea. One way to cut costs is to develop a small wheeled carrier to increase the number of cars per wagon. There is a large North/South used vehicle trade to countries on the Mediterranean, sometimes higher than the South/North movement of new cars. Nontheless competition between the two modes may change present routes, and therefore affect ports remote from the Tunnel. In regard to bulks, movement by small bulk ships is very cheap. Competition by rail will be difficult, unless large volumes between dedicated terminals are moved.

CONCLUSION 4.

45. This is the biggest challenge to existing Ports. S.N.C.F's. will to expand into this market should not be under-estimated. Their development of the Multifret illustrates this. Green pressure will help to force this change. As will a lack of investment in U.K. motorways. Bulk traffics between dedicated terminals is likely.

PASSENGERS.

46. Will passengers with or without cars transfer to the Tunnel. There is no doubt that foot passengers, currently about 2.5m a year, will consider using through trains. To travel surface from London to Paris now involves carrying luggage onto a train at Victoria, onto a coach and then onto the Hovercraft at Dover, and then onto the train at Calais. Compare this with a through train. There isn't a comparison. The time saved is less important than the reduced hassle. Although not relevant to this Conference, a through train service is very likely to attract passengers currently travelling by air. It has been mooted (by S.N.C.F.) that Frankfurt could be become the European airport for international traffic, with onward travel throughout the E.E.C. by high-speed train.

47. Accompanied Cars. Many of the route decision arguments marshalled for freight traffic will also apply to cars. There is little merit in driving extra distances merely to use the Tunnel. One exception to this is bad weather. Changing weather patterns are obviously with us. Hurricane force winds, although not occuring very frequently, will create apprehension, and divert traffic into the Tunnel.

CONCLUSION 5.

48. Foot passengers are very likely to be lost to the ports. Accompanied cars will not travel long distances just to use the Tunnel.

THE CHANNEL TUNNEL - FULL-BORE FOR 2000?

49. The Tunnel is only one more competitor for vehicles. It will only take such road traffic as it can attract through lower charges, and shorter crossing times. Cross-Channel traffic is increasing, and therefore the market share gained by the Tunnel will increase numerically. The increase in overall traffic will mitigate any effect on Ports.

50. Only if the will and the investment to create a high-speed rail network to at least B.R. W6, if not U.I.C. 'A', is there, will the Tunnel begin to increase its market share to the point where ports might be affected.

5. Changes in UK trading patterns

S. FARRELL, PhD, Coopers and Lybrand Deloitte

Introduction

The last 25 years have seen major changes in UK trading patterns, centred around the development of North Sea oil, productivity increases in British agriculture, and the dramatic expansion of trade with Europe. They have reflected both long-term structural changes in the UK economy, and unexpected disturbances from outside.

In the next ten years the pattern of UK trade will continue to change, but the driving forces will be different. They will include environmental protection, the integration of Eastern and Western Europe, and the next steps towards international economic cooperation. Some of the changes can be foreseen, although there is debate about their scale and direction; others remain unpredictable.

For UK ports, there are three questions which are of paramount importance:

- will UK trade continue to grow as quickly as it has in the past?
- what will be the main changes in its commodity composition and form of transportation? and
- will changes in the geographical balance of UK trade enhance the importance of some ports, whilst accelerating the decline of others?

These questions form the basis of the analysis which follows.

Ports into the next century. Thomas Telford, London, 1991

Trade Growth

The growth in UK trade over the last 25 years has been very variable. Excluding bulk fuels, it has averaged around 2.5% pa. in tonnage terms. In the 1970's, however, the growth rate was only 0.5% pa, whereas in the 1980's it has averaged over 5% pa. There have also been substantial variations from year to year.

Although the Government would no doubt wish the expansion of trade to be attributed to sound economic management, there are several other factors at work. These include:

- the growth in Gross Domestic Product and its impact on trade;
- the one-off effects of joining the European Community;
- foreign exchange earnings from North Sea oil;
- the growth in international trade in services.

The following sections outline their contribution to trade growth in the 1980's, and consider whether or not the trends of the 1980's are likely to be continued in the 1990's.

Economic Growth in its Relationship to Trade

Over the last 15 years the annual growth in real GDP has varied from -2.01% to +4.7%. Much of the variation is due to business cycle effects, which seem likely to be with us for a long time to come. When compared with our European neighbours, our long term GDP growth rate of 2.4% pa appears respectable if not outstanding, although it is disappointing compared with the equivalent rate of 6.4 % pa achieved by Japan.

A more interesting phenomenon is the steady increase in trade as a proportion of GDP. In 1960 the value of UK imports and exports each amounted to around 15% of GDP, whereas today this figure is around 25%. This is not something unique to the UK - it appears to be a general feature of economic growth. Nor is it something for which there is any apparent ceiling - in the Netherlands, which has always been much more dependant on trade than the UK, imports and exports each account for around 55% of GDP, and the proportion is still rising.

Membership of the European Community

All of the countries in the European Community have seen trade expand as a result of their membership. Academic studies suggest that for manufactured goods membership of the European Community has increased trade (from all sources) by between 10-30%, making the creation of trade a more important effect than its diversion from non-EC countries. Agricultural output and trade have also been considerably expanded.

The initial effects of EC membership have now worked their way through the system; it is, after all, eighteen years since Britain joined the Community. But the process is far from complete. Whilst the free movement of goods and people has been largely achieved the next phase, focusing on the coordination of national economic policies, has still to take place.

The results will be less visible - assuming that Britain takes part - but still highly significant. Many observers expect there to be a further impetus to trade arising from:

- coordination of macro-economic policies. This should lead to stability of exchange rates, alignment of inflation rates and better management of the business cycle;
- removal of qualitative restrictions on trade (non-tariff barriers); and
- transfer of attention from intra-European trade barriers to strengthening Europe's trading position with the rest of the world.

Two other changes could, however, have adverse effects on trade:

- standardisation of prices through more rigorous application of competition rules and harmonisation of taxation and subsidy policies. At present, prices of consumer goods vary from country to country by an average of 15% (before tax) and 19% (after tax), positively encouraging trade;
- development of a social charter for workers. This may lead over time to more uniform wage rates, employment structures and industrial relations, reducing the advantages of specialisation and leading to a further

concentration of industrial investment in the countries with the largest domestic markets.

Thus the "European factor" will continue to affect UK trade, but its effect will be more muted than in the past unless closer ties with the economies of Eastern Europe produce a new round of trade expansion in the 1990's.

Eastern Europe

The population of Eastern Europe (400 million) is larger than that of the European Community (330 million), but its total GDP is just over one-third that of the Community. It is dominated by the USSR, which accounts for around 70% of its population and income, and 45-50 % of its trade.

Table 1

EASTERN EUROPE : KEY ECONOMIC INDICATORS

	USSR	**East Germany**	**Poland**	**Hungary**	**Czecho-slovakia**	**Romania**	**Bulgaria**
Population (m)	280	17	35	11	16	23	9
GDP 1986 (US$ bn)	790	110	74	24	94	45	29
GDP per capita (US$ '000, 1986)	2.8	6.4	2.1	2.2	5.9	2.0	3.2
Trade 1986 (US$ bn)							
imports	103	42	11	9	21	11	16
exports	107	42	12	9	20	12	14

Source: Euromonitor "European Marketing Data and Statistics" 1988/89

East Germany, which seems likely to be the first country to be admitted to the Community, has an economy whose output is broadly comparable in scale with that of Belgium, and a per capita income which is comparable with Spain or Ireland. Its initial impact on UK trade will occur through unification with West Germany and the effect which this has on West German inflation, the value of the Deutschmark, and the competitiveness of West German goods.

Its long-term impact on UK trade will, however, be rather small : if East German per capita income were to increase over 10 years to reach the current level of West German per capita income, and the UK were to account for the same share of East German trade as it does of West German trade, the net effect would be an increase in total UK trade of around 2.5 %

Poland, whose economy is the most open in Eastern Europe, offers better short-term prospects for UK trade. It has the potential to produce goods for which there is a demand in the UK, such as coal and processed foodstuffs, and is a market for consumer and investment goods requiring a medium level of technology. There are still strong cultural links with the UK, and Poland has made more progress than its neighbours towards political stability.

Throughout Eastern Europe, however, there are constraints which will prevent integration from achieving an immediate rapid growth in trade with Western Europe. There is a need for investment before sufficient goods of a suitable quality can be produced for export. There is a need to develop a sound export base to finance the growth of imports. There is a need for training to improve the quality and efficiency of the labour force, and a need for price and wage reform to develop the large potential market for consumer goods. All of these changes take time.

So although attention will be focused on Eastern Europe during the 1990's, as it was on China during the 1980's and the Newly Industrialising Countries of S.E Asia during the 1970's, it may be at least another decade before the current events in Eastern Europe work their way through to the UK port statistics.

North Sea Oil

North Sea crude oil accounts for around 50% by weight of UK exports, but a surpisingly small share of UK foreign exchange earnings: in 1988 only 4%. This is partly because it is still a low value commodity, even at present prices, and partly because oil revenues are small in relation to service sector earnings.

Although oil production in the UK sector of the North Sea is planned to peak in 1993/94 at around 375,000 tonnes per day, industry sources expect it to decline rapidly thereafter, so that output by the year 2000 could be as low as 160, 000 tonnes per day, less than half the production rate achieved during the mid-1980's.

Of course the effect of this decline could be offset by a substantial increase in oil prices - who knows what consequences political change in the Middle East and other parts of the world will bring. But the fact is that the UK could become a net importer by the end of the decade, substantially reducing our ability to pay for other imports.

Table 2

NORTH SEA OIL

('000 tonnes per day)	1980	1985	1988
Production	220	350	313
Exports	105	218	193
Imports	123	74	95
Net foreign exchange earnings (£ m pa)	308	8101	2785

Source: IEA "Oil and Gas Information" 1988

Trade in Services

Some of the shortfall in foreign exchange will be made up by increased earnings in the service sector. Invisibles now account for almost 50% of UK foreign exchange earnings, and this proportion will increase both as a natural consequence of economic growth, and as a result of the liberalisation of international trade in services.

International trade in services within Europe is poorly documented, but is believed to be around half the value of trade in goods. It also appears to be increasing faster, as attention moves towards free movement of capital, standardisation of professional qualifications and practices, and transnational mergers in sectors such as construction, banking and insurance.

The growing importance of trade in services is recognised internationally, through its inclusion in the current round of GATT negotiations. The potential for trade expansion is large, as the service sector in many countries is still subject to considerable Government regulation. The UK is one of the world's largest exporters of services, and with prompt action stands to be one of the principal beneficiaries of deregulation. The expansion of service sector earnings needed to finance import growth is, however, large, and it would not be surprising to see UK trade in the year 2000 increasingly dependent on inward capital flows - foreign investment and short-term borrowings - in much the same way as the United States today.

Individual Commodities

The commodity composition of UK trade in the year 2000 is likely to be dominated by agricultural and energy policies, both of them underpinned by growing concern about the environment. At the same time intra-industry trade - imports and exports of very similar products - is likely to remain one of the fastest growing sectors.

Agriculture

Bulk agricultural products - cereals, sugar and animal feedstuffs - represent around 12% by weight of UK non-fuel trade. They account for an almost equal share of imports and exports.

Trade in agricultural products has radically altered since Britain joined the European Community, with a progressive decline in imports and a major expansion of exports. This reflects the comparative efficiency of British farming in relation to other parts of Europe, and the stimulus to production caused by price levels far above the world average.

But the Common Agricultural Policy, which provided price guarantees for over 70% of European agricultural output, is now absorbing around 1% of the GNP of Member States. Established initially to achieve self-sufficiency in foodstuffs and preserve the social structure of rural communities, its result has been higher prices for consumers, an obligation on the part of taxpayers to purchase production that nobody wants, and accusations by non-European countries of dumping on world markets.

Reform of the Common Agricultural Policy, like the ending of the National Dock Labour Scheme, carries with it an aura of inevitability, although the pressures for postponement are equally great. What form will this process take?

There are several ways forward, each of which has different implications for UK trade:

- a continuation of guaranteed purchases, linked to a price which falls automatically in response to overproduction. Because the UK is a relatively low cost producer of most items, this should lead to only a slow fall in agricultural exports, with diversion to non-European markets as intervention prices move closer to world market prices; some agricultural imports could rise slightly in response to lower European prices;

- a continuation of guaranteed prices, linked to production quotas. This would cause exports to fall more dramatically, particularly if the quotas were to discriminate against countries such as the UK which are less dependent on agriculture and have expanded their output relatively recently;

- measures to increase production of crops in which the European Community has not yet achieved full self-sufficiency, such as maize and animal feedstuffs. The impact on UK trade will depend on the ability and willingness of UK farmers to respond; providing that the price incentive is sufficiently large, and there are no technical constraints, there is no reason to doubt that an appropriate response would be forthcoming;

- payments to take land out of crop production. A substantial increase in the area devoted to forestry, for example, would have both commercial and environmental advantages, and would also be compatible with the increase in demand for recreational space. The effect on trade would be a double one, the immediate reduction in cereal exports being followed at a much later stage by a reduction in imports of forest products, which represent a large deficit item in European trade;

- the creation of new uses for agricultural products through the development of bio-technology. This is attracting much research effort, in Europe and elsewhere, and could be one of the areas in which there is a major breakthrough by the end of the decade.

Two other factors will have a large effect on the development of agricultural trade: climatic change, and the expansion of agricultural output in Eastern Europe.

Much has been written on subject of climatic change, but no firm conclusions can be drawn. Although temperatures are forecast to rise very slowly, with significant change becoming detectable only over a period of 30-40 years, the impact on crop production will be magnified by year-by-year variations in weather patterns; even small percentage changes in production can give rise to major swings in world trade. Countries whose climate is less predictable than our own have traditionally experienced years of feast and famine; could this become the pattern in Western Europe too?

And how will Governments respond? We usually think of dramatic measures imposed far away from home - the preservation of the Amazonian rain forest, for example - but if public concern about the environment becomes a major feature of the 1990's, the term "green" agriculture may take on a new meaning. Financial support for farming methods which have an ecological as well as a commercial basis, large increases in the price of water used for crop irrigation, and the transfer of land to recreational use could have an effect on British agriculture as pronounced as that already caused by EEC membership.

The effect would be enhanced if agricultural developments in Eastern Europe were to lead to export surpluses on the scale of those coming from the United States. This may lie many years ahead, given the scale of social reform which is required first, and is dependent on world weather patterns, but could produce a change of global significance.

Energy

The key objectives of European Community energy policy are well known:

- to reduce the ratio between energy and GDP growth to 0.7;
- to stimulate the development of renewable energy resources;
- to increase the use of coal and nuclear energy in electricity generation;
- to reduce the share of oil in primary energy consumption from 45% to 40%;

- to establish more transparent and "fair" market conditions and pricing policies for competing energy sources.

The consumption of energy, in electricity generation, industry and transport, is also the largest single cause of atmospheric pollution, so that energy policies by the year 2000 will be heavily overlaid by environmental considerations and the need to meet stringent (and expensive) fossil fuel emission standards.

But UK and European policies do not always coincide, and there are two characteristics of the UK energy market which make it in some ways unique. The first of these is privatisation, and the second is the UK's position as a major energy producer.

The privatisation of the UK electricity industry will have a major effect on trade in fossil fuels, as electricity accounts for around 40% of primary fuel consumption. Several forces are at work which appear to pull the industry in different directions as far as energy supplies are concerned:

- in the short term, increased competition between electricity suppliers, combined with discriminatory pricing, may raise the overall level of demand. But in the long term, the earlier introduction of more efficient generating plant may reduce fossil fuel consumption below the level that would have occurred in a nationalised industry;

- in the short term, the new generating companies will concentrate on establishing their positions in the home market. But in the long term, electricity itself may become more important as an internationally traded commodity, with stronger linkages between the different European grids leading to some displacement of coal and oil movements;

- in the short term, there is likely to be substitution of gas for coal as a basic fuel source, partly because of changes in availability and price, and partly in response to new power generation technology. But in the long term, the construction of more multi-fuel power stations and flexible fuel purchasing policies may bring the prices of the different energy sources closer together, resulting in more stable fuel consumption patterns;

- in the short term, the termination of guaranteed supply contracts with British Coal will open the door for increased coal imports, but in the long term this will accelerate the restructuring of the British coal industry, perhaps enabling it to recover some of its initial losses in market share. The restructuring process will be even faster if a re-elected Conservative government places coal privatisation high on its agenda.

Time is obviously a very important factor in establishing the scale of change, and lead times in the electricity industry have traditionally been long. But providing the privatisation process is largely complete before the next change of Government, it is likely to stimulate some major new investments in the UK ports industry.

The UK's position as a major energy producer is being threatened by the depletion of North Sea oil and gas reserves. This is likely to increase interest in energy conservation and renewable energy sources, but will have only a limited direct effect on total trade volumes as the complex pattern of imports and exports gives way to a growing dependence on imports. Some ports will inevitably experience dramatic changes in traffic volumes and earnings, which could affect their future commercial structure, but for UK ports as a whole the most important effect will be the general constraint on trade imposed by reduced foreign exchange earnings.

Manufactured Goods

In the last two decades, UK trade in manufactured goods has risen very much faster than trade in raw materials or basic commodities. This is reflected in the types of cargo which are being handled in UK ports, and has occurred in spite of a substantial increase in the unit value of manufactured goods.

	Average growth in UK trade (tonnes) 1965 - 1988
Container/RoRo/conventional	3.9%
Semi-bulk	1.3%
Bulk (exc fuel)	1.3%
Fuel	2.0%

Several factors explain why we both import and export even simple commodities such as beer. One is the importance of economies of scale, and their effect in reducing the range of products supplied by national manufacturers. Another is technology, which generates a constant succession of new products protected by patents, supply agreements and trade marks. And a third is the dominance of world trade by multi-nationals, whose strategies to reduce costs whilst securing supply lines and maintaining a presence in all major markets lead to complex flows of intermediate products.

But will these factors be as important in the year 2000? The answer seems likely to be "yes", although they will be reinforced by a fourth factor - the growing emphasis which consumers place on quality. This is perhaps the one development which could lead to a strong revival of British manufacturing, and reduced pressure on the balance of payments. But it is also a trend which will benefit producers in areas such as Scandinavia and Japan, where quality is already deeply embedded in the national culture.

The success of the UK in quality management will determine whether its first effects appear in imports or exports. But whichever is the case, a continued growth in trade seems likely to be the result.

Geographical patterns of trade

The geographical pattern of UK trade has, in the past, had a significant effect on which ports have flourished, and which have not. It has contributed to the balance between East Coast and West Coast ports, and between large and small ports, although the latter has been partially obscured by the effects of the National Dock Labour Scheme.

The extent of the changes which have taken place can be seen in the following figures, which exclude fuel.

Table 3

CHANGES IN THE RELATIVE IMPORTANCE OF BRITISH PORTS 1965-88

	West Coast	East Coast	South Coast[(a)]	Total	Large Ports	Small Ports[(b)]	Total
1965	45%	26%	29%	100%	79%	21%	100%
1975	34%	31%	35%	100%	65%	35%	100%
1988	27%	30%	43%	100%	55%	45%	100%

Notes:

(a) Felixstowe to Poole
(b) Ports handling over 1.0 million tonnes of cargo in 1965

Source: British Ports Federation "Port Statistics"

The three factors that are most likely to affect the geographical pattern of UK trade in the year 2000 are:

- international exchange rates;
- industrial growth in developing countries; and
- the continuing fall in the real price of sea transport.

Some observers expect the next phase of economic integration to involve the emergence of large currency blocks, centred around the US$, the Deutschmark, the Yen and perhaps eventually an East European currency unit. As currencies within each block stabilise, the relationship between the key currencies becomes the basis of structural readjustments in world trade. If this is true, the potential fall in the value of the US$ against other key currencies and action to remove the trade deficit could lead to a gradual reassessment of North America's position in UK trade.

TRADING PATTERNS

Third World industrial growth could bring about two important changes in UK trading patterns:

- more balanced trade with Asian countries as their domestic markets grow, absorbing output that would formerly have been exported, and lowering import resistance in countries such as Japan;

- an acceleration of trade with India, South America and Southern Africa.

The growth in trade with smaller trading partners may, however, bring about changes in shipping patterns similar to those that have taken place on the Europe-Far East routes, rather than acting to the advantage of the medium-sized UK ports which have benefitted from this traffic in the past.

It is perhaps shipping developments, rather than trade developments, which will have the greatest long term effect on UK ports. Overtonnaging and falling freight rates will maintain the pressure for lower port charges, whilst larger ships will lead to a further concentration of business at ports able and willing to meet demands for new investment.

6. Fishing — the changing scene

A. G. HOPPER, MRINA, Sea Fish Industry Authority

The British deep sea fishing industry has a long history extending back at least 600 years. It has had good periods and lean periods and has built up some great traditions. However, as we move towards the 21st century, some changes are inevitable. We have become part of the European fishery in the last decade and we can no longer see our country as having a wholly independent fishery. Our demersal resources are fully exploited or even overfished but our pelagic and shellfish resources are capable of better exploitation although even here there are some threats. The industry must survive as we all need food from the sea, but it will depend on sound management policies to control what we take from the sea and how we can renew these resources. It will depend also on reorganisation, including modernising the infrastructure and ports to capitalise on our geographic position which is in the centre of the European Community's fishing grounds. The U.K. could become a major force in the changing pattern of fish supplies in Europe, if it plans ahead.

1. Introduction

Most of our fishing ports can trace their origins back into antiquity, and their layout and facilities have grown in a haphazard way often limited by space. They have developed to serve the needs of the local community rather than to fit the framework of fish supplies and distribution in the U.K. let alone those of the wider European Community.

As an island too, we are blessed with many ports, harbours or beach sites where fish is landed. Indeed according to Seafish surveys there are over 270 different places from which fishing vessels operate. Realistically many of these are small and have few facilities, but they do handle as much as 20% of the nation's fish supplies and cannot be ignored. There are 40 fishing ports with proper quayside facilities, most with a fish auction market or

Modern practice 1990s

Production line

Expedition centre

Fig. 1. Disposition of the major UK fishing ports

some form of organised selling and a range of services for the fishing fleet. See Figure 1. It is these that we should address first.

The political geography of the fishing industry has changed substantially in the last quarter of a century; probably more rapidly that at any time in our history. Some of the factors creating change relate to the recent past, whilst others are just starting to take effect. They are:-

- The reduction in fishing opportunities available to our fleets as a result of the 200 mile Exclusive Economic Zones (EEZ) imposed in the 1970s.

- The Common Fisheries Policy (CFP) of the 1980s.

- Decline in the stocks of the more popular species in the N.E. Atlantic and especially in the North

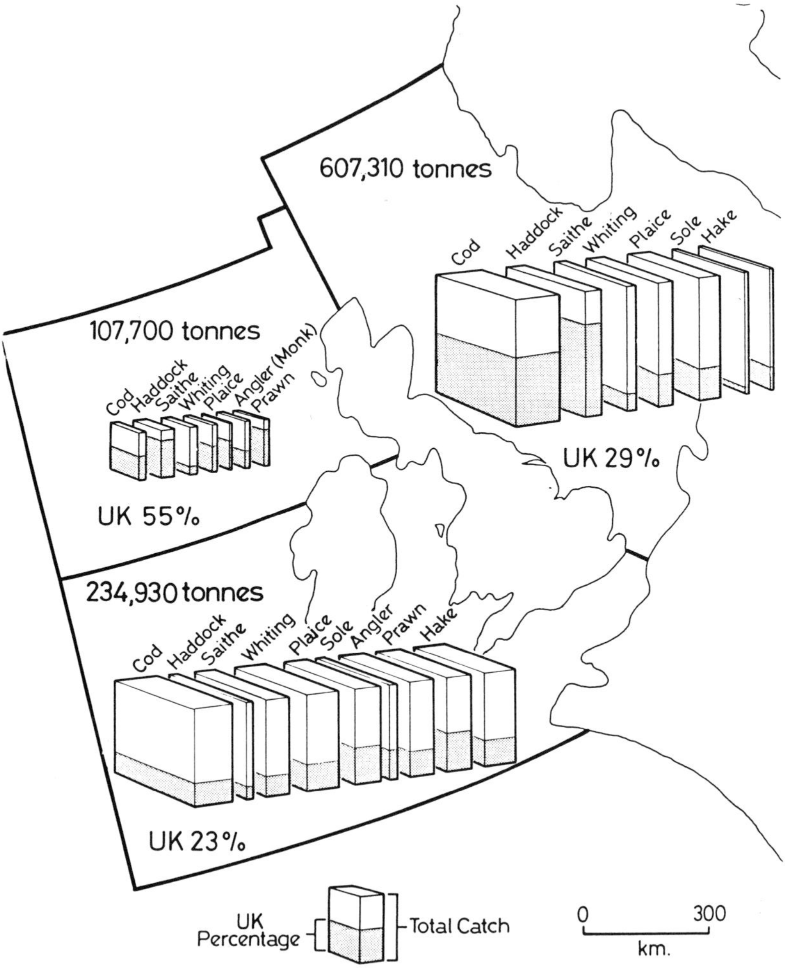

Fig. 1.1. Total allowable catch EC waters 1990
Demersal species

Sea where the total allowable catch has fallen 30% in five years. Most of the stocks we depend on are fully exploited. See Appendix 1.

- The dominance of imports in our national supplies of fish and fish products which is now 54%. See Appendix 2.

- The overcapacity in gross tonnage and horsepower of the fishing fleet in relation to the resource opportunities. The need is to reduce this capacity by at least 10% and adopt rigourous management measures to control over-exploitation of the resources.

- The growing trend towards the internationalisation of the fish trade which must accelerate with the advent of the Single European Market from 1992 onwards.

All of these factors need to be considered in planning ahead. A new investment in major port facilities in the 1990s has to be basically a sound project which will still be operational in 2050 or beyond. It will need a lot of thought and not least a considerable act of courage to spend what could be several million pounds on restructing a port or harbour.

But to do nothing to our ports would be to admit to lack of vision, and it could result in the U.K. being left on the sidelines of the European Community. What fish we can catch could be easily transported onto the Continental mainland, and then re-imported as high value products from more successful centres elsewhere. We have to keep a close watch on countries such as Denmark and Holland who have become nett exporters of fish and fish products. These countries have a small domestic market but their modern and efficient processing industries are geared towards the Community market as a whole and their demand for raw material is considerable.

There is a view that many industries will undergo extensive rationalisation once the effects of the SEM are felt. The fish industry of Europe already has overcapacity in relation to opportunity, but it will be the fish industries of those Member States who can secure supplies and offer service and efficiency who will emerge as the winners.

2. The U.K. Fishery in the 1990s

2.1 Supplies

The relevant key facts about our industry are as follows:-

- Current landings by British registered vessels in 1989 were:-

demersal fish	305,557
pelagic fish	272,863
shellfish	86,005
total	664,425

- There has been a steady decline coupled with a shift of emphasis from demersal fish to pelagic and shellfish since the mid 1970s when total landings were:-

demersal fish	579,000 tonnes
pelagic fish	222,000 tonnes
shellfish	67,000 tonnes
total	869,130 tonnes

- In 1975 10% by weight of our fish supplies were imported. By 1980 this had risen to 30% whilst today 54% of our supplies are imported. Further rises in import levels are to be expected through the 1990s, although our fish consumption is expected to remain fairly constant at around 1.0 million tonnes of whole fish. This is equal to a per capita consumption of around 7kg per year of processed fish.

2.2 Other Factors

Employment U.K. Totals (1987 statistics)

Processing Sector	21,000
Ancilliary Trades	19,700
Fishermen (fulltime)	17,000
(part time)	5,000

Fishing Fleet U.K. Totals

Under 40ft	6,232
40-80ft	1,700
Over 80ft	253
	8,185

Two UK ports in the 1970s

Grimsby

Scarborough

2.3 Analysis of the Trends

An important factor in the last decade has been the growth of imports from the Nordic countries - Norway, Iceland - and also from Canada. To a large extent this has been a substitution of our traditional favourites such as cod and haddock. There is also a trend to import more fish from tropical and sub-tropical regions especially shellfish. The world catch is increasing and should reach 100 million tonnes by the year 2000 but in the N.E. Atlantic it is declining. The U.K. is unlikely to return to the near self sufficiency in fish supplies of the 1970s. Those countries in the European Community best able to secure raw material supplies will be able to maintain viable industries in the future. Fortunately for the U.K. it has a buoyant domestic market and considerable skills in buying and selling fish and in processing. There is every reason to believe there is the vision to be one of the winners.

Coupled with the supply problem is the expansion of international trade in fish and fish products. Although a considerable volume of fish goes direct from the quayside into processing and the domestic trade, more and more is coming into the country in various forms either for the domestic market or for re-export to the Community and elsewhere. The large processors and distributors no longer see the U.K. fleet as critical to their supplies nor the U.K. consumer as their only outlet for sales. The range of products are now aimed at the consumer on a worldwide scale and it matters less and less whether they originate in the N.E. Atlantic or the Pacific.

The consequences of this are that the traditional relationships between the fishing port and the processing industry will inevitably change. The concept of a resource centre starts to emerge which consoldiates activities in fewer but more competitive places and which have the buying strength to attract supplies of raw material both from U.K. ports and imports; and the facilities to produce quality products for the international market. This concept has already emerged on Humberside, in Grampian Region and at our nearby North Sea neighbours Boulogne, Zeebrugge, Den Helder and Bremerhaven. A further trend will be the emphasis on quality health and hygiene in the fishing industry. One of the principles of the SEM is to set standards in health and hygiene in the food industries and this includes special regulations for fish and shellfish.

Modern practice 1990s

Chilled display hall

Plastic fish boxes

A resource centre exists where entrepreneurial skills are available to bring together raw materials from a variety of sources. These may be direct landings at a major port, or attracting supplies from nearby small ports and harbours. It will also attract landings from foreign vessels, and, most importantly from imports. The aim will be to maintain a balanced varied supply of fish and fish products throughout the year. See Figure 2.

The relative strengths of a resource centre will be :-

- proximity of abundant and stable fishing resources
- continuity of direct landings
- physical capacity and quality of facilities
- size and stability of demand on the auction market
- local processing capacity
- local cold storage capacity
- ready availability of containerized imports
- proximity to major European urban markets
- relative location within the European network of fish distribution
- availability of entrepreneurial skills, trained management and labour and a committment from regional and government offices to helping the centre within E.C. rules
- adequate public and private sector finance

During the 1990s it is likely we will see the development of a network of international resource centres which will dominate the distribution of fresh and processed fish throughout Europe including what we knew until this year as the "Eastern Bloc".

Whilst these standards set the ground rules it will be public demand for better standards which will determine the level at which they will become established. Seafish have been campaigning for better health and hygiene standards throughout the industry since 1984 and some important changes have been made such as the introduction of plastic fish boxes. Ultimately however it will be the impact of Regulations and the public pressure which will inevitably change many of the practices in our ports.

Further trends which will influence our thinking in ports and harbours are the changes in the operating patterns of the fishing fleets and the type of vessels in the future.

The U.K. has through circumstances built-up a large fleet of small vessels of under 12m length. These vessels are limited in range and will want to continue to operate from the small harbours and landing sites around the British Isles. Some contraction of this fleet seems inevitable as the vessels come under economic pressure from declining resource opportunity, increased costs, especially in inshore waters, and for many the difficulty of obtaining berths in traditional harbours which have been developed as leisure marinas. Indeed many fishermen merely continue fishing today to pay off bank mortgages on the boat taken out in more profitable times.

The Government has introduced new measures to encourage capacity aggregation in order that some of these small vessels will be taken out of service and replaced with a lesser number of larger vessels. The U.K. must maintain a balanced and diversified fleet able to safety exploit all the resources open to it.

3. Resource Centre Concept

The resource centre is not a new concept, it is merely a recognition of what is happening in the more efficient sectors of the Fish Industry at present. It was first suggested by David Symes (ref. 1) and describes in broad terms what is happening in major centres in Europe at the present time - either spontaneously or through deliberate planning.

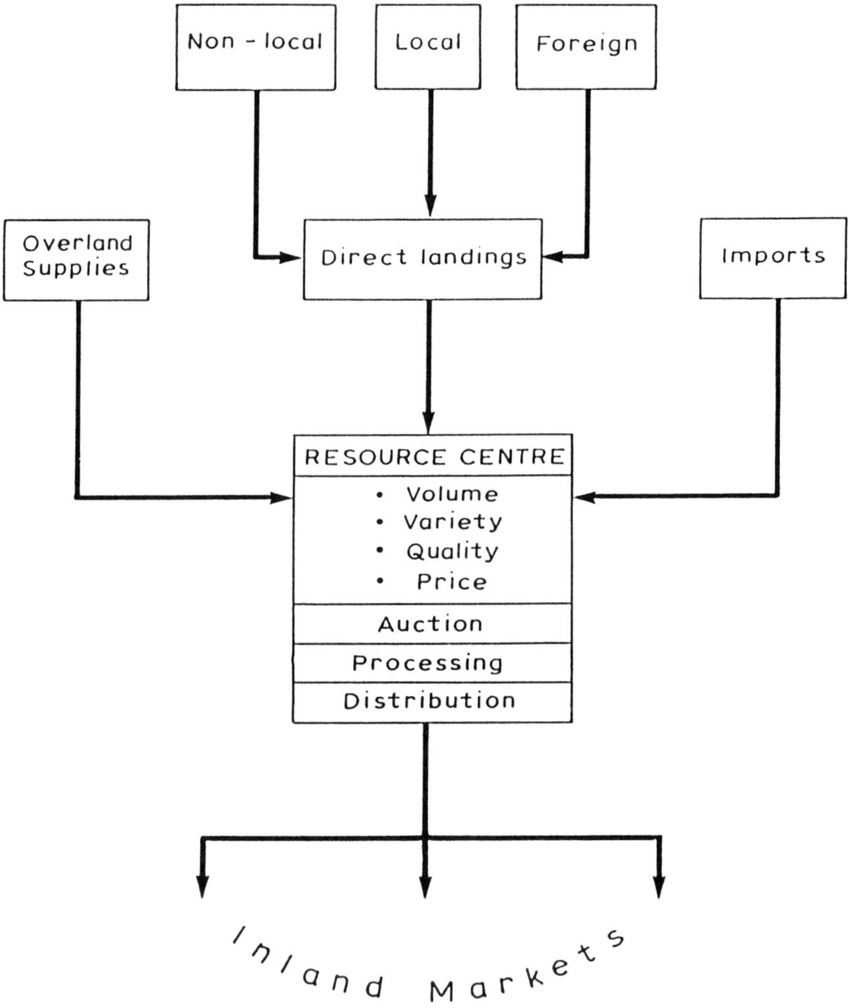

Fig. 2. Coastal Resource Centre

The U.K. has two resource centres on Humberside and in Grampian region which are already significant in the context of Europe. Others on a smaller scale exist at Fleetwood, Newlyn, Lowestoft and Shetland, whilst certain ports which in the past have been important may well face an uncertain future.

The keen demand for fish in the 1990s must lead to consolidation and the ability to attract supplies. The resource centres too must be able to handle and create a diversity of products and have the ability to promote these in the market place. This will mean making use of some of our lesser valued species such as pelagic fish for which we still have access to large quotas, but unfortunately we are letting these go cheaply as a raw material to other countries.

The role of the small port, however, cannot be ignored but it is believed that many will become feeder ports into the main supply as well as serving the local trade. Catching fish and being able to freely sell it as one wishes is still seen as an inalienable right of man, and a free rather than controlled choice will remain for many years part of the U.K. fishing industry. However, the hygiene standards whether by statute or consumer insistence could compel much of our fish to pass through a recognised centre where it can be properly packed and labelled. This will certainly be the case with most shellfish.

4. Elements of a Strategy

Strategic planning is not an action which sits comfortably with either the U.K. Government or with the fishing industry. It is possibly more acceptable in other Community Member States such as France where there at least seems to be a greater sense of forward planning and committment by national and regional government to the fishing industry than in the U.K. Contrary to popular belief there is not necessarily any more grant aid available but what is available is well directed.

For the U.K. if strategic planning is not acceptable then a strategic overview is needed, at least, to see where the industry is likely to be in ten years time and where its best opportunities lie. Seafish have already embarked on this work with a Prospect 2000 and by setting up a working group to look quite critically at our major resource centres and the supply and demand patterns in the SEM.

This strategic overview will take the following form.

4.1 Prospect 2000 will aim to identify the shape of fish supplies and distribution in Europe by the end of the decade. It will also try to make reasonable predictions about the state of the N.E. Atlantic resources given that management and conservation measures will be at least effective in stabilizing the stock levels. It will also analyse consumer trends which will be more and more away from the consumption of the whole fish or fillet into a variety of fish products drawing upon some of the presently under utilised species. Finally it will examine the demographic and social changes of the 1990s which could have far reaching effects on the industry. One of these could be an acute shortage of skilled and managerial personnel in the mid 1990s.

4.2 The role of our existing resource centres should be critically evaluated to judge their strengths and weaknesses and how they fit into the supply and distribution network of the future. Each will have to be rated for the positive strengths listed in Section 3. Already Humberside and Grampian are well placed to play a major role in Europe. Other centres are less dominant and will have to accept a lesser role and some will not be able to secure the fish supplies they need and may disappear. A most important factor will be the availability of capital and grant aid to help improve the infrastructure and to properly manage the use of these funds.

4.3 The capacity and structure of the U.K. fishing fleet needs to be evaluated: not only for the shape that will emerge purely as a result market forces, but to determine the shape of fleet which will be able to best exploit those resources available to the U.K. both in the N.E. Atlantic and elsewhere through fishing agreements with third countries. The licensing system and existing rules based length have reslted in a very large sector of the fleet being restricted to inshore fishing or heavily exploited areas and only able to fish about 150 days per year. On the other hand the U.K. has only a limited capability to take up quotas in Arctic waters, and South Atlantic, and none off the African coast.

The U.K. needs a structural policy which restores this imbalance by encouraging the building of new vessels or the modernisation of others whilst at the same time reducing fleet capacity.

4.4 Much more needs to be done in making positive use of the undervalued resources especially pelagic fish and shellfish. These resources are by and large exported as raw material to other European resource centres and some of this material comes back in the form of added value products. The U.K. resource centres can do more with the fish available to them and the recent decisions to build onshore pelagic processing plant at Peterhead is welcomed as a positive step in this direction.

4.5 The importance of the small ports cannot be ignored but too many of them are faced with having to provide services to the fishing industry which the industry for their part cannot afford because the low level of fishing activities either due to quotas or the limited size of the fleet. A partnership needs to be worked out in these ports between the users, including fishermen and the leisure industry, and the owners to reach a satisfactory working relationship. To often there is little or no dialogue between all sides except through the press.

Conclusion

There is a trend towards increased concentration of facilities for fish production at a smaller number of locations which are well geared to supply the wider European markets. This is especially true of ports surrounding the North Sea Basin and the Channel. To remain viable each of these has to fully exploit its locational advantage, the ability to assemble a large volume of raw material of a diverse nature and to have a progressive outlook with a favourable climate of support from local authorities and government. Such centres will become winners in what could become a very hard fought game in the new Europe.

The role of minor ports should not be seen as lost cause but the fish resources are finite and for many there may be an inadequate revenue to sustain them in the future. Minor ports which can work out the right partnership with fishing and leisure interests against a realistic expectation of activity and preferably linked to a major resource centre will also have a chance of being winners in the game.

Access to capital and grant aid and wise use of such finance will be vital factors in both resource centres, ports and minor ports.

Postscript

Finally on a somewhat sober note Sea Fish have recently completed a study of the Western Isles fishery. Here there is a large fleet of small boats mostly under 10m in length which are inadequate to properly exploit the resources available to them There are some 38 harbours or landing places which have had little investment during the present century and efforts to establish processing facilities onshore have by and large been unsuccessful. There is also a shortage of capital and entrepreneurial skills and skilled labour. Buyers only visit from the Western Isles when supplies are not available elsewhere. As a consequence the fishery which could be a major contributor to the economy of the Isles is unable to meet its full potential. The will to succeed exists but not the cohesive planning or the finance.

No one would like to see the British Isles gradually become the western isles of Europe, and it is up to all of us in fisheries to see that this is not the case.

References

1. Seafish Report No. 268 (Technical Report). Fish Supplies and Processing Capacity in the United Kingdom. Part 1. (Joint Seafish-University of Hull Study). April 1988.

2. Seafish Report No. 374. Perspectives on the Future of the European Fishing Industry and Fish Distribution Systems. April 1990.

3. Seafish Report No. 337 (Technical Report). Development of a Strategy for British Fishing Ports. July 1988.

4. Seafish Report (un-numberd). Fish Processing in the U.K. - an economic analysis. January 1988.

5. Seafish Report No. 276. Fish Supplies and Processing Capacity in the United Kingdom. Part 11. (Joint Seafish-University of Hull Study). April 1985.

6. Seafish Report No. 338 (Technical Report). Peterhead Harbour - a development strategy. August 1988.

7. Programme for the Improvement of Facilities at Fishing Ports in the U.K. 1988 - 91. EEC Regulation 2321/88. MAFF Publications.

8. Amin Rajan: 1992 A Zero Sum Game Industrial Society Press 1990.

APPENDIX 1

Total Allowable Catch (TAC) and Quotas

The International Council for the Exploration of the Sea (ICES) through its Advisory Committee for Fisheries Managment (ACFM) assesses each year the state of the main pressure stocks in selected areas. For this it draws heavily upon the reports from the scientific establishments in each maritime country and its own experience of stock management which goes back to 1902. The ACFM reports to the Fisheries Directorate in Brussels who through their own Scientific and Technical Committee recommend the TAC for each species. The Council of Fisheries Ministers then decide on the exact levels and this is made known each December for the following year.

The national quotas for each species reflect traditional fishing patterns. For example the U.K. has 72% of the haddock catch in the North Sea, but only 45% of the cod catch. Quota managements then becomes the responsibility of the Member State.

The 1990 figures for the TAC and the U.K. share are shown in Figure 1.1. The trend in the North Sea has been downward and the fall has been a dramatic 30% since 1985. Other areas are more stable.

Overfishing is only part of the problem. High levels of discards of small fish, natural biological changes, poor recruitment and seal predation are others. Pollution is often stated to be a major factor and no doubt contributes in certain areas. Unless there is some reversal of pollution trends in the North Sea this could become the 'last straw' for the fishery.

The ultimate solution is a combination of management, enforcement, conservation and reduced levels of pollution in all areas.

TABLE 1A
North Sea TACs and U.K. Quotas - 1990 and 1985

Species	1990 TAC	1990 U.K.Quota
Cod	105,000	45,180
Haddock	50,000	36,280
Whiting	125,000	29,260
Saithe	120,000	11,440
Sole	25,000	1,070
Plaice	180,000	50,300
Hake	2,310	420
Herring	385,000	61,150
Mackerel	0	0

Species	1985 TAC	1985 U.K. Quota
Cod	250,000	107,530
Haddock	207,000	129,500
Whiting	160,000	65,400
Saithe	200,000	16,250
Sole	22,000	940
Plaice	200,000	52,940
Hake	2,200	520
Herring	6,000*	68,190
Mackerel	37,000	330

* S. North Sea Only

APPENDIX 2

U.K. Landings and Imports of Fish and Fish Products in selected years 1969-1989 (tonnes)

	1949	1959	1969	1979	1989
U.K. Landings					
demersal	803,000	718,000	728,000	369,000	306,000
pelagic	220,000	155,000	175,000	403,000	273,000
shellfish	22,000	24,000	51,000	64,000	86,000
Totals	1,045,000	897,000	954,000	836,000	665,000
Imports (whole fish equivalent)	588,000	473,000	476,000	753,000	1,075,000

Note: These figures have to be adjusted for conversion to fish products and corrected for exports. The nett result is that 54% of U.K. consumption is now imported.

APPENDIX 3

Vessel Licensing Scheme

In the U.K. it is a requirement for all vessels over 10m registered length to posses a licence. It is not the same in other Member States although various restrictive schemes do exist to prevent the fleet exceeding its quotas.

The license scheme restricts further entries to the fleet of vessels above 10m, but there is no buy-back scheme for anyone wanting to leave the fishery to reduce fleet capacity. Licenses however may be sold or transferred.

Currently the scheme in the U.K. is under review and three types of licences are proposed in the future:-

pressure stock
non pressure stock
miscellaneous species

Licences will be issued to vessels with a proven track record in each fishery. Up until now only pressure stock licences have been issued. Once the licences are issued there will be no further allocations but fishermen may transfer licences to a new vessel provided it is not one of a greater power or tonnage, and the older vessel is removed from the register. It is also possible for a fisherman to aggregate more than one licence into a new vessel, again provided the older vessels are taken off the register. In aggregation there has to be a loss of aggregated capacity of 10%. The capacity is measured by a formulae linking vessel size and engine power.

In simple terms it will be possible to acquire three small vessels with a pressure stock licence and build one larger one provided the new vessel does not exceed 90% of the capacity of the three small vessels.

The scheme is not applicable to vesels under 10m and this has resulted in a proliferation of high powered high capacity vessels of just under 10m.

Discussion on Papers 1–6

E. LOEWY, Sir William Halcrow and Partners, Ltd

Legislation must take account of the problem of overweight trucks and containers and the false documentation of dangerous cargoes entering the UK on passenger and freight ferries.

The EC social programme has to be resisted whenever it appears merely to be a socialist intervention, especially in UK ports where it would seek to re-introduce elements of the Dock Labour Scheme.

Import duties are a form of indirect taxation and should therefore not be augmented when the UK is reducing direct taxation in favour of consumption charges.

Legislation and rules for improved shop safety should take account of the recent Which report on ferry safety in design and operation.

Acceptance by ship's captains and pilots of shore controllers instructions in port approaches requires these people to see themselves in the same light as airliner captains and not as independent persons.

Port authorities must not declare over optimistic, but false, shipping channel dimensions which their dredging programmes have not achieved (cf Royston Grange collision on Buenos Aires port approach 1976).

J. WRAY, Associated British Ports

Is the British Ports Federation bringing pressure to bear to equalize subsidies throughout the EC.

I. W. DAND, BMT Fluid Mechanics Ltd

Mr Finlay discusses legislation with respect to ship design and operation. Legislation, especially with regard to matters of safety, is important, but can only be effective if policed properly. Does Mr Finlay see himself and his colleagues in the role of policemen and, if not, who does he consider to have this role?

Regarding the pilotless ship, if by this Mr Finlay means a ship with an un-manned bridge moving in pilotage waters, controlled from the shore, I believe the realization of this to be a long way off. Ship manoeuvring in the confined waters of a port must be very precise and information about the ship's state at any instant must be very accurate. At present the means of automatically determining that state, and the ability to predict what it will be in a few seconds time, are insufficiently accurate for use in a port approach, unless carried out by a human being. At sea, auto-pilots and un-manned bridges are a reality; in a port approach they are, as yet, unable to cope with the rigorous demands placed on them.

However, the increase in shore-based VTS control is making ship approaches to ports similar, in a limited manner, to aircraft approaches to an airport under air traffic control. But in both, the human is still a vital link in the chain and will remain so for some time.

A. TOMS, G. Maunsell and Partners
In view of Mr Finlay's comment on driverless ships, should the port authorities not be insistent on vessel standards. This would avoid the risk that other parties might consider suing the port authorities as a result of loss from poorly prepared or operated vessels. Could Mr Sharples give a view on this?

D. PALMER, Tees and Hartlepool Port Authority
The implications of proposed European legislation regarding maximum working hours for the labour force (European harmonization of legislation) are that crew levels on board port vessels (dredgers) which often work 12-14 hours/day, will have to increase adding to the cost of part operation. What is being done to reduce this impact or resist the intrusive legislation?

E. LOEWY, Sir William Halcrow and Partners Ltd
If Eurotunnel fails financially it will not be SNCF alone who will complete the project, but also Bechtel.

Could ABP be more effective in older port redevelopments if Grosvenor Square Group were completely independent of ABP?

M. THORN, Hydraulics Research
I support Mr Loewy's general comments that the port user is influenced by the quality of service. I see many ports in the UK and overseas, and frankly many UK ports present a very poor service to the individual user. For example the car ferry facility at Portsmouth provides inadequate and poor quality waiting facilities for the large number of car ferry users arriving there. By contrast, the ferry port at Plymouth has an excellent terminal, but the ferry port is difficult to find via a tortuous route through poorly signed backstreets. It is these things that influence the

individual user to choose one port or another, or to transfer to the Channel Tunnel.

Mr Hooper has shown how fish handling is better arranged through enclosed, chilled and hygienic buildings. However the fish market is a significant tourist attraction in many small fishing harbours. Can these two aspects of the fish handling and marketing be reconciled?

A. D. M. BELLIS, Consulting engineer
It has already been mentioned that there is scope for rationalization of the fish ports (or resource centres). Is there likely to be a case for rationalizing general cargo and passenger ports in the next century?

A. TOMS, G. Maunsell and Partners
Mr Baker illustrated the problems facing Eurotunnel, having funded a large development and needing to earn income to pay off even the interest. Mr Hopper advocates future investment for the fishing industry and Dr Farrell intimates that interest led inflation is detrimental to prosperity. Does Dr Farrell consider that future devaluation of our currency will be used as a measure to combat inflation and encourage prosperity, now that high interest rate policies have been shown to be so detrimental for future investments?

H. MUIR, Dover Harbour Board
In support of Mr Baker, there has been a significant move of freight to rail since the opening of the new train ferry berth at Dover in May 1988. So it is, perhaps, doubtful that there will be a shift from road to rail of any significant size on the opening of the Channel Tunnel.

There is no reason why landside activities at the tunnel should take less time than at an efficient ferry port. Therefore, the saving of time is likely to be only in the cross-Channel journey time.

Does Mr Hopper consider that the suggested improvements in fish handling (processing, distributors etc) make fish unaffordable?

J. WRAY, Associated British Ports
Does Mr Hopper consider that the new EC regulations regarding fish handing and his proposal to create coastal resource centres will result in the demise of the small fishing ports and the creation of a few large port/coastal resource centres?

D. GLYN-WOODS, Mowlem Civil Engineering
Mr Baker's paper has brought the financial implication of the Channel Tunnel into sharp focus and added to our

knowledge of the issues involved. It also raises a question on the economic viability of the Channel Tunnel on the basis of the figures presented. Mr Baker suggests a revenue of £559 million in 1993 and £962 million in 2013. We are not sure what the final cost of providing the tunnel will be, or the ratio of equity to loan capital. However, at a cost of £7 to £8 billion, it appears highly unlikely that the revenue in 1993 will pay interest charges in that year, and doubtful if it will do so in 2013.

I trust that his comments on SNCF's 'sack of money' available to make a take over bid will not become prophetic.

N. FINLAY, Paper 3

In reply to I. W. Dand, first, I would like to establish I am an 'independent surveyor' with no affiliation either to a national body or a classification society. I am responsible for my own actions and to my clients who pay me for the work I do on their behalf.

Safety, is quite rightly the responsibility of a national authority or their appointees and in Britain this responsibility falls on the marine branch of the Department of Transport. They see that the legislation laid down in Acts of Parliament and sundry regulations are enacted and have the power to arrest vessels if they do not conform to the safety standards laid down for a particular ship. Once arrested, vessels can only put to sea when all the safety requirements have been met. Unfortunately we do not have sufficient DTp surveyors to monitor the situation properly.

It is my opinion that a greater hazard to safety today is the number of ships' crews which for various economical and other reasons contain several nationalities with different mother tongues. Difficulty in understanding one another is common and in difficult or dangerous emergency situations the problem is magnified. On several vessels where emergency situations have arisen and got out of hand, enquiry verdicts have stated that the danger and resulting damage could have been minimized had the crew members been able to understand one another properly.

With regard to pilotless ships it was not my intention to suggest that vessels would enter ports or similar areas with no one on the bridge, rather I was suggesting that with the variety of technology available today, ships could enter navigable waters under the command of their own officers with a 'talk in system' from port radio or radar control. It is my belief that with the shortage of merchant navy officers who normally join the pilot service, the time is not too far off when it will be difficult to recruit pilots. It is with this in mind and knowing how aircraft are controlled in similar difficult circumstances that I believe it is possible to dispense with the services of pilots. I agree with Mr Dand that the human link in the chain is necessary and as an ex merchant navy officer I confess that an unmanned bridge fills me with deep apprehension.

R. G. BAKER, Paper 4
Mr Glyn-Woods referred to my surmise that SNCF might have a 'sack of money' ready to make a bid for the tunnel's assets if Eurotunnel failed because interest charges and operating costs could not be covered by revenue. In mid-1990, media comment cast doubt on whether the Tunnel would ever be finished. My comment on SNCF was made to illustrate my very firm belief that the Tunnel would be completed and operated whatever the difficulties on the way. Mr Loewy reinforced this by his comment that Bechtel might be involved, in such an event.

Mr Thorn is right to draw attention to the effect which poor terminal facilities can have on traffic. Calais is another example at the moment. The hassle which bad approach roads, lack of signs, and delays at the terminals generates will undoubtedly lead customers to consider using the Tunnel. I think also that frequency of services is an important factor. The possibility that arriving half an hour late, might lead to a six hour wait for the next ferry is a deterrent to using that port. Mr Muir makes the same point indirectly, when he states that an efficient ferry port will handle traffic as fast as the Tunnel terminal. That ought to be true, but it is the overall efficiency of the port, ferry, operator and highway authority compared with the efficiency of the tunnel operation, and highway authority which will determine which mode is chosen by a user.

DR S. FARRELL, Paper 5
In reply to Mr Toms, since British entry into the European Exchange Rate Mechanism, the scope for using currency adjustments as a tool of economic management has become more limited. If inflation is to be reduced

to West German levels, for example, it seems likely that there will first be a period of recession, with a reduction in consumer demand and a significant increase in unemployment.

A. G. HOPPER, Paper 6
In reply to Mr Thorn, tourism and fishing boats and the colourful trade have always been compatible. Indeed, many harbours such as Scarborough, Looe, Oban and others would lose much if they did not have a fishing industry.

However, we have to recognize that fish is a food and under new regulations we have to be much more circumspect. We can allow the public into enclosed areas or walkways and, with creative planning, we can probably make the fishing industry more of an attraction than the haphazard way it takes place at present. This could include heritage buildings, aquaria, information, guided tours and much more. It will be essential, however, to keep the public with their street clothes, smoking and pets away from direct contact with food.

In reply to Mr Muir, there will inevitably be increased costs in handling and distributing fish in conditions that are much more tightly controlled. Fish price depends very much on demand and scarcity and it is the latter (scarcity) which will play the greatest part in the future. Fresh fish will be most vulnerable to increased handling and distribution costs because of the need to keep it within a tighter temperature regime of 0-4 °C. There will be radical changes in the future as a result of scarcity. It is possible meals will contain less fish in future rather than becoming unaffordable.

In reply to Mr Wray, the Privatization Bill and the changes in fishing opportunities will affect many of our ports in the next ten years. Many provide fishing facilities because they have a statuary obligation to do so. The Privatization Bill may permit them or the new owners to reconsider this and they cannot be blamed in taking a harsh attitude if they are obligated to show adequate revenue on their assets.

There is excess fishing capacity in all EC fleets when related to opportunity and unless there is a conservation policy introduced to all these fleets which does work, the opportunities will not improve. For the UK the excess fleet capacity is estimated at 40%.

It will be very sad to lose fishing interests from some of our ports and devastating to the communities who have known no other livelihood, but there are many issues stacked against them. Unfortunately, there is not a clear picture of who will be the winners and who will be the losers.

It is my suggestion that each region in the British Isles needs a strategy for change which looks into the opportunities for the region, the best means of meeting these in terms of fleet, harbours, processing centres and taking every opportunity to retain cohesive fishing communities. A fishing industry does not exist because there are fish in the sea. It exists because men are willing to go and catch it, whatever the weather or the difficulties may be.

7. Regional situations: the release of port land for redevelopment

D. J. GRIFFITHS, Grosvenor Square Properties Group plc

SYNOPSIS. The growth of high productivity cargo handling methods, larger ships, and changing economic circumstances, have all contributed to the release of port land for alternative development. As we approach the end of the century this pattern will continue, providing more opportunities for well-planned, comprehensive urban regeneration projects. Such projects will become more relevant as environmental concerns counter development pressures on "greenfield sites", particularly in the South East. Coupled with appropriate public sector assistance where necessary, the redevelopment of redundant dockland areas throughout the country can play an important part in providing for future economic and social needs.

THE HISTORICAL CONTEXT

1. The purpose of this conference is to look ahead to the year 2000 but in order to predict (or guess) the extent and nature of the redevelopment opportunities in our ports we must first look back at what has happened and what is happening now.

2. We are today in a continuing period of change and evolution for ports throughout the world. The resulting changes have in some cases, such as the London Docks, led to major closures and redevelopment opportunities. However, the release of port land for development does not always go hand-in-hand with the decline of the port or its traffic. Indeed, the opposite is sometimes the case. (Southampton cargo tonnage increased sixfold from the 1950's to the mid 1980's.)

3. Historically, the Industrial Revolution was a major turning point for the country resulting in an expansion of trade with the rest of the world, but with Britain remaining as the major destination or point of origin. It was then that many of our major enclosed port complexes were first constructed. But ports were different, depending upon the nature of their trade. In South Wales, for example, Cardiff and Barry were built to

export coal which required substantial areas of quayside land but little in the way of buildings. Compare this with Bristol, Liverpool or London, where we still have in existence today many of the substantial multi-storey warehouses required to handle their cargoes of tobacco, wool and cotton, and a wide variety of general goods.

4. Up to the Second World War and beyond, the growth in trade resulted generally in an expansion of the number of ships required with a consequential increase in the supply of quay space and labour to service the vessels.

5. Two further "Revolutions" have however taken place latterly which have had a profound effect upon ports and have resulted in the release of land for redevelopment. The first is the growth of air passenger transport, and the second the introduction of unitised cargo handling (containerisation).

6. The effect of the first is self-evident and as a result, ports such as Southampton and Liverpool lost substantial amounts of traffic. Southampton alone saw its international passenger throughput drop from 830,000 in 1946 to 118,000 in 1986. Ship passenger traffic - not only in Southampton - is now effectively limited to cruise liners and ferries with the latter being concentrated on the shortest sea routes.

7. The second revolution, however, is by far the most important in terms of opportunities for redevelopment. The growth of high productivity practices such as containerised traffic, bulk cargoes and specialised vessels, for example, large car carriers, has substantially reduced and changed the berth requirements. A general cargo ship of 10/15,000 tonnes might previously have required up to 5 or 6 weeks in port to load and unload. By comparison, a 20,000 tonnes container ship today can require only 2 days.

8. The intensified use of the quay is obvious from these figures but increased productivity has resulted in a greatly increased need for land to service the berth. To take full advantage from this, ships themselves have increased in size, therefore demanding larger dock entrances and deeper draught quays. Where these have not been available or could not be created economically, the old port facilities have become out-moded, redundant, and consequently released for other uses.

9. Changing economic circumstances have also influenced the release of port land. In some cases, facilities were specifically developed for particular trades which have since declined, such as coal in South Wales or fishing on Humberside.

Figs. 1 and 2. Cargo handling at Southampton - the old and the new.

REDEVELOPMENT PATTERNS

10. There has been a growth of primary manufacturing industry in other countries leading to changes in our own industrial base, and to the nature and form of our import and export trades. Coupled with this has been the decline of many heavy engineering operations, such as shipbuilding, again resulting in the release of what could be described as port land, principally on the Clyde and Tyne estuaries.

11. Finally, Britain's international trade is now much more heavily weighted in favour of the EC and the rest of the European mainland. Consequently those ports on the south and east coast have generally increased their trade at the expense of those to the west.

THE PRESENT SITUATION

12. Having examined the historical reasons for the release of port land for redevelopment, we must look at the present. Will recent legislation, for example, lead to an increase in the future availability of land? Since 1979 we have had a continuous period of Conservative government which has been promoting increased competition, increased efficiency, and greater self-reliance for all sectors of the economy. We have seen the privatisation of many businesses previously in public ownership, including ABP in 1983. But many other ports are still in public ownership through local authorities or trusts, and in some cases their continued operation is only made possible by public sector support. This was certainly true of London and Liverpool which were supported by direct government aid for many years.

13. One particular factor which previously affected the efficiency of many ports was the National Dock Labour Scheme which was eventually repealed in July 1989. Repeal of the legislation has enabled the "scheme" ports to offer the same flexibility and economies in the use and cost of labour which previously only applied to the non-scheme ports. Since July last year, ABP has seen a significantly increased level of business enquiries, and in some cases land which was previously being considered for development or other non-port uses has been returned to the port. For example, in Southampton, 5.9 hectares of surfaced land has been added to the container port to provide increased storage and handling, and just up-river a 21 hectare site which had planning consent for industrial and warehouse development and which it was intended to develop for non-port use has been returned to ABP's direct control. This general picture is repeated elsewhere in the country. In the Humber new river berths are planned at both Hull and Immingham, and in South Wales land and facilities which were recently under-utilised are now attracting new business.

14. I anticipate that this process will continue and those ports that are well-placed to offer modern up to date facilities will expand and prosper in the future.

15. There is undoubtedly over-capacity in the UK port industry as a whole - some comments I have heard refer to as much as 25%. If the present government policies continue we may well see the enforced privatisation of local authority and trust ports in the future, or at least continued pressure on public sector finances which will ensure greater accountability and increase pressure to reduce costs and therefore close uneconomic facilities. This will lead to the release of more land for alternative uses. Moreover, the investment required to create modern cargo handling and port facilities is substantial and the creation of capital profit and income from the re-use or redevelopment of redundant areas is an essential part of the overall business. Freed from public sector constraints, the management of these ports will certainly want to explore all the options available to them to ensure that they obtain the maximum use and value from their property assets.

16. The Channel Tunnel may also cause changes, particularly to the Channel ports, but there is a separate paper on this subject which will undoubtedly deal with the subject with more authority than I can. Nevertheless, we are already seeing the introduction of new ferries and improved port facilities on the Channel routes, as well as the first steps in rationalising the number of routes and ports with the redevelopment proposals for Newhaven and Folkestone announced earlier this year.

17. Finally, ports can be affected by physical changes, such as siltation, which may lead to closure or prevent commercial operation. For example, the closure of Preston as a commercial port.

CHARACTERISTICS OF PORT LAND

18. Port land displays certain general characteristics which influence the form and style of development for alternative uses.

19. Most obvious is the availability of water and water views. In fact, the water area may in some cases exceed that of the land itself. It seems that people have an unerring attraction to water and this, coupled perhaps with increased affluence and the growth of leisure activities generally, has led to an enormous increase in the popularity of waterside locations for housing and business. Where waterside homes can be associated with marinas or, even better, dedicated private berthing as at the Hythe Marina Village on Southampton Water, substantial

premium values can be obtained. The water attraction and the opportunity to create a different environment to that available in the town centre is also of value in the commercial field where premium rentals have been obtained for waterfront properties in a similar manner to the landscaped business park.

20. The size of the site, which is often large in relation to other urban developments - and in many cases in single ownership - allows the creation of a comprehensive range of facilities for residents, visitors, workers, and employers, in a style and with an atmosphere which is not achievable in the city centre. The development will often not have an immediate relationship with surrounding buildings and therefore there are less constraints on architectural style and scale of buildings. Canary Wharf in London's Docklands is perhaps the best example of how these opportunities and characteristics can be used to the full.

21. But Docklands also illustrates two other important characteristics of port land. Firstly, it is expensive and difficult to develop. It is almost certainly going to be reclaimed or other made-ground. There will sometimes be massive existing structures and previous industrial uses may have left soil pollution or contamination which must be treated or eliminated. New services will also need to be brought in, perhaps over considerable distance. As one of many possible examples, the total infrastructure cost for the redevelopment of Greenland and South Docks in Southwark, London, was £11.25 million for a total site area, excluding water, of 48 acres, or about £234,000 per acre. Affordable perhaps in high value areas - but elsewhere? (Source: Davis Langdon & Everest - Ref. 1)

22. Secondly, there is the question of accessibility. Ports generally have only a 180° hinterland and this must have an effect on access and the relative attraction of the land for particular uses. For example, distribution warehouses are much better placed in a central location inland. I am sure we are all familiar with the perceived transport problems of London Docklands as a result of continuous press comment and perhaps also from personal experience. Certainly millions of pounds are being invested in works designed to alleviate the worst situations. But accessibility is a key factor in any business or individual decision to relocate. Healey & Baker in a recent survey said that 58% of office staff now travelled to work by car. Equally important, although there has been an improvement, less than 30% of tenants classify their present car parking provision as "good". (Ref. 2). In port areas we have the opportunity to provide up to the minute transport and other

communication links and these will be a vital part of all development schemes in the year 2000 and beyond. With the South East becoming increasingly congested, and with the rapid growth in telecommunications and information technology, business will increasingly turn to other regions to satisfy its property needs.

23. Finally, all port areas have one other characteristic which does not always afflict other development sites but which can have a significant impact on the timing and manner of redevelopment. This is the enabling Act of Parliament which may need amending or repealing if closure or alteration to an existing harbour is required. The Harbour Acts, which are of general application, impose further procedural constraints and both provide extra opportunities for opposition and objection which may only be tenuously linked to the works proposed.

24. But what of the form and style of development in 2000? Will we see significant changes from today? First generation developments in port areas were generally of a piecemeal nature and often involved initial public sector renewal of infrastructure. Housing, marinas, smaller scale industry and employment uses, hotels and catering as well as other leisure uses, were on the "standard list" together with retailing in appropriate locations. Examples can be seen in London Docklands, on the Isle of Dogs, Preston to the North West, and Swansea, South Wales. In all these cases public sector authorities took the lead, invested in infrastructure, and brought in the private sector to undertake the development itself. For reasons of public accountability, this often led to a situation where sites were marketed with a view to obtaining the maximum price, which is not always commensurate with creation of the best scheme. Nevertheless, the "profit motive" is in my view perfectly proper and should not be ignored by the public sector which should certainly be seeking the best value for money in all areas.

25. Early schemes, Surrey Docks in London for example, also tended to fill in redundant docks to create additional land without real consideration of the value of that water or water view to the eventual development. Although there may be circumstances where it is still, on balance, appropriate to remove the water and other redundant structures, there is and will continue to be an increasing desire to retain such physical features where possible.

26. There will be an increasing move towards leisure uses within waterfront redevelopment schemes. Not just the marina or boat park with museums and waterside walks, but a whole range of attractions and activities of a financially viable nature that bring much more life to the area and increase the length of the active day beyond the 9 a.m. to 6 p.m. period which is still commonplace in many city centre areas. Leisure is after all becoming an increasingly important part of all our lives as living standards continue to increase and hours of work potentially fall further. (Personal disposable income in the UK grew by approximately 23% from 1984 to 1987, or 5.3% per annum compound.) (Ref. 3). At the same time, the Tax and Price Index, apart from a short period in 1985, was well below 5%, only climbing to that level again at the end of 1988 (ref. 4). There are, of course, regional variations with the highest incomes in the South East and the lowest in Wales and Northern Ireland.

27. Our expenditure on leisure activities alone continues to grow at a faster rate. Over the same period, according to the Henley Centre for Forecasting, the market value of total UK leisure spending increased by 31% (ref. 5).

28. In spite of the current financial climate, I see no reason why these general trends should not continue to the end of the century and beyond.

29. Where schemes are "leisure led", these initial attractions, because of their high profile, can generate a higher public awareness and increased commercial confidence in the location. Other elements can then be added. The site can be marketed as the best residential location and also the best office location offering facilities and an ambience that cannot be matched elsewhere. Each individual element must not be considered in isolation, however. A comprehensive approach to planning the redevelopment will become increasingly important. This is to ensure that each part is not only successful in its own right but contributes to the success of the whole.

30. I referred earlier to the desire to retain existing water features where possible but the water area is a valuable part of the total site and must be used to best advantage. One way of achieving this is to build over the water and there are many examples of this, but perhaps the future will see us building <u>on</u> the water using purpose designed floating structures, not simply a traditional ship. This year the country's first floating hotel has been opened on an inland waterway at Northwich in Cheshire and as technology advances no doubt we will

see further examples. However, the viability of such projects must be carefully considered. The UK property investment market is very conservative and unless there is a remarkable transformation, floating structures will have to be appraised on the basis of much higher returns than comparable land based projects.

FINANCIAL CONSIDERATIONS

31. It goes without saying that all private sector development projects start from the premise that there must be a profit at the end of the day. It is vital that when considering a potential new project we carry out a careful financial appraisal. The concept and the dream are, in themselves, very important but must be tempered by harsh commercial realities. Equally, we must balance the pressures for short term gains against the prospects for longer term success.

32. In many cases the successful redevelopment and regeneration of port land will require the creation of a whole new level of values for the area. In order to do this the early phases may well be "loss leaders", especially where there is a need to clear the land and provide new services and other facilities for future development. The higher values are required to offset the high costs that I referred to earlier but values vary and, in general, decrease with distance from the South East, except in the case of retail values which tend to decrease with distance from the major shopping centres. But existing values, and even sensible projections for the future, may not be sufficient to offset the costs of these urban regeneration projects and in that case public sector assistance is essential if the project is to proceed. Because costs are relatively static and values decreasing, it follows that, in general, greater public assistance is needed the further we travel from the South East.

33. Grant assistance at present is available to the private sector through:-

(a) City Grant - administered by the DOE, it is aimed at large scale projects and priority is given to schemes within the 57 Inner Area Programme (IAP) authorities.

(b) Derelict Land Grant - available outside the 57 IAP areas. Grant is payable at a rate of 80% within the Assisted Areas and designated clearance areas. Elsewhere a rate of 50% applies.

(c) The Urban Programme - concentrated on smaller projects, it is available only in IAP or other designated areas. It is mainly used to finance local authority assistance to industry.

34. Other sources of assistance exist, through Urban Development Corporations which promote development, for example, by land assembly and the provision of infrastructure; through tax incentives, as in Enterprise Zones; within the Assisted Areas and Development Areas with discretionary grants to manufacturing industry; and through other bodies such as Regional Development Agencies and Tourist Boards.

35. Financial assistance is also available from EC sources but normally is channelled through central or local government. It has been aimed mostly at providing infrastructure and to assist in restructuring after industrial decline or change. The availability and importance of EC development aid to the UK appears to be declining.

36. The future of public sector assistance is of course a political issue and will depend on the policies of the party in power. Assuming that the present government remains, within the UK we will see a continuation towards even greater reliance on the private sector. Grants are no longer available automatically and each application will need to present a well argued case demonstrating, in advance, the real benefits that will be achieved. The emphasis is on greater "value for money" maximising the leverage of private investment, and the creation of new jobs and homes.

37. There are, however, some areas where the "market" may not be able to respond and where the private sector will not wish to pursue redevelopment. If adequate public sector investment is not available then development will not occur in those regions.

Fig. 3. St. Andrew's Dock, Hull before reclamation with derelict land grant aid.

THE ENVIRONMENT

38. We are seeing an increasing concern for the protection of our environment and without doubt this will continue into the future. The redevelopment of large areas increasingly requires a consensus approach, not only with the local planning authority but also with the local population, local business interests and a wide variety of environmental pressure groups. As developers we must be aware of these trends and ensure that our proposals and methods of presentation are suitably responsive. It is no longer enough simply to draw a red line around a site in support of an outline planning application. Much more is required illustrating the form and style of development proposed and assessing its impact on the economy and environment of the area. Impact studies are already required by law in some North American States and it may only be a matter of time before the same occurs here.

39. One particularly topical example of environmental concerns is the passage through Parliament of the Cardiff Bay Barrage Bill. The proposal to enclose the Taff and Ely River estuaries has been especially controversial on a number of counts:-

(a) the loss of tidal mudflats and the impact on bird life;

(b) the potential problems of water quality in the lake;

(c) the potential damage to property as a result of rising levels of ground water.

We wait to see whether the final point will be resolved early next year when further research on the subject should be presented to the Secretary of State. If approved, Cardiff Bay will be one of the major port development and urban regeneration projects of the 1990s and continuing beyond 2000.

40. Moves to reduce or prevent further development in the Green Belts and other rural areas will continue and will ensure a healthy demand for alternative sites within existing developed areas. As a result, there is likely to be increasing pressure to move industry and employment opportunities away from the congested South East. Building technology must also respond to environmental pressures with greater energy efficiency and new materials to replace those that are considered dangerous to health and safety as well as those from "non-renewable" sources such as tropical hardwoods.

41. Nor must the needs of the consumer be ignored. More attitude research is being undertaken to find out what the customer wants, sometimes with uncomfortable, but nevertheless valuable, results. The occupier is becoming more discerning, requiring better spatial standards, and a better general environment. Information technology will also continue to impose increasing demands on building design and specification.

42. All this suggests that there will be an even greater emphasis placed on marketing - as distinct from advertising - in the future. Not only will it be necessary to ensure acceptance of the development proposals in the first place but later on continued marketing and good management will be necessary to ensure that the completed project retains its position in the marketplace. This will be especially true for those developments, such as shopping and leisure, which need to attract visitors.

CONCLUSION

43. Much of the evidence for the location, extent and form of development in the year 2000 is with us already. Present trends to greater efficiency in port operations, increased financial pressures from central government, and potential privatisation will all combine to ensure that ports must make the most effective use of land assets. Greater environmental awareness will lead to more redevelopment within existing built areas and to new standards of building as well as the introduction of alternative materials.

44. We will demand continued improvements in our quality of life and have more time and money to devote to leisure activities. Port land offers unique opportunities to meet all these needs with well planned comprehensive schemes providing a full range of opportunities for leisure, for housing, and for employment. Many of these schemes are identified or underway today. For example, redevelopment of Southampton waterfront, the Cardiff Bay project to which I referred before, and the several schemes proposed on Tyneside, Teesside, and in London, Liverpool, and Glasgow.

45. Current events in Eastern Europe suggest that our economic ties to the Continent must continue to grow if we are to take full advantage of the opportunities there. This will put continued pressure on the South East resulting in demand for more development in the Regions which may need support and encouragement from central government where the private sector judges development to be potentially unprofitable.

46. Finally, we have all learnt from the experiences of others and the development industry is no exception. Waterfront developments and other projects, especially in North America, have been the model for similar schemes here. I'm sure that we will continue to draw on this experience. We must, however, beware of false comparisons. Living standards, national characteristics, climate, and local economic circumstances, may be considerably different. We must learn with care and ensure that our product is not just a copy but a "British original" incorporating only the best and most suitable ideas from abroad. In that way we will ensure continued success for the future.

REFERENCES

1. DAVIS LANGDON & EVEREST. Initial Cost Estimating - Infrastructure. Building Magazine 11th May 1990, p. 67.
2. HEALEY & BAKER RESEARCH SERVICES. National Office & Business Space Survey 1990.
3. REGIONAL TRENDS 24 - Table 12.6, p. 139. HMSO 1989.
4. SOCIAL TRENDS 20 - Table 6.5, p. 100. HMSO 1989.
5. HENLEY CENTRE FOR FORECASTING. Leisure Futures, Spring 1990 - quoted in Financial Times article "Roller-Coaster Ride for Leisure Groups", 12th May 1990.

8. A canal and port interface

M. D. JAPES, FICE, MIWEM, and T. F. PHILLIPS, BSc, MCIT, MCIM,
British Waterways

SYNOPSIS. This paper traces the historic background to the canal and port interfaces, identifies some examples of economic stress in survival against changing transport modes and investment needs and points to the probable forward courses for those docks to the year 2000.

HISTORICAL CANAL SYSTEM

1. In the middle of the 18th Century the Duke of Bridgewater developed a barge canal mainly for transporting coal from the Worsley Mines. The resulting Bridgewater Canal was the first canal built with public subscription. The new barge transport enabled the 7d per hundredweight price of coal in Manchester to be halved. This was what inland navigation systems were all about and led to canal investment mania. During the next 100 years canals were promoted throughout the country. These linked mineral resource or agricultural areas to industrial and town centres, as the transport mode of the industrial revolution.

2. Most of the inland system was for barges of about 7'0" beam and 20/25 tonnes capacity. However, many of the river fed navigations which linked to the four major estuaries of the Thames, Severn, Mersey and Humber were used by vessels at least twice that beam. Ports were developed close to the point where the navigation met the estuary to facilitate trans-shipment of cargoes to and from sea going ships.

3. In 1948, the canal companies existing at that time were nationalised. One specific exception being the Manchester Ship Canal Company. In 1962 the British Waterways Board was formed and since 1988 has traded as British Waterways.

4. Four canal/port interfaces (Figure 1.) are worthy of closer examination as each has adapted to measures of

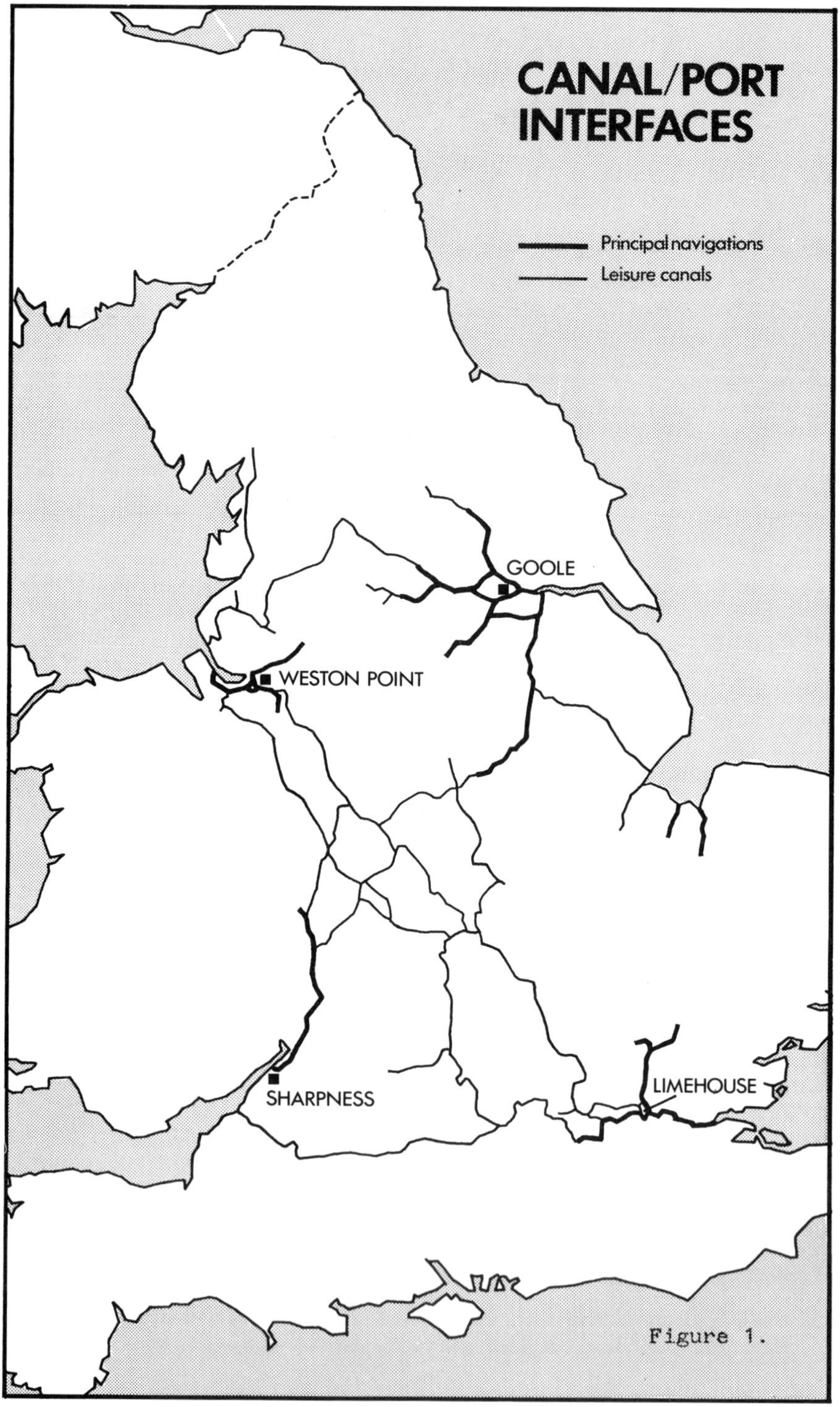
CANAL/PORT INTERFACES
Principal navigations
Leisure canals
GOOLE
WESTON POINT
SHARPNESS
LIMEHOUSE

Figure 1.

change which still continue in the struggle for commercial success.

5. Limehouse Basin was the old Regents Canal Dock. Access from the Thames was through a single ship lock in a period over the top of the high tide in the Thames. Maximum ship size would have been about 800 dwt and the impounded dock had been built with a large open water space and narrow quay areas, ideal for transferring cargo between ship and barge, particularly narrowboats. These could pass through the Regents Canal and via the Grand Union Canal to Birmingham and the north Midlands. As narrowboat carrying declined, the docks turned to using road transport, but the constraints of the site meant that this was never successful. 'Decasualisation' in 1967 soon led to the closure of the docks in 1969, except for the scrap metal terminal.

6. Sharpness Dock is the most upstream dock of the Severn Estuary and is therefore dependent on movements of ships on the tide for access through the tidal basin and lock into the dock level. The dock has four main quays which can receive 8000 dwt ships. From Sharpness to Gloucester some sixteen miles is a ship canal capable of carrying 1000 dwt ships mainly for oil products and timber. Beyond Gloucester, the River Severn can cater for 280 tonnes motor grain barges which, until recently, journeyed to Tewkesbury.

7. The Mersey estuary canal interface is at Weston Point Dock, Runcorn, poised between the Manchester Ship Canal and the Weston Canal which links with the Weaver Navigation to Northwich. Entrance is through a balancing dock, Delamere, held at a level approximately 300 mm above ship canal level. A knuckle restriction and mitred gate lay between Delamere and Tollemache Docks and above a swing bridge was the Old Basin and the Weston Canal. The docks were in this way sectioned into three operational areas all surrounded by quays but with portal cranes working those on the east side only.

8. At Goole, the Aire and Calder Navigation and other commercial inland waterway arms in the north east canal and river navigation system interface with the Associated British Ports complex in that town. Goole Docks, for example, had for a long time an infrastructure allowing inland movement of goods by road and rail as well as by waterway. It retained its backbone of business, which was the half million or so tonnes of coal moved yearly into the docks along the Aire & Calder Navigation by means of 'Tom Puddings'. This was a system allowing some 500 tonnes of coal to be moved in coupled barge units carrying

35 tonnes of coal apiece and the barge train pulled by tug. The barges were lifted by steam driven hoists so that the cargo could be tipped directly into the ship's hold. Invented in the 1860s by the engineer W.H. Bartholomew, the fleet ran profitably until closure only four years ago. In the period from 1965 Goole gained momentum and a greater business activity created by the increase in trade between the east coast ports of Great Britain and the continent of Europe.

CHANGES IN TRADE

9. Both canals and ports have seen changes to match with developments in trade and in transport. Up to the 1960s such changes were relatively slow and freight carrying in narrowboats continued, on a declining scale, right up to this time. The mid 1960s saw the beginning of containerisation on a wide scale; a development accelerated by 'decasualisation' of the dock workers in 1967.

10. At Weston Point and Sharpness Docks the flow of business brought to the docks by barges and narrowboats declined and by the early 1960s very little use was made of the docks for cargo handling. However both ports began to concentrate on using road transport for inland movement and prospered in the decade between 1965 and 1975. During this period trade through Sharpness showed a seven-fold increase.

11. Goole, Sharpness and Weston Point followed the general changes in the ports business which have taken place over the past 25 years and this has brought its own pressures both from the point of view of the market and of the maintenance and operation of the docks. The events that shaped the trade was brought about by two principle factors: the move to containerisation and the joining by Great Britain of the European Community.

12. In 1965 containerisation was a feature of trade only between Ireland and Great Britain and these trade routes led the market in the new business. Ten years later the traditional regular liner services to all parts of the world were largely containerised, including both deep sea and short sea services. 'LoLo' and particularly 'RoRo' became buzz words in the industry. Containerisation spelt death to the traditional lighterage business as practised on the Thames, Humber and Mersey. Such business relied on break-bulk cargo liner services operating on a regular scheduled basis. Henceforth barge movements meant cargoes being moved in bulk in craft with a capacity of up to 500 tonnes. This led to a dramatic change in the fortunes of

the waterway business, with British Waterways canal tonnage dropping from 7 million to 4½ million tonnes by 1980.

13. The accession of Britain to the Treaty of Europe led to a restructuring of the shipping industry, with an increasing concentration on trade with Europe, rather than the rest of the world. From around one-third of the market for imports and exports, Europe now counts for over half. This feature has been accentuated by the dominance of Rotterdam and Antwerp as deep sea terminals from which feeder services have brought goods to UK ports. The east coast ports in Britain grew and prospered, while many west coast ports withered.

14. Ships also became bigger, responding to economic pressure and the demand for bigger import and export freight consignments. The 750 dwt ship built in the 1950s became the 1000 dwt ship in the 1960s and the 1500 dwt ship in 1970s. 1980s building has been limited, but this sector now includes ships up to around 3000 dwt, many with low superstructures to assist deep penetration of inland waterways.

15. Intense competition in the ports led to rate 'wars' in cargo handling. Lower rates could only be profitable if investment was made in efficient new handling plant. Larger ships with bigger holds necessitated improved cranes with a bigger load carrying capacity, however this meant heavier cranes with higher quay loadings leading to problems on the quay surfaces and in quay wall stability.

16. The dock at Sharpness (Figure 2.) was limited by the dimensional constraint of its access lock to ships of about 2500 dwt but in the early 1970s to enable the dock to compete with the reduction of smaller sized ships, the tidal basin was used as a extension of the lock to enable larger and longer ships into the dock. In effect from the head gates of the lock to the tidal gates of the basin became one integral lock. Such use has had its penalties, firstly the water level fluctuations occurring in this period in the basin area has caused movement of water through the original rip rap protection to the soils which bank the basin at the higher water levels. The subsequent and repetitive draw down of water levels causes stripping out of fine material leading to slump of the rip rap. This has been repaired with concrete slab work but cracking exposes gaps through which this erosion continues with concentrated pump action. Secondly the increased quantities of water which need to be passed from the lock and its sluice culverts to the dock have generated excessive scour at the toe of the tidal basin side slopes

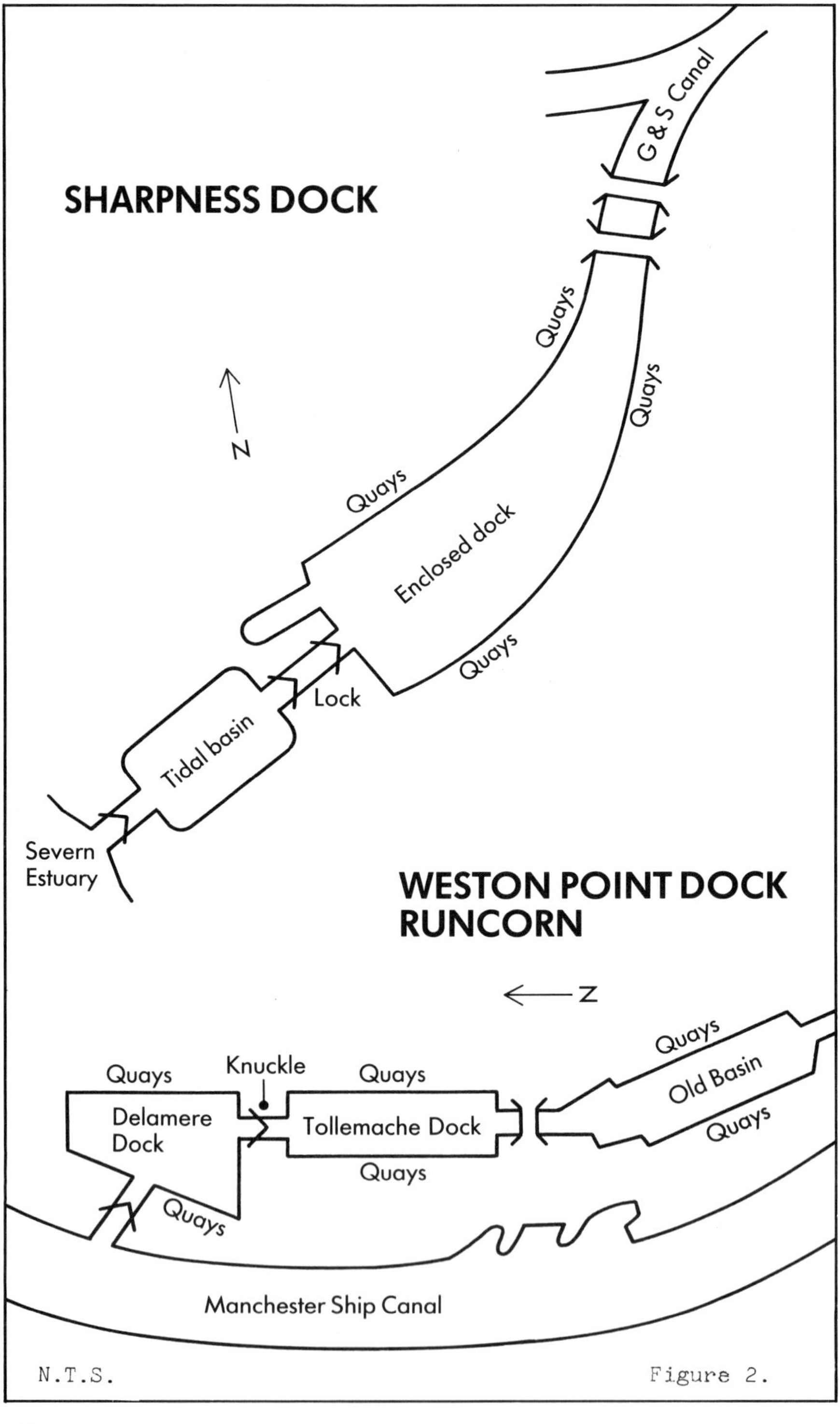
SHARPNESS DOCK
G & S Canal
Quays
Quays
N
Quays
Enclosed dock
Quays
Lock
Tidal basin
Severn
Estuary
WESTON POINT DOCK
RUNCORN
N
Quays
Old Basin
Quays
Quays
Knuckle
Quays
Delamere
Dock
Tollemache Dock
Quays
Quays
Manchester Ship Canal
N.T.S.

Figure 2.

which coupled with the foregoing problem has caused extensive sums to be spent to date in securing continuance of operation by maintaining the basin side slopes.

17. At Weston Point (Figure 2.) the problem was that the entrance gates to Delamere Dock from the Ship Canal were angled at about 70° to the line of the canal. With the quest to accommodate ships of increased dimensions vessels were constrained in their manoeuvring by the presence of the knuckle. This led in 1973 to the removal of the mitred gates at the knuckle and the knuckle itself. This enabled Delamere and Tollemache Docks to run together at one level as Delamache Dock above the entrance gates and with a common quay wall of 270 metres length on the east side, designed for the rail mounted portal cranes and a limited quay surcharge of 5cwts per sq ft.

18. Whereas this work enabled larger ships and deeper draughted ships to visit the dock, the quest for achieving improved turn round times led the dock management to abandoning the portal cranes in preference for heavier tracked mobiles. Unfortunately constant abuse of recommended quay edge safe working and loading criteria led to settlement of the quay and eventual failure of the quay wall. In 1986 this quay was stabilised by the installation of raking steel anchors.

19. However, the excessive construction costs of the two projects together with soaring crane costs and reducing dock throughput led to closure of the dock by directly operated BW arrangements and the setting up of a lease arrangement under which a private operator took over the activity. This in turn failed in early 1990 since when no shipping has been operated at the dock site.

THE NEED FOR INVESTMENT

20. From the days of the short lived 'National Plan' of the 1960s, there have been calls for a government policy on UK transport. Such calls have been continually resisted by whichever government was in power at the time and that remains the case today. However the clear objective of governments has been to improve the road infrastructure and this has led to the encouragement of road transport as the primary inland freight mode. The improvement of roads has led to the development of bigger (high tech) vehicles carrying heavier pay loads. The combination has been unbeatable in competitive terms, particularly compared with the capital starved infrastructure of railways and waterways.

21. Docks and shipping have fared no better. Governments have refused to subsidise ports and their development. Calls for help in the shipping industry have largely gone unheeded.

22. Such a situation is in stark contrast to that which exists on the European mainland, where governments have invested in transport infrastructure as a matter of direct policy. Massive investment in ports, for example Rotterdam and Zeebrugge, on land reclaimed on the seaward side of the port, have allowed the European ports to take over the principle business of Europe, relegating British ports to taking feeder services in many cases. The contrast between Britain and Europe in this context could not be greater. Shipping in Europe has perhaps not fared as well, although cabotage, or protection of trade, is still endemic in most of the European countries. It is very unlikely that the circumstances will change quickly even though Europe is supposed to have a free market after the end of 1992!

23. Nevertheless there are some splendid examples of new port investment in Britain, financed from private capital. Felixstowe is a prime example of such a development, which has led this once small terminal to become Britain's major container port. Likewise, Dover has become the gateway to Europe for wheeled transport. However the sheer number and spread of ports around the country and the intense competition which has existed between them, has seldom generated sufficient profit for reinvestment in port infrastructure. The ports on the west coast of Britain have been particularly badly hit because of the concentration on the European market for trade, which has left them largely isolated. Market forces, helped by environmental considerations, have led to the closure of a number of small ports, such as the recent example of Exmouth. These are generally marginal operations, catering for the smaller size of ship, themselves rapidly disappearing; an example indeed of market forces at work. Investment in new infrastructure in the face of declining markets is difficult to justify.

24. The former canal ports are good examples of the market forces which have brought us to the position we find in 1990. Goole and Sharpness remain busy active and generally profitable ports, with land surrounding them for industrial development, thus helping them to bring new business to use the docks. Goole, particularly, is very well located on the edge of the motorway network feeding the industrial heartland of England. Sharpness has a new road linking it with the main A38 and the M5 and avoiding narrow roads through built up areas. As a result the land

around the docks, until very recently almost entirely agricultural, has been redesignated for industrial development and has already attracted industry which will bring new traffic through the docks.

25. The examples of Goole and Sharpness are instructive. Goole, being on the east coast and geographically well located has a market niche in the operation and cargo handling of ships in the range up to 3000 to 4000 dwt, carrying mainly bulk cargoes and utilising rail, road and waterway transport for inland movement. Sharpness, on the less favoured west coast of Britain, has developed, just in time, a new industrial base which can take it into the 1990s with some level of confidence; again as a small port within a market niche.

26. Limehouse Basin is in the course of phased development by a joint venture partnership between the Hunting Gate Group Limited and British Waterways, comprising a mixed development of residential accommodation, offices, retail use which include a chandlery, public house/restaurant, community use and leisure use. Boat moorings, a marina and associated facilities will be retained in the basin. Weston Point Dock is also currently unused, although still potentially a viable small port operation capable of accepting ships up to around 2500 dwt. It lacks land for suitable associated port development and hardly has a unique position in the market. It is indeed like a number of other wharves and docks on the Mersey Estuary, looking for a tenant.

THE FUTURE - 2000

27. Can the experiences of the past decade be used to predict what will happen by 2000? Clearly environmental considerations are going to play an even greater part in the decade to come, but how much difference will this make to the events leading up to the new millennium? Higher standards of living and industrial growth are still the watch words. The Europe of 1993 and beyond, with the frontier controls down, may well assist such a development and will certainly increase the movement of goods between the member countries. Gross Domestic Product (GDP) is generally considered to be the best single predictor of traffic levels and it should not escape attention that both Germany and France already have a higher GDP and corresponding traffic levels than Britain. Economic growth therefore means more freight traffic, and with 80% of freight already going by road there is no panacea to be had in directing road freight to rail and water. Nevertheless any shift in the balance will help and it is

almost certain that extra encouragement, through government grants and other incentives, will be given to rail and waterway freight to assist in bringing additional business.

28. The bigger ports in Britain are already looking for major development and this has been greatly assisted by the ending of the Dock Labour Scheme. The very reason why the traffic moved up river may well see a reversal. However much of the upriver business is at small wharves and ports which are efficient and relatively modern in terms of capital investment in the infrastructure. Growth in trade arising from decisions of the European Community and from policy of continued growth, should ensure that the efficient and well managed ports and upriver wharves will survive and, indeed, flourish. The major ports are likely to invest in, for example, bulk handling terminals for 'Cape' size ships of 110,000 dwt. More business will therefore enter the United Kingdom direct without the need for trans-shipment at continental ports.

29. However a sizeable shake out can reasonably be predicted of ports with infrastructure which will require massive maintenance expenditure. East coast ports and operations can generally be expected to survive more easily than those in the west. Market forces may in the end be the best answer, although this will be a bitter pill for many businesses. It should still be a cause for concern in Britain that infrastructure investment on the European continent is likely to continue on a massive scale through government agencies, despite the open barriers and continued emphasis on 'level playing fields'.

30. For the waterways themselves the trends which became clear in the 1980s will continue into the 1990s. Those waterways that are navigable by ships in the range from 1200 to 2500 dwt will be in the right competitive league to stay in the freight business. Similarly those inland waterways that can accept barges of at least 500 tonnes capacity can also expect continued business and will benefit from some of the government incentives for industry to find alternative means of transport. These initiatives will reflect the environmentally friendly barge, each of which replace nearly twenty lorries with their noise and air pollution problems. There is very little case to be made to invest in enlarging waterways if the capital has to be found from private sources and interest paid on the principal, with the provision for depreciation. Roads will continue to be built on current account, thus attracting no capital charges. The 'playing field' between the three transport modes in Britain will remain anything but level and the waterways will remain

firmly undeveloped to modern class IV and higher European standards.

31. New waterway business will require new barges which will only be built if an adequate return on capital can be shown. The emphasis will be on improving productivity through, for example, specialised barges operated on a push-tow principle which will maximise both the size of craft using the waterway and craft utilisation. On busy waterways there will be a greater use of automation of control systems and these should speed the movement and flow of craft.

32. The result of the above is the likely continuation in active freight mode of the most well developed waterways. An example of the navigations that should prosper are those leading into the Humber Estuary; namely the Rivers Ouse and Trent and the Aire & Calder and South Yorkshire Navigations. These waterways will also benefit from the development of bulk cargo terminals on the estuary from where barge transport to power stations and industrial plants in the region will provide a major boost to waterway freight.

33. The Thames should continue its important role, provided wharves can somehow be kept from being developed for purposes other than cargo handling. Indeed, as a general principle, land must be available adjacent to waterways for industrial development and this must receive the encouragement of local authorities. Otherwise even the best freight waterways of Britain will clearly decline. Government money might well be considered for keeping suitable land for industrial development, where it might otherwise go for investment which would be more profitable in the short term.

34. Low superstructure sea-going ship already provide the versatile transport form for inland penetration on larger waterways; these will prosper and numbers will grow. Both the specialised ships and conventional ships up to 3000 dwt will continue to trade profitably and to meet the growing volume of business across the North Sea. Smaller ships, many of them now age expired, will not be replaced. This will lead to closure of some of the docks and small wharves around the country which can only accept ships up to 1000 dwt. Unless specialised new business can be found for them they will, by the year 2000, have been redeveloped for purposes outside the freight industry.

35. In the last twenty, but significantly in the last ten, years increased demand has existed for the application of the growing free time of the populus. The

shorter working week, unemployment/redundancy, early retirement, a healthier nation of long life expectancy have all made their contribution. Much of this free time, possibly due to our island existence, is attracted to water and related activities.

36. Leisure uses of waterways have in this period significantly increased in the areas of fishing, towing path walking and cruising. In fact, a 20% growth is recorded in these activities in the last three years. To match the cruising growth additional facilities are required for mooring and marina type developments. Old dock facilities are ideal, providing deep water and secure mooring areas.

37. In parallel the combined effort of government led initiatives to raise environmental standards of inner cities and the advent from the mid-1980s of significant enhancement of both commercial and residential property values with the promotion of the 'added value' of the use of water in a development setting has caused an 'explosion' of development with water and leisure adjuncts which in their turn threaten freight options for the future use of old dock areas.

38. Limehouse is an example of development for new non freight purposes which is likely to be reflected at other docks in the next decade. This takes advantage of the enhanced property values of water-associated land and the rise in demand for boating and water-based leisure activities.

39. Of the other canal ports, Weston Point will see new development for light industry on much of its area, but the larger dock could still offer scope for commercial cargo handling. Sharpness will continue to trade within its specialised niche market, much assisted by the adjacent industrial development. A major increase in traffic may well require massive investment in the wharf and dock infrastructure and this again will be unlikely to generate a favourable return on investment without a generous grant, or through ploughing profits from property and land development into port operations. Marina and leisure developments would be a logical development outside the main port.

40. Goole, again operating in a narrow but on-going market area, should continue to prosper. The close association with the waterways will assist both docks and waterways in maintaining a good level of business into the next century. New industrial development within the port area should yield profit which can, to some extent, be

ploughed back into the business to ensure a sound infrastructure.

41. In summary, therefore, the canal/port interfaces will only survive in their transport role if the market opportunities remain and if there is also a will and commitment to provide the supporting investment to modernise the business. Intervention by government is likely in the form of grants for barge and associated infrastructure, where the environmental benefits are of sufficient strength. If such criteria do not apply, and this will be the position in many cases, property development values will dictate an alternative development with water-based leisure and commerce.

9. Waterside development in old docks

P. LACEY, FICE, FIStructE, FIHT, FFB, FRSA, Ove Arup and Partners

SYNOPSIS A quick resume will be made of the reasons why dock basins have become dilapidated and unused. The potential of such land, water and banks will be discussed and will include the amenities of water, access, services and the proximity to large communities. The initial filling in of old docks has been stopped and such sites have become a subject of regeneration. The residential waterside developments, leisure use, marinas and restoration of old buildings will be examined. The future use of old docks will be assessed and will include:

- Regeneration of previous developments consistent with the improvement of the economic climate.
- Increase in leisure use, water quality improvement, water sports, heritage and boat parks, conference venues, inner city parklands and sites for non-water sports.

INTRODUCTION

1. New techniques in cargo handling, ship design and changing economic climates and patterns have caused the progressive closure of many of Britain's older docks.

2. Why have dock basins become dilapidated? What has happened and what does the future hold? Firstly then why have docks and dock basins become dilapidated and unused?

3. Dock areas have always been large walled areas. Security has generally been high and they have not been people places as we know the term today as the public has not been able to access the river frontages. What has been left is vast hectares of urban desolation in prime parts of the city and mostly with direct access to the sea either by river or canal systems. Even this important route has been ignored for many years. The residual areas were not tidied up but left with decaying buildings and sub-structures. Figure 1.0 shows such a site, Salford Docks, Manchester Ship Canal, 1957 and Figure 2.0 shows just up canal Pomona Docks.

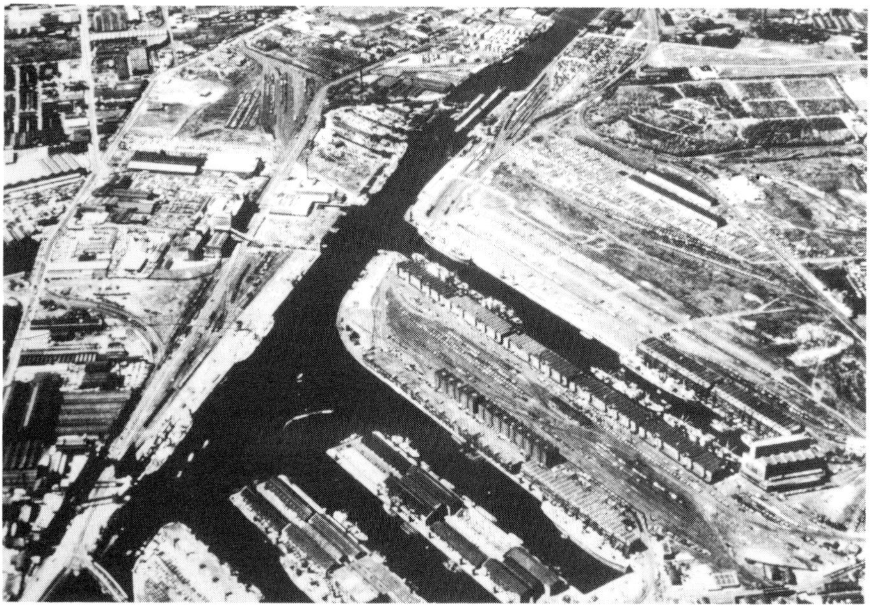

Figure 1.0 Salford Docks, Manchester Ship Canal 1957

Figure 2.0 Pomona Docks

4. Dr E F Schumacher wrote "Small is beautiful" in 1973 and it is a phrase that has been repeated many times since then. This phrase has not however applied to the transport industry where the quest for ever more economy of scale in the transport of goods and passengers has resulted in larger planes, trucks and ships.

5. In the 1950's the first jet passenger plane carried 40 passengers, 20 ton trucks were restricted to 40 mph and 10,000 ton general cargo ships plied the seas at a stately 8 knots, 10 with the more modern vessels.

6. With cross channel ferries now in the 12,000 - 15,000 ton range and container ships of 60,000 tonnes travelling at 25/26 knots it is not difficult to see how the size of ships has changed dramatically and with the change the need for deeper water alongside the unloading berth. These days it is not uncommon for a minimum of 12 metre water depth to be specified.

7. With the need for deeper water and ever faster turnaround times demanded for increased efficiency, a natural trend for ports to move down river towards the sea took place. In the United Kingdom the London docks gave way to Tilbury, whilst Southampton and Felixstowe both with 24 hour deep water and quick access to the open sea, thrived.

8. The change to containers also produced another effect. Instead of offloading cargo into barges for onward transhipment further up river or via canal to quayside warehouses for unpacking, sorting and distribution, containers could be loaded onto lorries at the port for delivery direct to the recipient. Thus changes in transport technology had a dramatic and lasting effect not only to the major ports themselves but the hearts of our cities situated on the network of rivers and canals that spread right the way across the country.

9. The process of ships and their corresponding docks growing in size is not new being more or less continuous and only restrained by the materials and skills available.

10. At West Ferry Circus, part of the Canary Wharf project in the London docklands, where design of a new 500 metre length of river wall is in progress, no less than 3 slipways and 8 docks are known to have existed. One of the largest, Union Dry Dock, having been built across and on top of older slipways and Lower Union Dock all now filled in. Until relatively recently, filling in was the usual treatment for many old docks with the space created being used for additional storage for the new larger docks being constructed. Often this was done without any real plan or strategy.

11. The mega jump in ship sizes producing new ports further downstream had a much greater impact on the old port areas. Whilst the shipping companies and port employers concentrated on keeping in business, the old areas now derelict were left to decay for a considerable time.

12. In the early 1980's when the economy began to improve and firms wanted to expand several individuals and companies began to realise that the old dock areas provided large areas of relatively cheap land, in many cases at or near the existing business centres. Businesses need people and people need homes. Marketing experts and others became aware that properties built near water with space and/or views across water could command prices two or three times that of a similar property on a typical estate and so preservation of the open water spaces became an economic proposition and a central theme for many developments. The problems of finding vast quantities of suitable fill material and removing silt from the derelict docks were also solved.

WHAT HAS HAPPENED

13. I have described how the economic climate changed, businesses wanted to expand and how the large open spaces of the old docks became attractive.

14. The existence of the City Airport with flights to and from the continent situated less than 20 minutes from the City centre gives some indication of the amount of space available.

15. The early developments tended to be of the light industrial type which gradually changed to offices then shops and houses.

16. To encourage businesses into the new areas the Government created development zones and the necessary infrastructure had to be provided which took time.

Figure 3.0 St Katherines Dock

Figure 4.0 Shadwell Basin Development

17. The residential developers emphasised the leisure use of the water areas and in many instances marinas were created, the backdrop of yachts producing a good maritime atmosphere whilst providing an income from the preserved water areas. In many cases this atmosphere has been enhanced by the refurbishment and renovation of existing port buildings either into pleasant offices and flats as at St Katherines Dock, shown in Figure 3.0, or the old Billingsgate Fish Market nearby. The Shadwell Basin Development is shown in Figure 4.0.

18. More recently Swansea and Hull docks were refurbished and revitalised by turning them into marinas with mixed developments. What is more astonishing is that although leisure craft were previously of minimal numbers both marinas are now at capacity.

19. Providing the basic fabric of the building is in sound condition it has been proved many times that refurbishment is economic and in many instances enables planning applications to be rapidly approved. Renovated docks are becoming the focal points for new business opportunities not only in London where Canary Wharf is well known but others in Limehouse Basin (Figure 5.0), Southampton, Port Pendennis (Figures 6.0 and 7.0), Liverpool, Newcastle and probably one of the most successful to date Salford Quays where part of the Manchester Ship Canal docks have been turned into a successful business, commercial and residential area. See Figures 8.0 to 12.0.

THE FUTURE

20. Where do we go from here. The potential of large or smaller tracts of land is still commercially attractive.
With the present climate of high interest rates causing a slow down in property sales it is inevitable that changes will occur, indeed are occurring. Many of the large schemes underway will be slowed down or in some cases virtually stopped until market demand picks up which financial experts tell us will be next year. In the meantime with smaller developers now fully aware of the development potential of waterside locations and the larger developers opting for smaller but more "exclusive" projects the search is on nationally for suitable sites. These will most likely be found along the 4000 miles or more of inland waterways and rivers. Once found I believe that office or residential properties will prevail with high quality developments being blended to match with the local environment.

Figure 5.0 Limehouse Basin

Figure 6.0 Port Pendennis

Figure 7.0 Port Pendennis

Figure 8.0 Salford Quays

Figure 9.0 Salford Quays

Figure 10.0 Salford Quays

Figure 11.0 Salford Quays

Figure 12.0 Salford Quays

21. The one major lesson that has been learnt is that good planning is essential for any waterside project to be successful. With water quality, pollution and environmental being the 'buzz' words of the moment, guidance is needed to comply with all the various authorities and legal requirements to be met. With the right guidance however these can and have been overcome to the advantage of all concerned.

22. The regeneration of old disused docks and run down river fronted sites has presented the engineer with a series of problems. Most of these problems are not new but have become complicated by the sites chosen, the type of redevelopment chosen and the time period. The schemes are getting more ambitious (see Figure 13.0 News Quays, Newcastle and Figure 14.0 Custom House Dock, Dublin).

23. Experience gained from developments of old docks and riverside sites indicate that many aspects need to be addressed.

24. The closing of existing basins and the need to produce new promenades or edges poses many design problems. Some of these are set out below.

(a) Depth of soft material overlying the dock bottom such as silt, mud, etc, which could cause problems when attempting to fill for the purpose of providing developable land.

(b) Composition of the soft material or any other dumped material in the case that toxic substances may be present or that methane generation in the future could cause a problem. Poor quality fill in existing basins or graving docks can produce problems with foundations.

(c) The existing dock or river walls with respect to their condition at present and the loading which they might be subjected to arising from the requirements of the development.

(d) The water level which may be either retained at a nearly static level or some intermediate levels between the tides.

(e) Proposed usage of the dock basin either for leisure or other uses. Any requirements for navigable access into the basin will need to be considered with those of (d) above.

Figure 13.0 News Quays, Newcastle

Figure 14.0 Custom House Dock, Dublin

(f) The quality of the existing water and the future standard of water quality needed by the development must be assessed.

(g) Position of buried obstructions, ducts and services which are very common in urban/dockland sites.

(h) Position of buildings or loads near existing walls.

(j) Design life required by authorities.

25. As most developments have water areas as part of their saleable ambience the engineer must consider the usage of these water areas:

- Are locks or retaining gates required?

- What water depth and retained water level is needed?

- How can these water areas which are retained have their quality improved to allow leisure activities?

- If bridges are required can they be of a permanent type with all the headroom and landtake problems or should a lifting or swing type be provided?

26. All these issues have their own engineering problems.

27. Looking further into the future, it is a well established fact that moving freight by waterway is the most fuel efficient method per tonne per mile with rail being more than 40% and road 300% greater. With the increase in traffic the Channel Tunnel and 1992 will bring it may be that with the roads clogged and the cost of new railways high, inland waterways may well become an economic way of moving freight once again. This in turn could lead to an upsurge of commercial waterside development or would it? I leave you to consider the point and come to your own conclusions.

28. Developable flat land is desirable. Serviced flat land near existing populaces and communications is more desirable. Water frontages will still appear worth that little extra capital. See Figure 15.0 Heron Quays.

29. Docks and dock lands and equivalent sites up canals and rivers will continue to become people places and targets for private/public sector development.

Figure 15.0 Heron Quays

Figure 16.0 Port Pendennis

30. When the economic climate is right more marinas/residential development will continue. It should be remembered that such marinas raise the quality of the old dilapidated docklands, increase employment and attract spending. See the Port Pendennis vista produced in Figure 16.0.

31. If this does not appeal then the areas should be landscaped using the water as a facility and turn them into people places until other planning strategies can be devised. Why not inner city parklands. From this would follow leisure use, water sports, heritage usage and sport facilities. It may be that regeneration of the present developments may occur. What is very clear however that all new uses or development schemes will receive rather special attention by way of Environment Impact Studies, not the least of these being water quality, noise, etc.

32. What has been made very clear since the London Docklands Development Corporation and Salford Docks schemes is that you need vision not planning by expedient.

33. My conclusions are as follows:

- People are being encouraged back to the waterfronts - that is good.

- There is better cooperation between architects and engineers - that is good.

- Engineers are entering professional teams formed by developers at concept stage - that is very good.

ACKNOWLEDGEMENT

34. I thank John Faulkner of the Maritime Engineering Department of Ove Arup and Partners for his help in preparing this paper and his help in our previous existence together.

REFERENCES

1. LACEY P. The Changing Face of Marina Development in the United Kingdom. PIANC Bulletin No. 59, 1987.

2. LACEY P. Urban Waterside Development in the United Kingdom. Ports 2000, Barcelona, Spain, December 1989.

3. HINDLE B R, JOHNSTON D T, KEMPTON R C, MORGAN J H. Salford Docks Urban Renewal: Design, Construction and Management of Civil Engineering Works. Institution of Civil Engineers Proceedings, Part 1, February 1990.

Discussion on Papers 7–9

A. J. VAUGHAN, Shoreline Port Authority
Could Mr Griffiths give an indication of rates of return achieved in the redevelopment of ports for housing/marina purposes. Assuming that these rates are higher than those achieved in some port operations, does he believe that the newly privatized shareholder-driven trust ports (to be) will themselves move away from port operations towards such types of redevelopment?

D. PALMER, Tees and Hartlepool Port Authority
What parameters do Associated British Ports adopt, in the opinion of Mr Griffiths, with respect to surplus port land, in deciding whether to reserve it for strategic port purposes or to develop it immediately for commercial non-port related purposes?

R. D. DAWSON, W. A. Dawson Ltd
I understand British Waterways has invested in enlarging the locks on the Rotheram Canal. Has this investment proved successful in increasing traffic on the canal?

P. S. LUCAS, Mersey Docks and Harbour Company
How long do the Authors expect the vogue for waterside developments to continue? Is the present downturn in the property market going to end the fashion?

I would like to return to two points made in reply to earlier questions. The first is the use of an income stream from a development to fund maintenance of a (canal) system.

The second is the difference in level between dock water and quay surface. It is important that, when considering development schemes, provision is made for the future maintenance of the quay walls and that this is associated as far as possible with income from the development. The cost of providing impounded water can present similar problems of cost allocation. Whereas certain developments may be able to justify the cost of minimizing leakage, the Merseyside Development Corporation, for instance, have opted for lowering water levels to approach mean tide levels. The object is to minimize impounding which would introduce silt into the system, which would in turn have to be removed.

D. COOPER, Associated British Ports Research and Consultancy Ltd
With the increasingly dry summers that we now experience, do British Waterways see a future for a national water grid in conjunction with the National River Authority?

S. M. THOMAS, Bertlin and Partners
I would like to add to the discussion on whether ports with land which is unsuitable for port use should sell it or go into joint venture for its redevelopment. It all depends on the situation. In one port in the British Isles where we are currently working, we felt that the option to sell would involve less risk and would provide immediate revenue; this could then be used for cleaning up or other modernization. In fact, cleaning up could well be a prerequisite to realizing the best sale value for the adjacent land. A further point is that some ports may be debarred by their constitution from joint venture participation in developments which are non port-related.

E. LOEWY, Sir William Halcrow and Partners Ltd
It is essential for urban housing port redevelopments to retain water level in old basins not more than 1 m below quay level at all times. How can this be achieved?

D. J. GRIFFITHS Paper 7
The rates of return achieved on property development vary with the nature of the development and for the land owner depend on whether he is a direct investor or simply selling a site. ABP are not housing developers and have realized value so far from land sales and profit sharing with other developers.

If the values or rates of return are greater than those in existing use for port operation, I am sure that any future privatized ports will act to maximize the value of their land assets.

In most cases the decision to release land for non port-related purposes is an obvious one because the land is unsuitable for future port use, for example, because of its size, location, or suitability for modern port operations. There are, of course, marginal situations and in those areas it is important to maintain a flexible approach, e.g. ABP have recently, because of the abolition of the National Dock Labour

Scheme, brought land back into port-related use that had previously been considered for alterative commercial development. The short answer is that the decision needs to address what is in the best overall interests of the company at the time.

I expect that the vogue for waterside developments will continue but none of us can predict what the future holds with absolute certainty. The present economic situation, however, will undoubtedly change at some time in the future and past experience suggests that there will be a continuing upward trend in land values and the attractiveness of waterside locations in the long term.

M. D. JAPES Paper 8

In response to the question by R. G. Dawson, it was unfortunate that following the Government's agreement to the Sheffield and South Yorkshire navigation improvement scheme, there was a major industrial recession in the UK. This had such a severe effect that the companies who are related to the identified tonnages, which justified the navigation improvement, collapsed before completion of the improvement scheme. Little traffic was in fact moving initially but there has been a considerable upsurge in recent years as a result of new tonnages identified for the navigation. However the scheme is still less than a commercial success as a result of the effects of recession.

In response to P. S. Lucas, the downturn in the property market will definitely affect the phasing of development schemes at the waterside. However the demand for the added value of a waterside situation continues together with the demand for mooring and marina facilities, which are not exclusively dependent on the property market. It is important that the income streams from developments depend on the success of integrated businesses, of which one element is property. In the experience of British Waterways, such developments would usually include a marina base, chandlery, pub, restaurant or hotel complex.

In a redeveloped dock area careful regard must be taken of future dock wall maintenance. In some cases the dock wall will be structurally integral with building development. Where the continued maintenance is not the responsibility of the navigation authority, transfer of maintenance obligation will be to the developer, who may be a joint venture company. In such cases, care needs to be taken to ensure the security of long-term maintenance funding in agreements entered into with developers.

To minimize the effects of silt drawn into the system the development at Limehouse Basin in London incorporates a smaller tidal lock suited to the class of vessels requiring access from the River Thames with sector lock gates designed to resist tow-directional pressures, a feature not incorporated in the original mitred gates.

In answer to D. Cooper, the use of the British Waterways canal system for a national water grid was investigated by the Water Resources Board many years ago and found not to provide an appropriate facility. The difficulty is that the transfer of large quantities of water around the country would depend as far as possible on gravity. Canals have summits and valley pounds which would mean either an enormous quantity of pumping or a mix of environmentally unacceptable aqueducts and very deep tunnelling works to effect the gravity system.

P. LACEY Paper 9

In reply to Mr S. M. Thomas, I repeat what I said in my presentation. In my view, unless there are enormously pressing reasons why land should be sold to others, then land owners should not give up the ownership but keep control of developments, re-use etc., and if possible, enter into a partnership with a developer and help shape, control and enjoy the profits.

Mr Loewy's question regarding retained water level in old basins has partially been answered by Mr P. S. Lucas. However, much depends on the level of the existing quay walls, whether they can be stepped down, the outside water levels and whether a locking system is used or not. Experience in docklands has given us a set of approximate rules.

	Type	Water depth	Cope to water level
Band 1.	Ornamental ponds	0.5 m	Below 1.0 m
2.	Basins	Exceeds 0.5 m	Below 2.0 m
3.	Basins	Exceeds 1.5 m	Below 2.0 m
(Edges protected by fencing. Grab chains at water level)			
4.	Basins, deep rivers, canals.	Deep water	N/A
(Fences, walls at least 1.0 m high)			

Examples of all these types can be found at Shadwell basin (Wapping), Greenland Dock (Surrey Quays), Glasgow Garden Festival, Western Docks (Wapping) and Easton Dock Canal.

10. Use of computers in future port design

R. H. BRIDGE, MA, FICE, MIEAust, PE(Singapore), MConsE, G. Maunsell and Partners

1. It is my intention to set out the case supporting the use of more complex reviews and analyses in Port Development work and to try to see in my crystal ball how this trend will go forward. Others will, I believe, be more specific on certain aspects and case studies of this work, but I will try to paint the broad picture to begin. First, it is appropriate to look at a definition of where a port should be situated. "A port is ideally where sheltered deep water directly connected to the open sea is adjacent to low level firm dry land which has direct access to an expanding hinterland."

2. What is so difficult and complex about that statement that causes us to feel we must use electronic brains to solve it for us? That definition has been consistently valid for centuries and man, being the opportunist that he is, has found most of the great harbours and ports of the world already constructed for him by nature. Exploitation of such natural locations has been the basis for significant impacts on human geography and has caused the establishment of both cities and nations. To illustrate this point it is only necessary to list the natural harbours of the world such as Sydney, Auckland, Hong Kong, San Francisco - there are many more. From these natural harbours grew the transport networks to service them and the trade routes to ply through them. These trade patterns in turn became the driving force which dictated the development and expansion of ports over the years. However as ships using them developed and changed, so the definition of the natural port had to be revised and extended. The words "deep water" could originally be applied to three to five metres (10 to 15 feet of old measure) while "access to the open sea" could be defined as 10km winding along a tidal river or estuary. This is a far cry from the present minimum depth of 15m for general cargo, while vessels carrying bulk cargo and oil require considerably more, and their access requirements are a sweeping well buoyed channel with sufficient width to enable these less manoeuvrable ocean-going vessels to pass.

(Their steering and propulsion are designed for efficiency on the open sea, rather than for nimbleness in docking.) Therefore as ports became developed and expanded, compromises had to be made and the old criteria for natural harbours had to be re-examined. In some cases existing harbours could be easily adapted to new conditions by extending the berthing line or by buoying an access channel. Frequently, however, the only solution to changing needs was to create a new port site where the basic definition of an ideal port site as stated earlier was not provided by nature.

3. A key element in modern port design is the sea to land interface, whether it is a shelving beach, a tidal estuary or a rocky shore. This interface is an ever changing balance between land and sea, which is in some cases very stable, but in others a fragile one and it is this that engineers have to consider when creating the missing features of the ideal port site. These may involve the improvement of "access to the open sea" by dredging or "provision of low lying firm land" by reclamation, or the provision of a "sheltered harbour" by breakwater construction. Any of these elements will affect the land-sea balance and it is their impact on this which is the main concern of port designers now and will be in the future.

4. Having examined the increasing difficulty of providing an ideal port it is easy to see why computing has been applied to solving the engineering problems. To show how useful a tool it has become, the following table indicates the relative magnitude of various design tasks associated with port design.

Table 1. Analytical capacity required to solve engineering tasks

Analysis of gravity retaining wall	1
Analysis of piled retaining wall	3
Analysis of wharf deck	5
Analysis of breakwater armour	20
Analysis of wave action and refraction	50
Analysis of tidal regimes	200
Analysis of siltation regimes	300

5. This table is a gross simplification, but it does identify the increasing complexities of various analytical problems. In the past there have been ways of short circuiting the total analytical requirements. Ideally this has also been supplemented by experimentation and by physical modelling. By this means the complexity of these problems has been addressed and reduced so that they might be more readily handled by the designers. But, as the analytical complexity of port design work has increased, so has the available computer power. See below.

	Year	Power
Initial Analytical Computing	1960	1
Desk Top Calculation	1970	1
In-House Main Frame Computing	1970	10
Desk Top Computing	1980	10
Higher Powered Main Frame Computers	1980	100
In House Desk Top Networked Systems	1990	500

Table 2. Increase in computing power available to engineers

6. This table is again simplified and I offer it, not as a computer expert, but as someone who has had to use computers and who sees them purely from the user's view point. Over the years they have had a considerable impact on the engineering profession. As you can see, their use stretches from 1960 to the present, a period of 30 years; this is a comparatively short time but during it we have moved from the ability theoretically to analyse basic port structures to the capacity for analytical modelling of complex wave, tidal and siltation regimes. The power of computing has kept us abreast of the increasing demands of modern port design. It is small wonder therefore that to achieve an economical design we frequently depend greatly on the computer. But at this point it is necessary to issue the statutory health warning: computers analyse, they do not think. At least those computers commonly available to engineers are not the thinking type, although artificial intelligence computing is going to be significant in the future when computers can be used to think as well as to analyse. Even then, however, their "intelligence" will only be that of the programmer.

7. To sum up, the extension of the use of the computer into port design is no longer merely analytical, but now also covers modelling. To my mind the implication of this is the

need to gather and have available accurate natural data: the data of wind, wave, soil, pollution, sediment, and topographical survey. Since we can now model so much of what we propose to do, it is pointless modelling the wrong thing. This does not of course mean that before any proposal is put forward, a year has to be spent on surveying; but it does mean that at the outset comprehensive modelling of the proposed locations of the port should be carried out. This model should initially be based upon the best assumptions drawn from the information available. The model should be constructed to accept the input of more accurate physical data obtained subsequently as the designs evolve and to confirm and record the appropriateness of the design concepts put forward and their robustness to perform against the physical information being fed into the computer.

8. I hope that I have shown the way that computers have graduated from analysers to modellers. This is not to say that analysis has been left behind. Analysis still needs to be done. It still proves the adequacy of specific elements of port design. But it is in modelling that I think the greatest strides have been made in the last five years and it is in modelling in which the greatest strides will be made in the future.

9. Now I shall turn to another subject, which concerns not the present use of computers, but a task for their future use. Most advances in design are driven by a need to limit the construction cost of a facility to one which justifies the feasibility of the project. One such area is the design of significant breakwaters. These are usually considerable in length but defined by relatively few dimensional parameters. Together with the obvious need to control construction costs, there is the opposite constraint of the possibility of failure of such a critical item. The events of the early 1980s when there were five noted failures brought out the need for considerable further study of the nature of breakwaters to understand their behaviour. Currently there is a significant effort being put in on the analysis of the breakwater cross section under the influence of wave attack. In the past this has very much been the preserve of the physical modeller, a situation which should continue because it is the performance of physical models that is always required to calibrate the ultimate theoretical analysis put forward. However it is hoped that before long the detailed complexities of the build-up of water pressures within the core of the breakwater will be tackled by computer simulation and therefore better understood, so that methods of alleviating this build-up can be found. Indeed such knowledge may well exist already in an academic form and encouragement is required from engineers for its commercialisation and application in the design office. An understanding of the core, together with the advances made

in the design of the armouring of breakwaters and revetments, will create a considerable advance in this technology.

10. Significant work is currently underway on the analysis of single layer armour units: these are the voided blocks which are placed regularly on revetments and breakwaters. These blocks appear to perform well both in model and in real life. However the theory behind their performance is not yet fully understood, and it is important that this should be thoroughly researched so that current installations can be further developed and new applications of the technology be made, based upon a proven theoretical analysis.

11. Now let me turn to the future and address port operators and owners. In all that I have said, I have talked only about the design of ports, but there are also many aspects of the physical operation of ports for which the computer is now significantly used. I would make the plea for all significant data concerning ports to be held in computer form. The days when computer data was restricted to a certain type of hardware or a certain type of program are now thankfully behind us. We can now establish large data bases of topographical data, ordnance survey information, etc. Now as ports are designed and built the data concerning their physical arrangement and services can be held on a computer, so that in the future when changes and expansion and modification are required, we will already have the data on the existing facilities available around which to base proposals for expansion and modification. Gone should be the days of the data base being rolls of drawings stored in a tin box which constitute the as-built drawings of the facility from 10 years before which have never been changed and updated since. This system should be replaced by the port managers' staff using a simple CAD system and a plotter on which they can continually have access to the up-to-date physical parameters and arrangement of their port. It is this sort of use of computers in the future that we, as designers, should be recommending to our clients.

12. When invited to talk on this subject, I asked my staff for a list of the areas where we, at Maunsell, use computers in the design of ports and related facilities. I was amazed by the list that arrived. I have tried to cover some of these areas, but there are many that I have not even mentioned. However to reassure you that these areas exist - and I am sure they will be mentioned by others - I can identify areas such as ship-handling simulations, marine traffic congestion models, modelling of container stacking and storing, port operations, analytical programs on the wave analysis of piles to compute potential pile-bearing capacities, to name but a few.

13. Are we slaves to the computer or efficient users of this powerful design and analysis tool? I hope if I asked for a vote on this, the result would be 50% for the former and 50% for the latter. If that were the result, we the designers are probably doing the right thing.

11. Port design—computerised techniques

T. McKAY, BEng, MEng, MICE, Peter Fraenkel BMT Ltd, and
M. BARRATT, BSc, MSc, MRINA, BMT Fluid Mechanics Ltd

SYNOPSIS. This paper considers how computerised simulation techniques can be used in port development projects, to quantify the effects of increased traffic and changes to the port layout. A traffic model is being developed which links delays and encounters to traffic volumes and operational limitations. Previous experience is mentioned in projects involving marine traffic simulation.

INTRODUCTION

1. There are very few things that can confidently be predicted ten years ahead. In the absence of any global catastrophe within that time scale, perhaps the best bet is increasing traffic congestion.

2. On land this is already commonplace in road traffic. In the air, traffic within European airspace is suffering delays requiring increasingly sophisticated organisation. Now some seaports are looking ahead and planning with a view to avoiding congestion effects.

3. BMT Fluid Mechanics has recently completed a number of consultancies concerned with proposed terminals or channel improvements, to establish that the expected traffic will be able to use them without undue delays or risk of incidents. We are now building upon this experience in simulating shipping traffic movements within ports.

THE PORT ENGINEER'S VIEW

4. Once a potential port expansion or development project has been identified, pre-feasibility studies generally involve transportation planning, traffic forecasting, economic evaluation and financial appraisal. Preliminary port planning activities lead to the preparation of an initial masterplan for the port and guidelines for port operations.

5. Scoping of future study needs will generally be carried out at an early stage with regard to such issues as navigation, marine risk and hazard assessment and environmental impact.

6. Prior to detailed planning the needs of the port project must be established with regard to projected growth of vessel

traffic and cargo volumes, annual turnover subdivided into commodity, size and nature of vessels which will use the port and the effects of likely trends in vessel design, cargo handling facilities, back up storage areas and land transportation methods.

7. It is then that the port planner, engineer and marine operations specialist must begin to work together in order to define the optimum configuration of the port in terms of land and water areas with regard to the following:

* Marine access to and from open sea.
* Port approaches, navigation channels and fairways.
* Shelter.
* Port entrances, turning areas and manoeuvring basins.
* Location and configuration of berths.
* Layout, size and nature of berth structures, mooring dolphins, etc.
* Requirements for capital and maintenance dredging.
* Land areas including bunkering, ship repair or maintenance facilities.
* Contingency planning.
* Aids to navigation.
* Potential phasing of future development.

8.The maritime specialist is called upon to provide input which will meet the requirements of the client and satisfy the needs of other interested parties which may comprise some or all of the following.

* Developers.
* Port or Terminal Operators.
* Shipping Companies.
* Statutory Authorities.
* Government Departments.
* Existing Port Users.
* Shore Based Communities.

9.All the above groups will have different needs and priorities with regard to proposed port developments. Key issues which must be addressed by the maritime specialist will include the following:

* Compliance with statutory marine regulations.
* Compatability with internationally recognised guidelines and procedures.
* Safety and efficiency of shipping operations within the port.
* Identification of marine support facilities and contingency planning measures.
* Vessel traffic management procedures.

10. In order to make firm recommendations with regard to the key elements set out above it is necessary to carry out a detailed examination of vessel traffic patterns within the port area and to and from the berths. The effects on these patterns of vessel movement which would be brought about by increased vessel traffic can then be assessed with regard to such issues as risk of collision, risk of grounding, delays due to vessels passing in transit or manoeuvring on and off

of berths. The effects of mitigation measures such as increasing navigable water areas or the establishment of revised vessel traffic rules can then be assessed and examined in cost benefit terms related to the overall port operation.

11. In the past, marine operations input at the planning stage has tended to be provided by individual specialists or specialist teams with a mixture of seagoing experience and background training related to pilotage, vessel traffic management or the functions of the harbourmaster. Such input remains essential to the port planning team but the rapid advances in PC based computer techniques has enabled computerised simulation models to be developed which can provide decision support to marine operations and port management specialists engaged in such work. Development of such systems, based on practical experience gained on the port planning elements listed above, is presently underway at British Maritime Technology Ltd.

MARINE OPERATIONS MODELS

12. Ports which aim to expand find it necessary to establish new berths and to increase the numbers and sizes of ships using the channels which serve them. There may be increasing demand on particular parts of the waterway because of land reclamation for extra berths, the volume of traffic generated by the extra berths and ships of increased size using limited channels. A number of needs can be identified:

13. Information on the sensitivity of the operation to changes in factors such as commercial demands, traffic loads, safety constraints and port developments.

14. The ability to plan and evaluate a response to future events.

15. The ability to compare alternative plans and quantify their influence on port efficiency (e.g. ship or berth delays), risk (e.g. the potential for ship collisions).

16. Identification of operational bottlenecks and a better overall understanding of the operation of the port and how the various internal and external factors interact.

TRAFFIC SIMULATION

18. Some of the necessary information may be obtained by traffic simulations of the type shown in fig.1. Based on projected traffic levels and route constraints, ship tracks are generated on a random basis and "encounters" are detected whenever two ships would approach within a chosen distance of one another in the absence of avoidance action (fig.2).This approach, originally developed by IRT in France, gives a good indication of conflicts and collision risks for the open sea. For harbours it is also useful in comparing encounter distributions for different layouts and showing the location of concentrations of traffic congestion.

19. For the particular example shown we have tracks of vessels approaching and leaving a proposed extended terminal

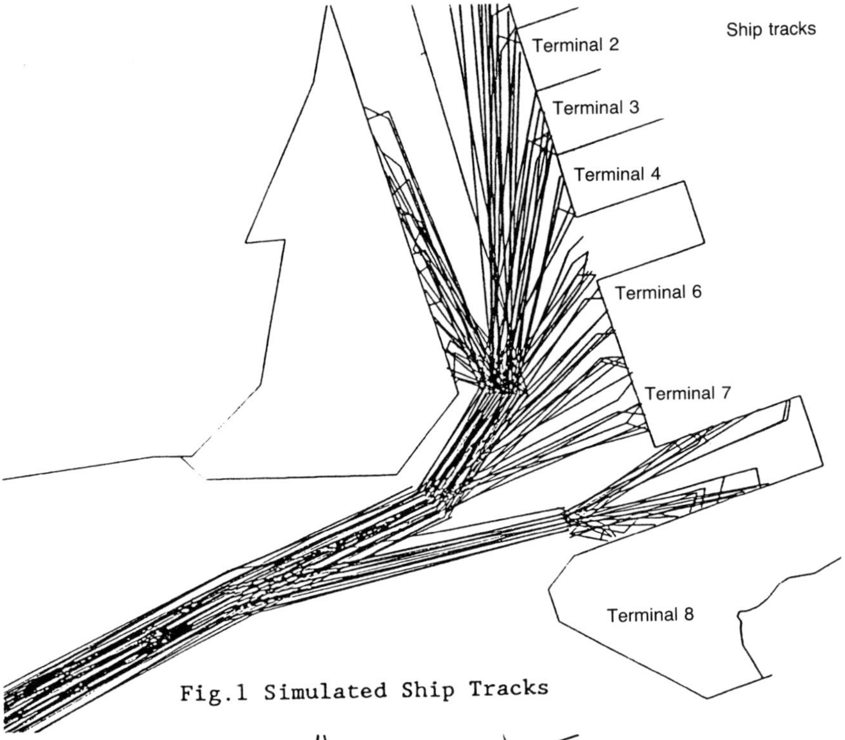

Fig.1 Simulated Ship Tracks

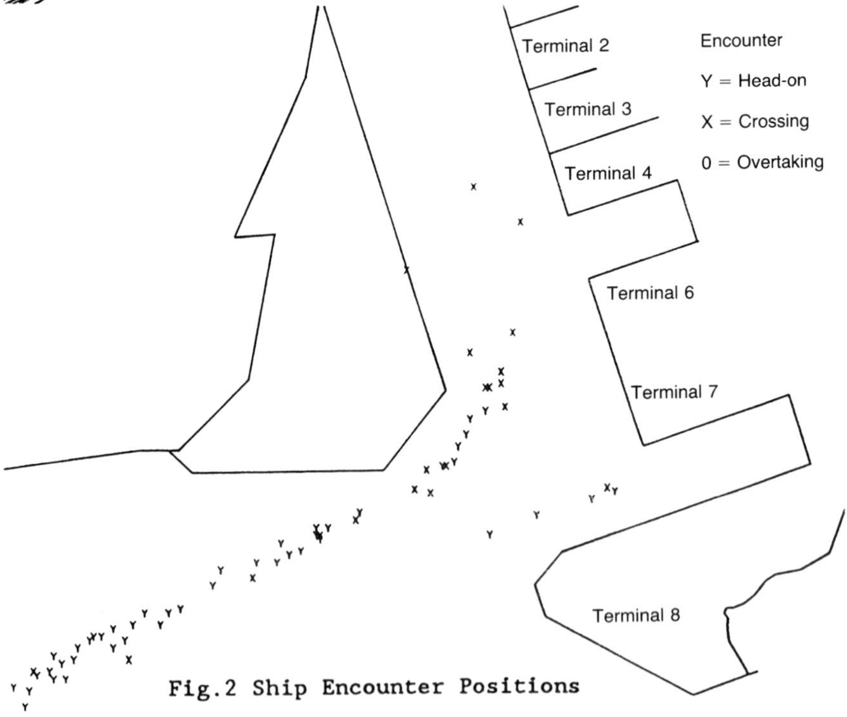

Fig.2 Ship Encounter Positions

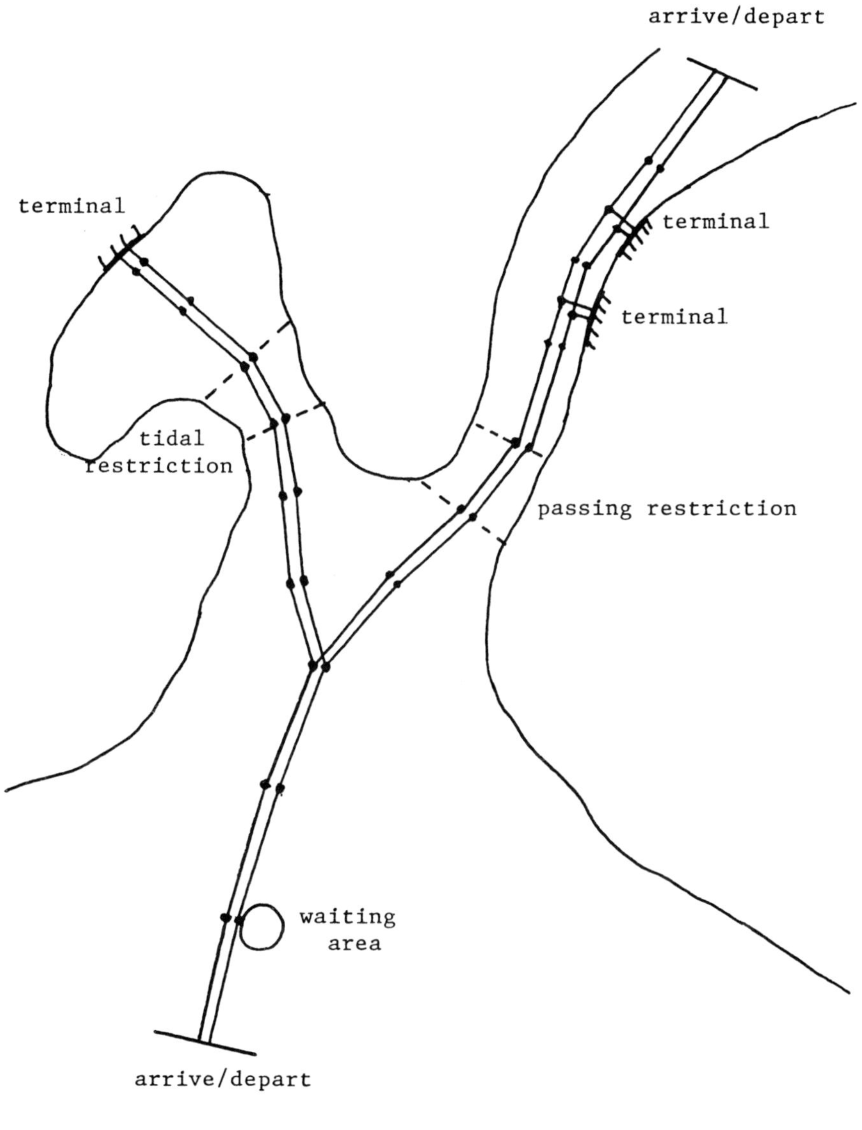

FIG.3 Harbour Route Network

- PORT DATABASE
  - TRAFFIC NETWORK
  - SHIPPING POPULATION
  - NAVIGATIONAL CONSTRAINTS
  - CONFLICT RULES
- SIMULATION
  - TRAFFIC GENERATION
  - MOVEMENT THROUGH NETWORK
  - CONFLICT RESOLUTION
  - PASSAGE RECORD
- ANALYSIS
  - DELAY STATISTICS
  - ENCOUNTER DISTRIBUTION
  - TRAFFIC DENSITY
- PRESENTATION
  - INDIVIDUAL MOVEMENTS
  - ANALYSIS DATA
  - PORT DATBASE

Fig.4 MARINE TRAFFIC PLANNER - STRUCTURE

layout. A compromise has been reached which should allow sufficient land to be reclaimed for cargo handling purposes without causing undue traffic congestion. Clearly the situation could be improved further if incoming vessels moving to the northern part of the basin could take the bend in a wider arc. Manoeuvring simulations can be used to investigate whether such courses are practicable in a range of weather conditions, with or without tug assistance.

20. In many cases it may be considered preferable to control the traffic to prevent encounters. The effects of congestion will then appear as delays due to vessels having to wait for a "slot". To some extent a situation similar to air traffic control could develop in the port and immediate approaches.

MARINE TRAFFIC PLANNER

21. BMT's port traffic simulation is being developed to include ship delays due both to controls and congestion. It represents a network of routes with ships moving under various passage restrictions (fig.3). These restrictions can include:

22. Berth availability - If no berth is available, an incoming vessel must wait at an appropriate holding location.

23. Tidal restrictions - some vessels may have to wait for an appropriate tidal slot to pass through particular channels.

24.Vessel encounters - It may be prohibited for vessels to pass under some circumstances; while one is swinging near a berth, or in narrow channels.

25. The simulation used in the traffic planner is thus essentially a queueing model based on a network over which ships travel for an extended period, building up statistics of waiting periods as an indication of congestion.

26. It is designed to apply to any port. The particular port is defined by input files which may be amended to represent possible changes in port layout or traffic volume.

MODEL STRUCTURE

27. The port marine traffic planner consists of the following main elements (see fig.4):

28. A database describing the port operations, the traffic volumes, the vessel types, their routes, the locations and characteristics of the berths, tidal constraints etc.

29. A simulation program that generates port traffic, according to the statistical or timetabled daily patterns described in the database, and tracks these vessels through the port area to and from their berths. When a conflict arises (desired berth, desired track, tidal limits etc.) then the simulation delays the vessels according to local rules.

30. Statistical analysis and presentation packages for the derivation and presentation of various measures of the port operation. These include the distribution of vessel delays and where they occur, and the number of ship encounters or

conflicts. A fast-time animated display of the port activity can either show the dynamic build-up of route traffic and delays, or the movements of individual ships.

OPERATION OF MODEL

31. The construction of the port database can be in itself an important step towards improved understanding of the port operation. The basic data of numbers and types of ships using particular berths needs to be supplemented by arrival distributions and service times at the berths. Radar or other information will establish the tracks followed, the speeds and manoeuvring times. Any traffic management, whether due to tidal limits or to passing restrictions, has to be stated without ambiguity. This stage may well point to possibilities for change which can be investigated by later runs of the model.

32. The simulation runs can continue for a long enough period to build up a representative collection of waiting times and/or ship encounters. Alternatively, a transient condition such as port evacuation could be modelled, with a range of initial conditions.

33. The post-simulation analysis will provide statistics of ship delays and encounters. For existing layouts and traffic volumes these would normally be at insignificant levels, but proposed developments could lead to effects which were not obviously predictable. The graphical display provides an immediate impression which may well point to sensitive features of the layout, such as a tendency to rapid build-up of queues. Subsequent runs can then investigate changes in an economical manner.

34. The estimation of the risks of the major incidents of collisions and groundings can also follow from the data provided by the planning model, used in conjunction with historical accident data from a wider area. In the absence of relevant historical information, the relative risks of different layouts can still be found from the model. Thus collision rates may be assumed proportional to encounter rates, and groundings to numbers of passages for a given channel geometry.

PROJECTS

35. The decision to proceed with the development of the port marine traffic planner has stemmed from the success achieved by way of traffic simulation modelling carried out by BMT Fluid Mechanics Ltd. on a range of port projects over the last two years. Key elements of these projects, which have been addressed by simulation techniques, include the following.

Port Development

36. Comparative evaluation of options for container port development including reclamation configuration, location and layout of berths, dimensions of waterways, basins and dredged

channels.

37. The simulation model was run for a range of scheme layouts for potential development given a forecasted growth in traffic. Comparative assessment was then carried out for each scheme with regard to potential delay times due to vessels passing, manoeuvring operations and random arrivals. Comparative evaluation of the schemes with regard to marine hazards, risks of collision, striking or sinkage were also carried out.

38. Finally, an assessment of the limiting capacity of the port was provided by carrying out a sensitivity analysis. Based on the earlier simulation work the effects of variation in numbers of berths, numbers of vessel movements and patterns of arrival were assessed. Advice was given with regard to the limitations for port development set against the requirements for vessel traffic control procedures.

39. The traffic simulation work also identified those areas where more detailed ship manoeuvring simulation was required in order to examine manoeuvring techniques and tug requirements for a range of environmental conditions.

Jetty Construction

40. Vessel traffic simulation modelling was used to examine the effects of a proposed bulk terminal development on passing vessel traffic and adjacent port users.

41. The proposed development was close to a water area which was heavily trafficked by a wide range of vessel types and sizes. The simulation model was run with and without the jetty structures in place enabling the effects of the development on nearby or adjacent shipping operations to be assessed.

Maritime Construction Operations

42. The simulation model was used to assess the effects of marine construction operations on vessel traffic movements within an existing port.

43. The construction work was associated with the installation of an "immersed tube" tunnel across a busy waterway. Construction elements included dredging, seabed preparation, tow out and sinking of precast tunnel section. The work was to be carried out over a period of about 6 months, each construction element resulting in the partial blockage of the waterway as the construction programme proceeded.

44. The results of the traffic simulation modelling included an assessment of the potential delays to vessel traffic, risks of sinking or collision and the identification of critical manoeuvres for further study by detailed simulation techniques.

12. Potential developments in merchant ship design

I. W. DAND BSc, PhD, MRINA, BMT Fluid Mechanics Ltd

SYNOPSIS The paper sets out to explore the possible developments in ship design up to the year 2000. The factors which affect ship design are first considered and it becomes clear that, because of these, ship design changes tend to be evolutionary rather than revolutionary. The possible developments in the design of various types of ship are then explored with special reference to their effect on ports and their operation. The paper closes with a brief consideration of some miscellaneous items relating to such matters as manning and ends with the view that while ships and shipping will exist in and beyond the year 2000, it is important to ensure that their key position in the commercial world does not diminish.

INTRODUCTION

1. Shipbuilding, and therefore ship design, has been going through a difficult period for some years. Fleets have been declining and Europe has seen the decline and, in some cases, the disappearance of famous shipbuilding companies. British Shipbuilders has come and, to all intents and purposes, gone while the demise of shipbuilding in Sunderland and the Clyde has been well-publicised.

2. With the decline in the United Kingdom of its shipbuilding has come a decline in ship owning and a change in port structure and activity. Docks which were once alive with ships on the Clyde, the Mersey and the Thames now have been re-developed to house the storm troopers of the new Britain.

3. But against this gloom can be set some notable areas of success. In Britain the ports of Dover and Felixstowe, among others, have considerable success stories to tell, the ferry, ro-ro and container ships which they service being active and innovative in both design and operation. With the demise of ship yard design offices, consulting naval architects have been active in Britain as much as in the rest of the world, servicing the demands of new design

and safety requirements of owners.

4. World-wide, shipping is still by far the most common method of transporting goods and in some areas, owning and operating ships and port development are very important components of a country's economy. One need look no further than to the present and proposed port developments in Hong Kong to see that this is so.

5. And, as a final note of optimism, it seems that at last, ship-building world-wide is moving out of the doldrums and is on the increase (ref.1).

6. So it is against an optimistic, rather than pessimistic, back-drop that this paper is set with the view that, not only will shipping and ports survive to the year 2000, they will do so with renewed energy and vigour. First, however, we must survey the constraints imposed on ship designers before we can discuss what ships will be like in the year 2000.

FACTORS AFFECTING SHIP DESIGN

7. There are certain unmistakable aspects of the basic design of a ship which ensure that changes are evolutionary rather than revolutionary. Some of these are now considered as they form an important background to any consideration of the design changes likely in the next decade.

Fitness for Purpose

8. Any ship is part of a transport system. It transports its cargo across water rather than land or air and must therefore be suitable for this job. Its design will therefore be governed by:

- the type of cargo (passengers, dry bulk, oil, break bulk, containers etc.)
- the amount of cargo
- the proposed route
- the speed required on the route to satisfy the demands of the transport system
- the designs of competitors for the same route or cargo.

9. Some ships must carry their cargo across the open ocean, some across narrow, sheltered seas. Although modern weather routeing systems can indicate the route least affected by bad weather, the ship must be able to withstand the motions and loads placed upon it by its environment. Therefore ships operating in sheltered waters will have design features which differ from those of ships operating in the open ocean. As an example, one may compare the shallow draught, low freeboard and high superstructure of the stern-wheeler river-boats which used to operate in the

calm waters of the Missisippi with the ocean-going vessels which use the port of New Orleans. (Fig.1)

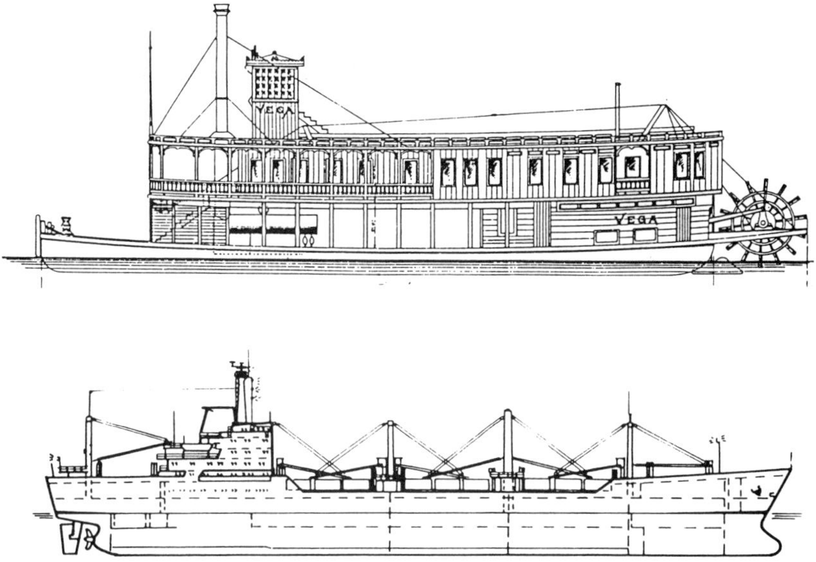

Fig. 1. Fitness for Purpose: a river-boat and a sea-going cargo ship

10. The demands of the environment will not change. The sea will be just as rough, the wind just as strong for future ship designs as they have been for those in the past.

11. The speed at which the ship is required to move in such conditions will be dictated by the commercial demands of her trade as well as the on-board energy requirements, and will have a major effect on design. The bulbous bow, the catamaran hull form, two, triple and quadruple screw forms have all been used by naval architects to balance the requirements of speed, power, capacity and the structural capability of the propulsion system. By the last of course is meant the balance that must be achieved between the power which must be absorbed by the propeller to produce a given thrust and the structural strength of the propeller itself when producing the required thrust and achieving the desired power.

12. Fuel costs and speed are of course closely related and in times of high prices for oil fuel, energy-efficient propulsion plants, or alternative, economic, means of propulsion may be sought. Wind-assisted propulsion has its

devotees at present and may find favour among the operators of commercial ships at the lower end of the size range.

13. The type of cargo is also a powerful driver of ship design. A ship may either carry 'mass' (oil, iron ore, coal for example) where the cargo density is high, or 'volume' (passengers, cars, liquified gas for example) where the cargo density is low. The former yields a ship with a large change in draught when empty compared to laden while the latter does not; the former often requires a high load factor at the expense of speed whereas with the latter a high load factor and high speed are often important requirements.

14. The activities of competitors can also directly or indirectly influence ship design. In the next decade competition will come not only from other ship operators, but also from other modes of transport. Air transport has, of course, captured much of the world-wide passenger traffic, but there is a substantial cruise market to be exploited. The Channel Tunnel will provide competition to the Cross-Channel ferry operators who are already responding with new, attractive designs to tempt passengers away from their subterranean rival. The extent to which the Tunnel will provide an attractive cross-channel alternative to road transport firms carrying goods from, say, Scotland to Italy, remains to be seen, but it is clear that ferry operators are not being complacent and are stirring to meet the challenger.

Legislation

15. Much of ship design, as with the design of aircraft and other modes of transport, is governed by rules aimed at ensuring a satisfactory standard of safety for ship, passengers and crew. Construction rules are set by the Classification Societies, stability requirements and others by the Marine Directorate of the Department of Transport (with international agreements through the International Maritime Organisation, (IMO) with the standing orders required by the operating and owning companies as additional constraints on design.

16. Although these design requirements evolve with time, they do so slowly and it may be assumed that they will be similar in ten years time to what they are today. Legislation governing design is often regarded as an encumbrance to designers, stultifying any originality and making the new ship very similar to the last. It could be further agreed that such requirements are the main contributors to the evolutionary rather than revolutionary changes in design.

17. This may be so, but it may be pointed out that in the

past, requirements imposed on designers have actually advanced ship design rather than retarded it. The classic example is the rapid evolution of the clipper ship which was brought about in part by the revised measurements of tonnage length in the 1836 Tonnage Law (ref.2). The famous 'Clipper Bow' was the result.

18. The present trend toward ships with reduced length/breadth ratios is virtually a direct result of recent legislation requiring improvements in ship stability. The safety of ro-ro vessels with regard to stability is presently receiving much attention and the improvements which are likely to be required will have a marked effect on the design of such ships in the future.

<u>Efficiency</u>

19. If goods are to be transported by sea, it must be done cost-effectively and efficiently. This translates in design to methods of cargo-carrying on board ship (e.g. bulk, containers etc.) and the means of loading/unloading. The advent of large-scale containerisation revolutionised merchant ship design in the 1970's as it also revolutionised cargo-handling ashore. The container ship was an important part of a complex transport system; it had to be efficient and so turn-round times in port were reduced as much as possible. A ship is not earning when in port and so rapid means of loading/off-loading are essential and are likely to become even more so in the years to come.

20. Efficiency of course also extends to operation. When fuel prices are high, a hull form that has the smallest power requirements compatible with the required speed and cargo capacity, is desirable. Bulbous bows are a convenient means of reducing power requirements in certain speed ranges so their inclusion in future designs is highly probable.

<u>Age and Obsolescence</u>

21. Although it is not suggested that obsolescence is built-in to a ship design, it is perhaps relevant to the future to note that much of the existing fleet of cargo vessels is old and will need replacing in the next decade. This is true for example of oil carriers and it will be of interest to see what, if any, changes in deadweight size will be made by owners in their replacement vessels.

POSSIBLE DEVELOPMENTS IN DESIGN

<u>General</u>

22. In the light of the above remarks possible developments in ship design over the next ten years are now considered. It should be stressed that this is, to a large

extent, a personal view and one which is, in some areas, deliberately contentious.

23. The main classes of ship type and their developments are considered in turn.

<u>Oil Carriers</u>

24. A world demand for oil and its products is presumed still to exist at the turn of the century. The vessels which carry oil are part of an energy transportation system which begins, for crude carriers, at the producer and ends at the refinery. The size and speed of crude carriers are parameters which are initially linked to this system and it is hard to see them change radically in the next decade. Figure 2 shows the distribution, by deadweight, of new-buildings and ships on order as at April 1990 from reference 3. These will be representative of the sizes of crude carriers in the world fleet at the turn of the century. Much of the existing fleet is comparatively old and it is clear from the world order book of 143 crude carriers over 60,000 dwt that an appreciable re-building programme is in hand.

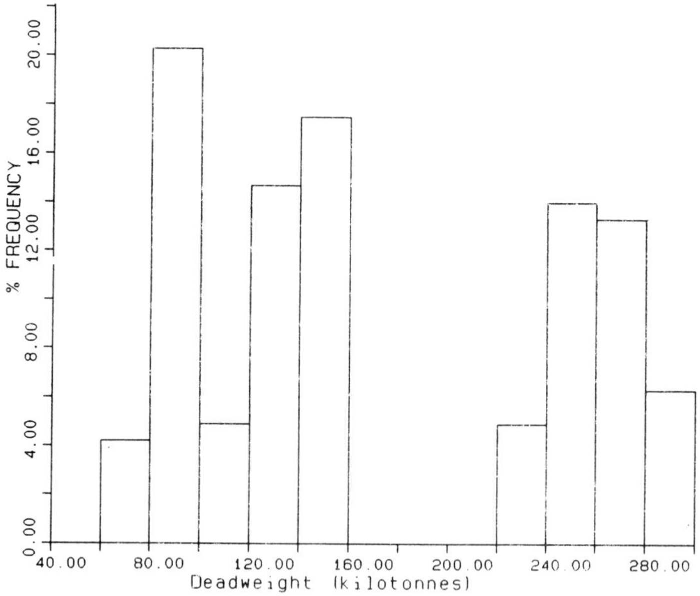

Fig. 2. Newbuilding Crude Carriers: April, 1990

25. It is apparent from the Figure that most new ships will be in the 80 to 160 kilotonne deadweight range with a further smaller, peak in the 240 to 280 kilotonne range. This suggests a move toward slightly smaller vessels compared to the common 250 kilotonne type developed following the closure of the Suez Canal in the 1960's.

26. The general trend in reducing length/beam ratios, due to stability legislation and evident in most cargo ships, may well be evident with such ships although the hydrodynamic problems of a tanker with a length/beam ratio lower than about 5.5 may provide a lower limit.

27. It is probable that ships in this class at the turn of the century will look similar to those of today albeit somewhat broader and perhaps shallower; they will almost certainly be powered by slow speed diesel engines and may well be designed to be more energy-efficient. This trend is already evident in some large bulk carriers (ref.4 for example) and generally means hulls designed to minimise drag (bulbous bows etc.) and large, very slow-revving propellers. From a port's point of view such ships may be less responsive to the rudder and more difficult to manoeuvre than their present-day counterparts. Increased beam may also require additional outreach on loading/off-loading arms and gantries.

28. Radical design changes in terms of shape and concept are not therefore envisaged. The submarine tanker, which has been proposed from time to time (ref.5 for example) is still not seen as a viable proposition.

<u>Bulk Carriers</u>

29. New buildings and orders of all types of bulk carriers from reference 3 are shown distributed by deadweight in Figure 3. The very large number of new ships on order in the 40 to 50 kilotonne deadweight range may be noted, but it may also be seen that a large number of ships over 100 kilotonnes deadweight are also planned.

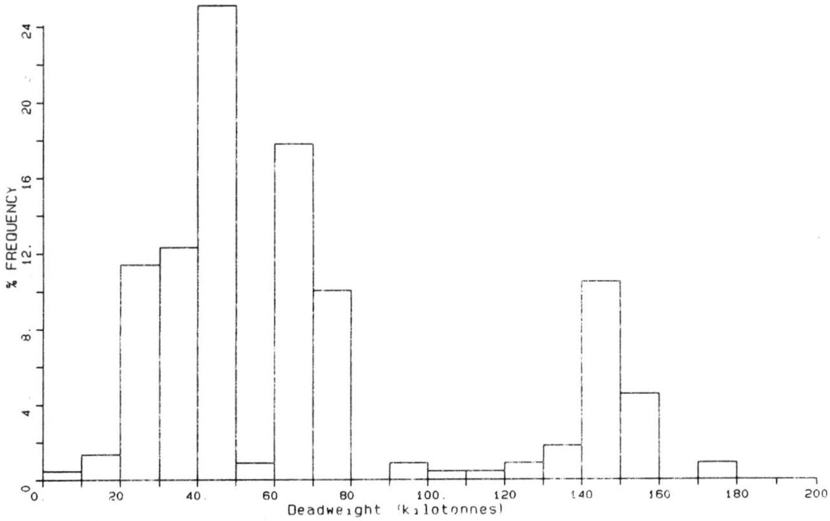

Fig. 3. Newbuilding Bulk Carriers: April, 1990

30. Remarks made above regarding hull design and energy-efficiency will apply to the larger bulk carriers and the trend toward lower length/beam ratios with, presumably, draughts staying the same or even reducing, will also apply.

31. But bulk carriers at the turn of the century may well have a much higher percentage of self-unloading designs. (Fig.4) Reference 6 points out the economic advantages of self-unloading and, for the smaller ships, this may be expected to be an increasing trend. The implications for port operations are clear.

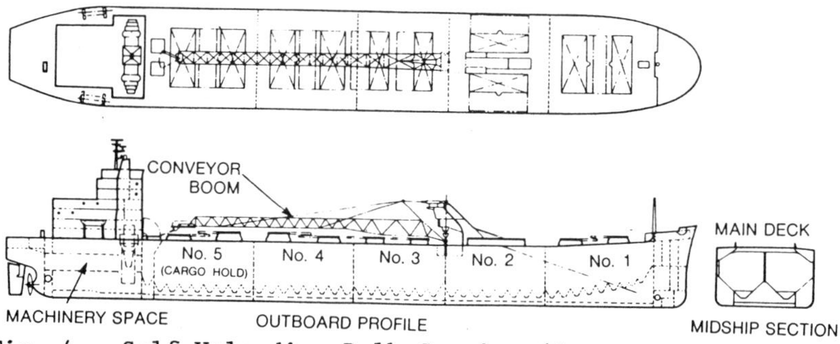

Fig. 4. Self-Unloading Bulk Carrier (Source: "Marine Technology", October, 1984)

<u>Gas Carriers</u>

32. Figure 5 shows the age distribution of the present LNG gas carrier fleet. It is clear that, whereas many of the 'middle' size LNG carriers are nearing the end of their operational lives, the large carriers are comparatively young and should be trading into the next century. This is borne out by the low number of LNG ships on order; in reference 3, of 558 new building tankers of all types, only 4 are LNG ships, three of which, are sister ships for the Australian North West Shelf Project exporting LNG to Japan.

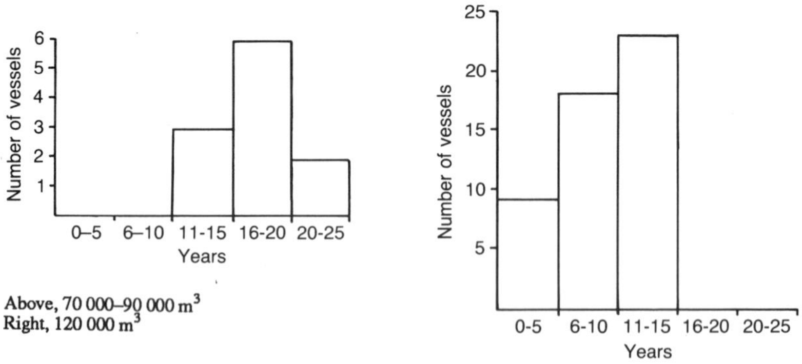

Fig. 5. Age of LNG Carriers, 1989 (Source: Gotaas-Larsen Shipping Co.)

33. Regarding LPG ships, some 9% of all tankers presently on order are of this type. Ranging in size from 1000 to 55000 dwt, it is clear that many such ships will exist at the turn of the century. Design developments on such vessels are likely to rest rather more with safety of operation than shape or size. The operator of such ships is presently heavily circumscribed from considerations of safety. This is likely to continue and even intensify as the maritime world becomes more safety-conscious. The consequences of an accident between a laden ferry and an LNG ship would be very serious indeed and the operation of such ships in close proximity within a harbour port is carefully controlled.

Container Ships

34. The container revolution changed the face of merchant shipping and cargo handling in port. It is a mode of cargo transportation that is here to stay, having survived where alternative systems, such as LASH, have largely failed. Massive developments in container berths are in hand, or planned, in the Far East (Hong Kong and Singapore), as well as those in the United Kingdom. The demand, therefore, for container ships will continue.

35. Two factors could well bring about design changes in the next decade. The first relates to the size of the standard container, the latter to the route taken by the larger ships.

36. The standard container presently has a width of 2.44 metres (8 feet) and there is a possibility that this may increase to 2.59 metres (8 feet 6 inches). If this occurs then clearly there will be a demand for ships which can accommodate either or both types. It is of interest to note that 17 of the present standard containers could be stacked side-by-side in roughly the same space as 16 of the wider container. Therefore if beam could be increased in container vessels to around 40 to 42 metres, both types of container could perhaps be carried.

37. Presently beam is limited to the Panamax value of 32.25 metres allowing 13 containers to be stacked across the deck. However, the 'post-Panamax era' is dawning with routes to the Far East from Europe entailing passage through the Süez rather than the Panama Canal. It would seem probable that, by the end of the century heavier, shallower-draught container ships will be afloat. The present maximum draught of around 13 metres may well not be exceeded if the ships increase in beam, although the possible powering penalties of too great a beam/draught ratio may not result in too drastic a reduction in draught.

38. If beam is to be completely unrestricted then the catamaran container ship becomes a possibility (ref.4) as indeed does its near-relation the SWATH (Small Waterplane Area Twin Hull) vessel. (Figure 6)

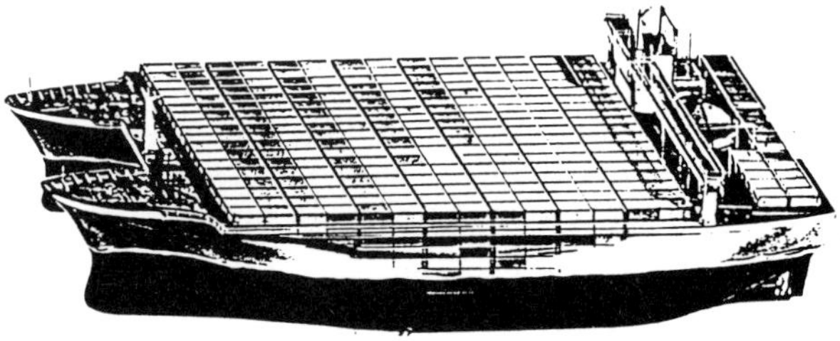

Catamaran Container Ship (Source: ref. 5)

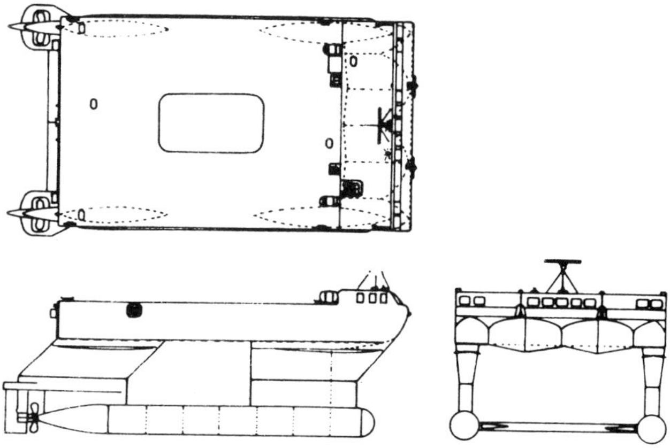

SWATH (Source: "Marine Technology", Oct. 1988)

Fig. 6. Catamaran Container Ship and SWATH

39. Even if the catamaran and SWATH vessels do not appear on the scene, the implications of the beamier container ship in ports and their operations could be profound. Container crane out-reach, approach channel and bend width are all affected as are the handling and manoeuvring characteristics of the vessel itself. Therefore present-day reclamations for, and the building of, container terminals should consider the manoeuvring of beamier vessels up to perhaps 42 metres beam if the larger container of the post - Panamax era are pursued.

Ferries & Cruise Ships

40. It is perhaps in the design of cruise ships and ferries that the most dramatic changes will occur. This will be in response to commercial pressures from the

Channel Tunnel and air transport and in legislative pressures aimed at improvements in the safety of passenger-carrying roll-on - roll-off ferries.

41. Commercial pressures have already given rise to the 'cruise ferry', the wave-piercing catamaran and the high-speed catamaran. The ro-ro concept in ferry design should still be with us in the year 2000, but somewhat modified in the quest for improved damage stability. This will almost certainly lead to increased beam, a theme which has run throughout this survey.

42. Ferries may also show an increase in size and speed, although the newer catamaran and wave-piercer designs still have some operational and design problems to overcome. It may well be that the newer breed of high-speed ferries - the catamarans and wave-piercers - prove to be more weather - limited than their monohull sisters with implications on port operation and congestion.

43. The carriage of large numbers of passengers on comparatively vulnerable craft implies strict safety measures in and around the ship, and presumably the requirement for ports to have appropriate contingency plans ready for a serious emergency will grow. Aluminium may well be used more and more in the lighter, higher-speed ferries with the consequences of any fire on board being at least as, if not more, serious than that on their steel-hulled counterparts.

44. At present the cruise ship industry is enjoying something of a boom (ref.7) and this may be expected to continue. Cruise liner size will be large and there will be a growing tendency for them to dispense with tugs whenever possible and be self-berthing. This will be a continuation of a trend already in evidence.

45. Turn-round times in port for the cruise liners of the next decade may be expected to be measured in hours rather than days with air-line style 'passenger and baggage processing.' The design of the ships will continue to be extravagant as they aim for the vacation cruise market.

Other Aspects

46. Other aspects of ship design may show marked changes in the next 10 years. On-board communications and electronic equipment will doubtless become more versatile and wider-ranging. As more automatic control of on-board systems is introduced, crew levels, already very low, may well reduce further with shore-based 'crews' communicating with ships in the fleet from a central base thus reducing the demand for specialist crew. The turn of the century may see ports having to provide 'berthing crews' to send

out to incoming ships to assist in line-handling etc. when berthing, because of the small permanent crew on-board.

47. The ultimate development of this is the 'crew less' ship. Already experiments are being carried out with remotely-controlled ships and, while the technology for this may already be available the demands of safety and the conservatism of the marine community may postpone its introduction for some time.

CONCLUDING REMARKS

48. Earlier in this paper the point was made that changes in ship design are evolutionary rather than revolutionary. There are certain unchangeable pressures acting on the naval architect which result in slow rather than rapid change; indeed there have been times in the history of naval architecture when design had completely stagnated.

49. Having said this however, we have seen, in the recent past, some remarkable developments in ship design and operation and, with the ingenuity of naval architects, there is no reason why this should not continue. That ships and shipping will exist in the year 2000 there can be little doubt; it is up to all of us to see that its importance in the commercial world does not diminish any more in the next decade.

REFERENCES

1. 'World Shipbuilding: A Market Poised for Rapid Take Off and Sustained Growth' Maritime Reporter/ Engineering News, December 1989 p.12-14.

2. MACGREGOR, D.R. 'The Tea Clippers, their History and Development, 1833-1875' Conway Maritime Press, 1983.

3. Newbuildings Supplement, Fairplay, vol.309, Issue 5557, April 1990.

4. 'HOEI MARU': A fuel saving VLBC from Kawasaki with MAN Propulsion' The Motor Ship, July 1983. p.27-31

5. SCHONKNECHT, R, et al: 'Ships and Shipping of Tomorrow' McGregor Publications Ltd., 1983.

6. JONES, R.M. 'Bulk Ships for the 1990's' PIANC Bulletin 1989, no.66.

7. 'Bright Future for the Cruise Industry' Maritime Reporter/Engineering News, December 1989.

Discussion on Papers 10–12

J. E. BAKER, Posford Duvivier

I would like to introduce the first new port to open in the UK in the past 20 years.

It has shown how derelict industrial land can be reclaimed and find a vital new commercial use to strengthen the UK's port capacity rather than be lost to leisure and housing developments - however desirable these may be. Its design and construction has incorporated modern technology and it has been built to budget and programme. It is designed to be one of the most automated container terminals in the world and to lead the charge for greater port efficiency through the introduction of automation to what is essentially a repetitive lifting, sorting and loading operation.

The timescale was daunting. Posfords were appointed in September 1988 and the planning and design had to proceed in parallel with the setting up of the client organization and the formulation of the design brief and operational strategy for the port. The first vessel alongside was required in under 18 months.

Fulfilment of this tight programme required a fast track approach but this also had to be achieved without compromising the financial advantages of competitive tendering. To minimize time between finalization of the design concept and start of construction four separate contracts were let; the first for reclamation commenced construction in just four months and the last for onshore work within six months of kickoff.

The civil works for phase I cost £27 million and were completed in just 14 months to programme and budget - an outcome viewed with considerable relief and some surprise by some of the battle-scarred bankers backing the scheme.

This result was all the more satisfying since the jetty had to be moved 50 m after the jetty contract award and the onshore equipment was changed from RTGs to RMGs during the onshore works tender period.

Fig. 1. The project now renamed Thamesport

Fig. 2. BP refinery. The previous site use was the tank farm and jetties for the BP Isle of Grain refinery from the mid-1950s to 1980; a short life for such a gigantic investment

Fig. 3. Reclamation, the site left cleared of tanks but derelict. 500 000 m^3 of granular fill were dredged off Harwich and pumped ashore in just 14 weeks. The largest heavy lifting equipment readily available was used to speed the demolition of the old oil jetties

Fig. 4. Taklift IV capable of lifting around 1600 tonnes

Fig. 5. Lifting part of a jetty

Around 600 tubular piles from 40 to 50 m long - some 27 kms of piles in all - were barged across the North Sea and driven in just five months.

We opted for an in situ design at tender stage but encouraged bids with precasting incorporated. The outcome only confirmed the different preferences of contractors. The two lowest bids were almost identical in cost but with one contractor wishing to proceed with the in situ construction and the other determined to use an element of precasting.

Fig. 6. Jetty under construction

The alternative with some precasting won the contract and Fig. 6 shows the full sequence of construction activities displayed. The tubular piles, in situ crossheads, precast deck soffit planks and in situ concrete topping with materials being handled by tower crane are visible.

On shore the client opted for rail mounted gantries for the container park since these offered the fastest operating performance and the opportunity to introduce automation. Further they encouraged the use of gravel beds which gave substantial cost savings over conventional paved container park areas.

Fig. 7. The gantry cranes, sleeper supported rail system, which showed a considerable saving on the alternative piled solution and a reefer gantry

Fig. 8. Vehicle loading bays with Tardi for drivers required for safety reasons when automatic loading

Fig. 9. Aerial view of terminal operation after the completion of phase I

Automation is being developed to programme and already there has been a successful trial of fully automatic box sorting within the stacks. The medium term goal is to introduce an automatic controlled vehicle (ACV) system from the quayside cranes to the stacks and then automatic road trailer loading; although this last operation is recognized as the hardest to complete. Design work is already well advanced for phase II and there are further phases to follow. This is a Supra Pamamax port being automated for the 20th century and I believe that we can be proud to have it in the UK.

D. PALMER, Tees and Hartlepool Port Authority

What sort of computer aid does Mr Bridge advocate port engineers should require?

D. PALMER, Tees and Hartlepool Port Authority

What does Mr Dand consider ro-ro ships will look like to the port engineer in the next century? Will they have wider single level single ramps or double level, double ramps?

K. MURRAY, Crouch Hogg Waterman

In general the relationship between the naval architect and the civil design engineer for port works is very good, but there exists a major point of dispute or perhaps more correctly an area where the civil engineer feels that the naval architect in his ship design ignores the problem he is creating at the ship/shore interface. I am referring to ferry vessels and the provision of belting around the exterior usually in the plane ofthe main deck. By concentrating load into the hull from external contacts at main deck level and utilizing this plan of strength to withstand the impact on the hull then, presumably, the hull and shell elsewhere can be of lighter plating and framing.

However, the belted vessel must rank as the most powerful demolition tool devised by man; it delivers a Karate chop below the knife edge into the shore terminal fendering. The cost of trying to provide fendering systems and facings to take these concentrated line loads and the resulting high maintenance costs in perpetuity suggest that more should be done by the ship designer to provide much deeper contact faces. Of six recently built ferry vessels the contact face of the belting varied between as little as 100 mm up to some 300 mm which results in extremely high contact pressure. What prevents the naval architect from improving this situation? Does he consider the cost implications on the shore side of these narrow belting? Will the changes which might come out of implementation of the SOLAS 90 recommendations enable a rethink of the berthing interface and perhaps provide beltings of metres rather than millimetres in face depth?

A. STIRLING, Posford Duvivier

How long does it take to set up Mr McKay's navigation model and obtain some results?

Further to Mr Bridge's paper, my firm had port clients who allowed and encouraged us to prepare port databases. In one case this saved time for a future development. I confirm that port databases are most valuable and useful and ports should set up such databases.

M. F. C. THORN, Hydraulics Research

Mr Bridge has referred to the use of computer models as a port planning tool. I support and recommend the trend towards in-house models of water flows and perhaps sediment movement for port strategic planning. It enables the port authority to ask and explore questions in close dialogue with other elements of port planning. However, I would emphasize two points which are often overlooked. Computer models are configured to operate in specific computer systems. If they are to continue to be usable they need to be maintained and updated as the in-house computer system evolves. They are also only as good as the physical processes built into them, and if the user does not fully understand how the model works it is easy to produce inaccurate or incorrect results. Therefore, although these models are a useful aid to strategic planning, the results for an evolved plan should be checked usingmore sophisticated models or more informed specialists.

I strongly support the plea for the collection and accessible archiving of port data. I am often surprised at how little data ports hold on their own local environments. Studies and evaluations of port developments may need information on local wave climate tidal characteristics sediment type and movement and a reasonable distribution of tidal water velocity data within the port area for a variety of tides. On today's timescales it is often impossible to collect adequate data of this type for a specific study, and I would urge port authorities to take steps to collect and keep information as part of the eventual port database.

A. TOMS, G. Maunsell and Partners
Some 20 year ago I wrote a computer simulation of vessel arrivals to Cyprus ports. At that time the tourist trade was to be increased and more ships were to be anticipated. The objective was to determine an optimum berth length to avoid excessive perceived queuing on arrival. The simulation, based on random arrivals and tailored to suit all the characteristics of the existing vessels, length, port duration etc confounded the engineers because often a large cruise ship would be followed soon afterwards by another. A very large berth would have been necessary to accommodate such vessels which was not acceptable to the client on cost grounds.

The problem was solved by the removal from service of the S. S. France which had been included in the statistics.

This comment is made to illustrate that too much reliance should not be made on even accurate modelling of situations. Perhaps the Authors could indicate if they have encountered similar situations.

E. LOEWY, Sir William Halcrow and Partners Ltd
How safe are new catamaran ferries in fire and collision situations?

R. H. BRIDGE, Paper 10
I see the need for a basic CAD system which can hold and amend a topographical computer model of the port area.

This could then be enlarged to include data on service layouts in the port area. Additionally there could be an offshore topographic computer model which would log and record seabed surveys and channel makers update for any maintenance dredging. There is also scope for a computer model or data base of sea states, tides and currents.

All of these computer models and data-bases fit readily on currentmidi computer systems, (as are no doubt used by the ports commercial department) and are rapidly being fitted onto networked PC systems (e.g. UNIX).

Little investment will be required by port engineers to network existing resources to provide the relevant computer support for their activities. These include the following.

Hardware: a combination of the currently separated computer system, which is probably already being used by the commercial and managerial aspects of the port operations, into a networked system.

Software: CAD and topographical data management software are now being marketed for small PC-based network systems.

Data base: utilities, ordinance survey and commissioned bathometric surveys will all provide data on a specific computer format to act as a basis for a specific port data-base.

Staff: a whole generation of computer-literate draughtsmen/technicians is now available to compile, modify and use these topographical data-bases.

DR I. W. DAND, Paper 12

Mr Palmer asked about the ro-ro vessel of the next century. The safety of ro-ro vessels, especially those which carry passengers, has received much attention recently and it is fair to say that, because of this, their design is likely to see significant changes in the next decade. More stringent intact and damage stability requirements will have to be met to increase the safety of such vessels without compromising their operation. This may well result in beamier ships, but will probably mean that new ships will have different internal arrangements to make them more secure against capsize.

It is probable that the double level/double ramp arrangement will continue to have attractions for short haul passenger/freight ro-ro vessels, provided this does not result in an unacceptably high centre of gravity.

It is perhaps worth mentioning a design feature, brought about by the more stringent stability requirements and which is already seen on some ships, and that is the addition of sponsons. These can be retro-fitted to existing ships to improve intact and damaged stability; they naturally result in an increase of beam, thus requiring more space at the berth.

Mr Murray makes a plea for more berth-friendly belting or fendering to be fitted to ships. This is, of course, a problem that can be looked at in two different ways. Belting can, as Mr Murray would have it, be viewed as 'the most powerful demolition tool devised by man'. On the other hand it can be viewed as the main protection for the ship when berthing. The belting is, as Mr Murray points out, generally positioned in line with the main deck, one of the strongest parts of the ship and that best able to absorb berthing load. Making the belting deeper, quite apart from adding weight to the ship and probably raising its centre of gravity, would transfer the berthing loads to other, less strong parts of the ship.

The SOLAS 90 changes may have some effect on this matter. Ships which are retro-fitted with sponsons may be able to provide a deep and sufficiently strong belting around the ship which could withstand berthing loads. However, berths in some areas pose difficult handling problems; in some cases the belting may have to be used as a bearing face to allow a ship to pivot on a dolphin, for example. In such cases it might be possible to provide inflatable rubber 'doughnut' fenders on the dolphin, but failing this it is difficult to envisage a sufficiently strong alternative to the present belting arrangements.

Finally Mr Loewy asks a very relevant question regarding the fire and collision resistance of the new catamaran ferries. These ferries are constructed mainly of aluminium and there has been a case where one was badly damaged by fire. However, as has been assiduously reported in the press recently, the Marine Directorate of the UK Department of Transport has been paying particular attention to aspects of fire and evacuation for such vessels. This has resulted in changes being required to their internal arrangements with regard to fire protection, especially in the engine room. For the moment it is understood that the number of passengers and vehicles carried has also been restricted by the department on safety ground.

The vulnerability of such vessels to collision has also been considred. The twin hulls have sufficient subdivision to allow the vessel to remain afloat after certain types of collision. Evacuation of all passengers has also been tested in live exercises.

Therefore a considerable amount of work has already been done to ensure that the new catamarans have an acceptable level of saftey. But it must be remarked that such vessels have many novel features which take them, in many cases, beyond the bounds of existing experience. Many aspects of their operation and safety will remain under scrutiny for some time to come.

13. General and bulk cargo

A. HOLLAND, Consultant

SYNOPSIS
Consideration is given to the situation in the ports of the United Kingdom, at the turn of the century, for handling general and bulk cargoes, reflected against the background of those factors likely to have the most significant effects on their development, location and operation.

BACKGROUND

1. In 1989, freight traffic through United Kingdom ports fell for the first time since 1981. The drop of 11 Mt. (2%) was due entirely to a 24 Mt. (9%) fall in the bulk fuel traffic. Other traffics increased by 14 Mt. (6%).

2. In that year, dry bulk traffics accounted for 119 Mt. (25%) of the 480 Mt. total figure, with the conventional cargo at 2 Mt. (0.5%).

Table 1. The major dry bulk cargoes.

	1989 (000's T)
Coal/Coke	26,000
Ores/Scrap	26,000
Aggregates	21,000
Minerals	16,000
Cereals	10,000
Animal Feeding Stuffs	4,000

These six categories total 103,000,000 T and amount to 86% of the 119,000,000 T total.

BULK CARGO FEATURES

3. There are a number of different features relating to these commodities.

(i) Coal/Coke. There could be significant changes in this commodity over the next 10 years. Currently approx. 2/3 of the U.K. requirement in domestically provided, with approx. 1/3 imported. Coking Coal as used in the manufacture of steel is, in the main, delivered to the manufacturing plants. There seems to be little prospect of any change in this situation. However, coal used for power generation could come from alternative sources in future. There currently exists an agreement between the CEGB and National Coal for supply until 1992. The privatisation of the generating companies will allow them to opt for the most economical supply, not necessarily from a national source. This could allow for foreign supply and a change in the 2/3:1/3 balance.

(ii) Ores/Scrap. This is predominantly an imported cargo, with a requirement that the port of discharge is close to the process point. This often results in the process companies having their own terminals.

(iii) Aggregates. In the main, this is a coastwise/domestic cargo: The boom in the building industry, particularly in the south-east, coupled with the increased difficulties in obtaining land based supplies, which have now become subject to much greater environmental considerations, has lead to a tremendous rise in the use of sea-dredged aggregates. The major companies in the trade are pursuing new terminal sites and new vessels and equipment are on order. The current high level of requirement seems set to continue for the next 10-15 years.

(iv) Minerals. Similarly to aggregates, mineral traffic is closely related to the needs of the building industry.

(v) Cereals. Of all the major dry bulk commodities, this is the most sensitive to a range of different issues. It is a commodity that is highly politically sensitive and subject to governmental controls (both U.K. and E.E.C.) Supply is subject to a range of effects due to weather and the quality and quantity of the harvest. Cereals are also price sensitive and the end user/supplier location is important for either the imported or exported product. Internationally the background to the commodity is one in which both developed and developing countries are seeking self-sufficiency. This aspect would indicate a decline rather than an increase in traffic.

(vi) Animal Feeding Stuffs. As with cereals, these are subject to change in governmental policies and trends are difficult to predict. However, there are no apparent indications of appreciable growth.

Table 2. The major dry bulk cargo ports.

	1989 (000's T)
London	16,200
Tees	10,700
Immingham	8,400
Clyde	5,900
Medway	5,900
Tyne	5,800
Liverpool	3,700

GENERAL CARGO

4. The graph at Fig. 1 clearly indicates the continuing decline in conventional general cargo from over 23 Mt. in 1965 to around 2 Mt. in 1989. The 1965 figure represented around 50% of the non-bulk cargo compared with less than 3% in 1989. There is nothing to suggest that this decline will not continue leaving general cargo at levels of less than 1% of the total figure.

U.K. PORTS

5. Various aspects have had, and will have, an effect on U.K. Ports over the next 10 years.

(a) The Abolition of the National Dock Labour Board Scheme.
(b) Size of Ports.
(c) Manpower.
(d) Identity.
(e) Freeports.
(f) Channel Tunnel.

6. Abolition of N.D.L.B. Scheme. Without doubt the biggest factor affecting the operations in U.K. ports was the abolition of the N.D.L.B. Scheme in 1989. Whilst the scheme was in place some of the smaller, and not-so-small, ports which operated outside the scheme had some advantages when competing with the scheme ports for certain traffics. There was a financial advantage of not having to fund the scheme, coupled with an 'emotional', and what was sometimes seen as a larger, issue of not having to employ registered men. This latter element had a 'stigma' attached to it, which came to the fore when investment proposals for port areas were being considered by transport or manufacturing interests. There was the very real fear that any new operation could be drawn into the 'registered net', if sited in or near to a registered port operating area. The abolition of the scheme has removed this difference, so that all U.K. ports will now operate from the same base - the 'level playing field' philosophy.

7. Size of Ports. Having set aside the 'unacceptable face' of the registered scheme, the ex-scheme (mainly major) ports should be able to offer services on the same basis as others - but now potentially with an added advantage. For the major ports their size should enable them to offer to customers a share of any benefits resulting from the ability to handle larger and different types of cargoes and vessels.

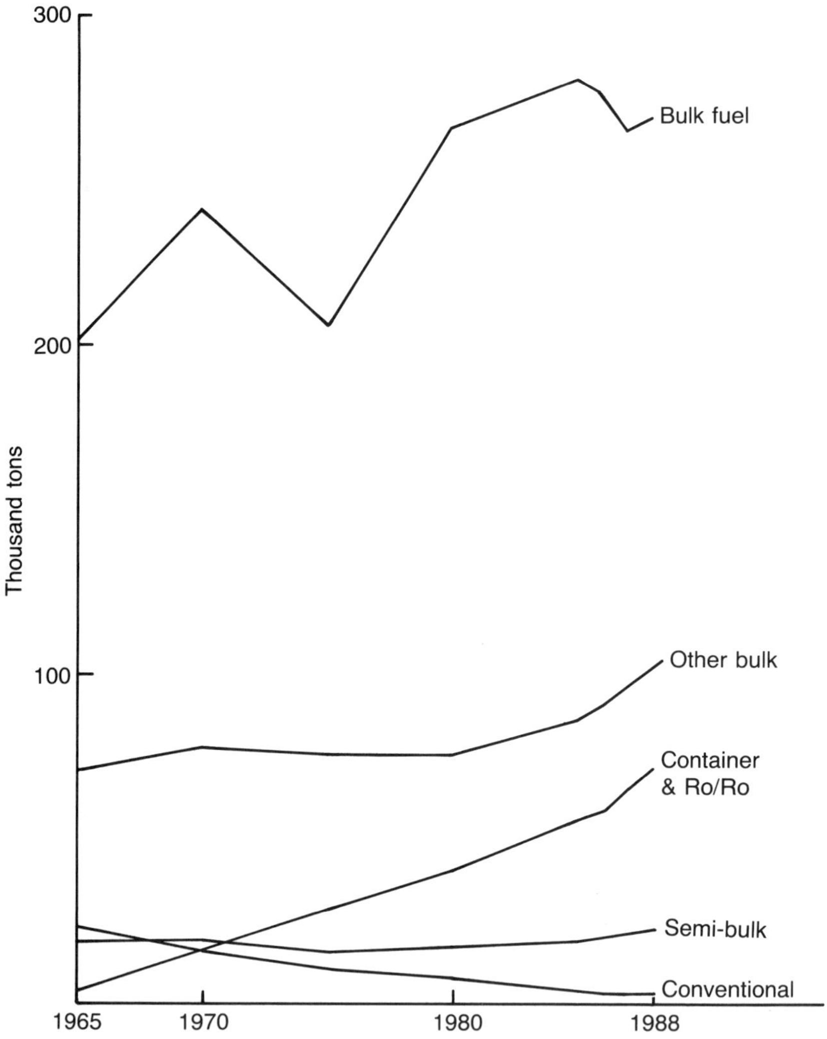

Fig. 1. Foreign and domestic traffic

8. Manpower. The abolition of the scheme was accompanied by a dramatic reduction in the numbers of port workers, particularly the cargo handlers. Competition between ports will ensure that there is a continuing effort by port managers to provide the service required by the customers with the correct level of manpower. Not only the correct level but also the most skilled and flexible. Flexible not only in their working ability but also in their approach to the job, and the use of equipment provided.

9. Identity. Over the years ports in the U.K. have had a changing view of the role they saw themselves performing or being asked to perform. In the early part of this century they were not only ship discharging and loading points, they also provided a whole range of services from storage and warehousing to sampling, labelling, blending, etc. During the 1950's and 60's the developments in containers, ro/ro, unit loads etc. the emphasis was on speed of handling through the port. Berths and quay areas were required to be kept clear to facilitate ship turnaround. Ports moved to the transit area philosophy, and cargoes were not encouraged to dwell in berth areas. As mentioned earlier the presence of the registered scheme in certain ports also discouraged thought of anything other than the simple discharge/loading, receipt/deliver operations.

10. Freeports. The introduction of 'Freeports' into the U.K. trading pattern as an encouragement to traders to move into port areas for some process activity and re-shipment can be seen as a move away from the transit area concept. Although in the view of some groups Freeports allowed nothing more than was already possible under existing regulations, their introduction seemed to fill a gap in the U.K. transport/trading pattern compared with our continental neighbours.

11. The Channel Tunnel. This is the subject of a separate paper. However, although the effects of the bringing into use this transport link are still unknown, and subject to a wide variety of speculations, it will not make the U.K. ports situation any easier and will certainly increase the competitive position.

EUROPEAN PORTS

12. The future position of U.K. ports cannot be considered without reference to our continental neighbours. There are two particular aspects:-

(a) Their physical situation.
(b) Subsidies.

13. Physical Situation. The physical advantages of the European ports cannot be denied. They lie at the mouth of, and service a huge natural hinterland which is the core of the E.E.C. commercial and industrial centre. In addition, for example, compare draught levels in U.K. and continental ports.

Table 3. Range of draught levels.

London, Liverpool, Southampton, Tees & Immingham	12.8 m - 17 m
Rotterdam, Antwerp, Hamburg & Le Havre	14.3 m - 22 m

14. Subsidies. If the position described above were reversed, and dredging were required in order that the continental ports would equate, or better, their facilities compared with U.K. ports, there is no question that government subsidies would be made available for them to do so. As it is, U.K. ports are on their own and are likely to continue their commercial battle with their continental rivals without governmental assistance.

1992 - THE SINGLE MARKET

15. With the coming of the Single Market in 1992, the aim is to reduce or eliminate barriers to trade. Most commentators anticipate increased volumes of trade as a result. Increased volumes will also bring increased competition between the U.K. and continental ports. However, because of the competitive imbalance caused by the subsidies, the competition among U.K. ports for national and international traffic will intensify. 1992 may also bring other legislation which may assist the U.K. position, e.g. the changes in the tender/procurement procedure, and these will be welcomed. However, the port subsidy 'hot potato', lately addressed by the U.K. Government in seeking transparency of accounts for port undertakings, is unlikely to be picked up and will remain the missing link in the single market legislation.

FACILITIES AND LOCATION

16. There is a school of thought that the U.K. already possesses sufficient or even a surplus port facilities. There is also the view that it does not. If the former view is correct, simplistically with a 'level playing field' even with some increase in traffic levels there will still be facilities available or underutilised. This is if the location is correct. The annually published B.P.F./ D.T.I. statistics draw information from over 90 locations. These range from the major ports (30 Mt. - 50 Mt. plus) to those handling under 100,000 T of cargo. Centres of population in the U.K. are in the South-East and Midlands. The increase in trade with the European Community (allied to the increased use of container and ro/ro modes) has resulted in a shift of emphasis of traffic to ports in the south and east (particularly the ferry ports) at the expense of those in the north and west. (See Fig. 2)

THE FUTURE POSITION

17. There are no indications that major new locations are required for port facilities. Environmentally, this type of development is unlikely to be approved. In any case, existing ports have the navigational facilities, operational arrangements etc. already in

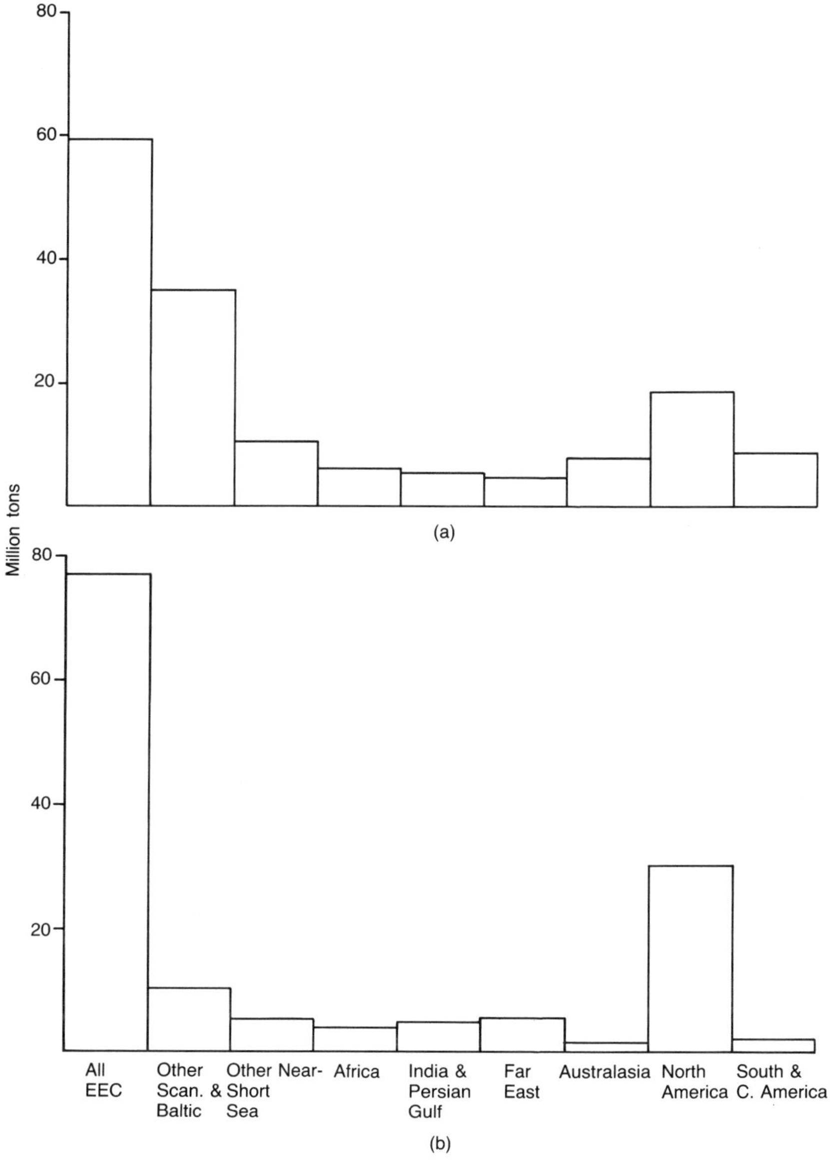

Fig. 2. Overseas trade statistics - 1988 - UK ports

existence. Because of the changing traffic patterns existing ports, particularly the larger ones, may well also have surplus land available for development.

18. In recent years there has been an increase in the size and number of the very large multinational companies able to exert financial influence. Many of these companies in process manufacture have increasingly been moving towards a 'just-in-time' manufacturing cycle where the transport leg for the raw material, shipped in bulk, becomes an integrated part of the total process.

19. The privatisation of U.K. ports is likely to be a major feature in the next 10 years. Surplus land values and the availability for plant/factory building close to discharge/loading point could make them an attractive proposition for purchase. In addition the existing ports have the existing shipping services for the onward transport of the manufactured product.

20. Port equipment is becoming increasingly automated, adaptable, remotely controlled and labour unintensive. It is also required to be environmentally and user friendly. Bulk vessels are capable of self-discharging and highly manoeuvrable, making them increasingly independent of other port services.

SUMMARY

21. Putting these elements together for U.K. ports at the turn of the century would indicate developments for general and bulk cargo in the south and east, within existing ports also providing other modes of cargo handling. The port equipment would be highly automated and adaptable e.g. containers and scrap, using integrated computer clerical systems and working 24 hrs a day, 7 days a week. The bulk handling area would service a major environmentally friendly industrial complex employing a small number of highly skilled, adaptable personnel. The port would be privately owned probably by a large multinational company with a substantial interest in one or more of the industrial processes.

Reference

1. The Dept. of Transport/British Ports Federation - Port Statistics 1988.

2. Ports of the World - 1988.

14. The future role of rail in British ports

T. J. HANSFORD, Railfreight distribution

SYNOPSIS. This paper seeks to answer the question - is there a role for rail in the future of port distribution.

RAIL OBJECTIVES

1. In terms of both the passenger and freight businesses is a qualified yes, but before expanding on the reason for my qualified response I think it is important that we set the political rules of the game straight. Neither the Passenger Business serving existing UK ports, nor any element of the Railfreight Businesses receive any form of Government subsidy and indeed these activities are expected to operate profitably, and to make a return on the assets employed.

2. It is important that you remember this before the environmentalists amongst us renew their deplorement of the increasing number of private cars and heavy goods vehicles on Britain's already congested motorway network.

3. British Rail is operating in a deregulated, market driven environment where customer choice, the quality offered, and the price to pay are the key factors.

PASSENGER SERVICES

4. Looking first at the passenger side of the business, British Rail will continue to provide services from the short sea and Irish ports such as Dover, Folkestone, Harwich, Sheerness and Holyhead, but with the accent being on a fast relatively cheap road transfer of customers from the port environment to an adjacent main line

station. Where port inter-changes already exist, such as at Holyhead and Harwich, it can make sense to continue to utilise them, but the days of special boat trains to cruise terminals such as Tilbury and Southampton are gone. With the advance of air travel the market has, not surprisingly, by and large disappeared. No more will we see the ticket clerk at Southampton accompanying the Pilot vessel out to meet the Queen Elizabeth with a stock of 500 first and standard class singles for the boat train to London.

5. Apart from the excursion market from the Kentcoast and East Anglian ports, upon which the impact of the Channel Tunnel is likely to be less noticeable than a change in Duty Free allowances, the chief existing classic passenger route is to and from Northern and Southern Ireland. Here again a steady decline has been experienced because of the improvements in air shuttle services and a more competitive airways pricing policy.

6. However, as Geoff Baker said in his paper we are busy digging a hole at Folkestone which will, when linked to France, give a much needed boost to the continental foot passenger market.

7. Within two years of the opening of the Channel Tunnel some 13 million passengers per annum will be travelling on international trains between the United Kingdom and mainland Europe. Around 30% of them will come from, or be travelling to, destinations beyond London.

8. The reduction in overall rail journey time between cities like Birmingham and Brussels or Paris will create a new market for railways in business and leisure travel which both BR and its mainland European railway partners plan to cater for with high quality through trains and good connecting services.

9. The international passenger service will capture its market principally from existing rail/sea, rail/air, road/air and coach/sea traffic.

10. In addition to diversion from existing transport modes, improvements in the quality of rail transport will generate traffic by diversion

away from other competing items of consumer expenditure, or by encouraging people to change to alternative destinations. These elements of traffic generation are taken into account in forecasting passenger flows. The forecasts also take account of the total projected growth in the economy.

11. Detailed assessment of both the passenger and freight marketing opportunities are incorporated in this brochure, a copy of which accompanies my speech notes which are available from the conference desk.

12. I am not prepared at this venue to become embroiled in any political debate about about the financing of the Channel Tunnel project, the high speed link, nor indeed this country's and railways approach to the venture as opposed to the attitude of our continental colleagues.

13. BR are continuing to examine options for a high speed link from the Tunnel the findings of which are expected to be announced early next year. Many of you present at this conference have I know already been involved in discussions either as proponents of alternative strategies or in a consultancy capacity.

FREIGHT SERVICES

14. My specialism as you may know is the freight market and may I say straight away that a decision about a high speed link for the Tunnel in no way impacts on RfD's ability to provide freight services to and from the tunnel from its opening date in June '93.

15.Investment in infrastructure, terminals, locomotives and wagons will exceed £300m and we confidently expect to triple our carryings from 2 to 6 million tonnes in the first 5 years of the Tunnel opening. Whilst I would not agree with Geoff Baker's assumption that we may attract business as a result of lower charges, the Tunnel, and the economics of a long distance rail haul, will enable us to compete favourably with the traditional road haulier; with block train movements from city centre to city centre. Speed rather than price is of the essence and we believe the majority of business will be of an intermodal nature in either the traditional ISO container or more likely the swapbody which has already made such rapid advances in main land European distribution.

16. It must, of course, be remembered that the capacity of the Tunnel is finite and currently RfD have pathways for 35, 30 wagon length trains each way every day.

17. We have examined the opportunities for a land bridge to Europe for the North Atlantic deep sea trades through Liverpool, or equally through Bristol, but by and large have discounted them for the very same economic and logistics reasons outlined by Geoff Baker yesterday. Having said

that, we recognise there may be land bridge opportunities from Ireland to the continent for up to 40,000 units annually and are making plans accordingly for such business.

18. Much has been made of the likelihood of a major deep sea line opting for one European port of call and feeding the UK via the Tunnel.

19. Together, with some of the major Far Eastern lines we have investigated the likelihood of them utilising the Suez Canal and choosing Marseille to off-ship all European boxes, but the logistics and economics of disgorging a 4000 TEU vessel at one entry port do not match up and there is also the question of Industrial Relations at a single entry/exit port to consider. Indeed many shippers favour their goods being handled either in the import or export direction through a port of their own nationality and we believe the greatest opportunity in deep sea terms, via the Tunnel, will be in the mode of 'vessel chasing', where a container which misses an export ship at Felixstowe can by rail through the Tunnel catch up the mother vessel at say Marseille.

20. Enough now of the Tunnel, for the objective of this conference is to discuss our UK port strategy. Even were we to fill the Tunnel each way everyday we would only cater for 14% of the cross channel freight market and I am firmly convinced there will be a continuing role for UK ports in terms of European distribution

particularly from the East coast. Indeed it is our intention, at least in the early years, and until the picture on dangerous goods becomes clearer,to maintain our Trainferry link via Dover/Dunkerque.

21. To return to the original question, but in relation to freight, is there a future for rail in ports inland distribution. The answer again is a qualified yes. Remember, of course, a port in railway terms is no different to any other private siding. To achieve a competitive edge against the road alternative we need to satisfy three key elements:-

1. Distance - the average length of journey for a heavy goods vehicle in the UK is around 90 miles. The competitive distance for rail against road for a single unit is now assessed as between 250 - 300 miles. This, of course, dramatically limits the market share available to rail.

2. A relatively high volume in tonnage terms to a minimal spread of destinations and.

3. To be able to offer the same or better service quality as our competitors.

22. Overall rail movements of traditional bulk imports and exports have declined over the last 10/15 years. There are, of course, exceptions to this, but by and large the bulk imports are low value commodities which move over relatively short distances. The ultimate destination of the goods dictates heavily the port of operation chosen.

23. Having said that, in the growth intermodal field, Railfreight Distribution are market leaders in the inland distribution of deep sea containers, with 35% of all import and export boxes utilising the Freightliner system. Over half a million containers each year are moved to and from the ports of Southampton, Tilbury, Felixstowe, Liverpool and more latterly the Isle of Grain.

24. The abolition of the National Dock Labour Scheme must improve our competitiveness against the subsidised Northern European ports such as

Rotterdam and Antwerp. I wish Leon Brittain every success in his harmonisation attempts in terms of port handling costs, although I remain somewhat sceptical about the outcome. Certainly if deep sea lines abandon a UK port and choose a Northern European port for the mother vessel call, it will reduce Railfreight Distribution's competitiveness in terms of inland UK distribution. Logistics dictate that the boxes from say Rotterdam would be fed via short sea services to the nearest geographic port to the containers final destination in the UK.

25. Raifreight Distribution is by nature parasitic in as much as we have to follow the vessels to the port of their choice. Whilst I welcome the initiative shown by developing ports, regrettably the gain of one shipping lines business through port X is usually at the expense of abstracting the volume from port Y. A greater spread of business from a railway point of view only results in increased infrastructure and resourcing costs for the same level of business. Ideally, and in true luddite fashion, I would like to see the ports of Southampton and Greenock or Invergordon as the main centres for UK trade. This would mean that it is a long way to get to anywhere and would improve our competitive edge in terms of distance. However in all seriousness we see no major change to the existing dominance of the four main UK deep sea ports, the development of the Thames Estuary Terminal apart.

26. I am a great believer in market conditions and fair competition. One pill I have always found difficult to swallow is the handling charge levied by ports against Railfreight Distribution, where container handling facilities are provided and operated by the port. I can well understand the wish of the port to recoup their investment outlay, and I fully understand the operating costs associated with running a rail container terminal. However, where the pill really begins to stick is when I consider the amount of road infrastructure, cranage and storage facilities which these same ports provide, at their cost, for my main competitor the private road haulier. The road haulier pays nothing for this facility which puts rail at an immediate cost disadvantage, and only has the effect of increasing the mileage band at which rail is

competitive against the road alternative. Not only does the road haulier get a free ride in terms of port handling, but he also benefits from paying an infinitesimal amount towards the nationwide road infrastructure through the medium of his road excise licence. As against this, rail picks up its total infrastructure costs, plus port handling charges on top, and this could be something the environmentalists may wish to consider.

SUMMARY

27. To summarise, yes there is a role for rail in Britain's existing and future port development. In both the passenger and freight context it is limited to where we can compete on price and quality with the alternative mode; and yes we do believe there is unfair benefit given to our competitors in terms of infrastructure costs and handling. Having said that, I know of no port in the UK, and I stress no port, with major development ambitions that would not consider the availability of an efficient rail link a pre-requisite to a successful marketing strategy for their facility.

15. The contractor's role in the promotion of port developments

W. G. STEAN, Balfour Beatty Projects

SYNOPSIS

Most port development in the next two decades will be privately or quasi privately promoted, and financed with private funds. Implementation time, capital costs, flexibility, development and construction risks, operation and maintenance costs will all be critically assessed. Contractors should assist in the optimisation of these factors through intimate involvement in project development and promotion.

INTRODUCTION

As the Balfour Beatty Group is the largest UK non-housing contractor I am looking to the other eighteen or so leading participants in this conference to indicate the shape and size of some future glorious development market for the Group's abilities in the ports' sector. I therefore do not propose to make any predictions of my own regarding the "what", "when", and "why" of the market, but to give some thoughts on the "who" and "how".

THE PROJECT PROMOTER

It is clear that the role of the contractor in the development of projects has primarily been dictated by the promoter's view of the organisational, contractual, and financial structures which will best procure the project. Indeed the shape of the whole industry has changed over time to satisfy the promoter's perceived requirements. Therefore, it is reasonable to assess the contractor's role in the next decade, and beyond, by first attempting to define who will be the promoters of the future, and what they will need from our industry.

The history of infrastructure development in the UK has gone through two distinct phases. The dynamic Victorian industrial growth lead to, and required, the enterpreneurial development of shipping, the ports and railways. The promoters of these developments were generally not distinguishable individually as businessmen, engineers or contractors - they fulfilled most or all of these roles. The projects were financed with equity and loans provided by investors and bankers based on their views of risks, returns and security.

As Government became a more dominant force, public expenditure increased significantly as a proportion of our gross national product. The State assumed the responsibility for providing infrastructure, health services, education etc. The funds for the capital works associated with these activities were provided by the Treasury and the assessment of risk and return became a much less significant concept.

For a period in excess of fifty years the fundamental principles of project promotion were changed. The methods of implementation required a different engineering and construction industry. The evaluation and design of projects was undertaken partially or wholly by governmental organisations supported on a closely defined and frequently narrow basis by consulting organisations. Construction was managed by these same organisations through the letting of multiple specialist manufacturing and construction contracts.

In theory this system should have resulted in high standards of specification and design, coupled with economical and efficient project implementation. In practice schemes became over-engineered with insufficient regard to cost, practicality and implementation time. Many projects were beset by construction delays and major cost overruns due to both design variations and the virtual impossibility of allocating responsibility and penalties for delay.

This inefficient system has been partially revised during the last decade. There have been four primary catalysts for this welcome redevelopment of the construction industry, all of which relate to my contention that the evolution of project promotion will result in changes to the contractor's role.

- privatisation has lead the affected organisations to assess their activities and developments in an increasingly commercial and aggressive manner.

- political insistence that the remaining State funded activities should adopt more market lead and accountable policies continues to enforce the adoption of more efficient development methods focused on cost, time, sufficiency of specification, appropriate use of assets.

- private promotion and financing of major infrastructure projects has resulted in a significant return to the careful assessment of capital cost, implementation time, commercial demand, financial return and risk.

- the massive increase in the private property development and housing sectors brought about by demands from the bouyant service, commercial and light industrial industries has fuelled the adoption of more commercially acceptable construction methods and conditions of contract.

To some degree the UK ports organisations have been less affected by these changes than other sectors of commercial life. It may be true that the economic imperatives have been less strong given the general over-supply of port facilities and a rapidly declining UK manufacturing base. However, two major events occurred during the penultimate decade of this century which may prove to be the key instigators of radical development during the 1990's and into the next century.

- the privatisation of Associated British Ports in 1983 formed an integrated private owner/operator with a 1988 turnover of £212m and balance sheet net assets of £265m.

- the abolition of the dock labour scheme on 3rd July 1989 enabled the scheme ports to compete both with the non-scheme ports and with their continental competitors.

ABP's responsibilities to its shareholders and the need to make a return on its sizeable assets forced it to look seriously at both its port operations activities and the disposal, leasing or re-development of its redundant land assets. The Government is now keen to encourage the publicly owned municipal and trust ports to follow the same privatisation route. The more commercially active of these organisations such as Tees and Hartlepool Ports Authority and the Dover Harbour Board will embrace the challenge.

The U.K.'s two largest current commercial port developments at Felixstowe Trinity Container Terminal and at Thames Estuary Terminals Isle of Grain site are both being privately promoted. It is also interesting that the senior management of the latter was drawn from the former. The recent investment programme at Dover and the Medway Ports Authority/Lion Hope stalled initiative at Sheerness are further examples involving semi-public organisations - both perhaps to become private?

A cursory assessment of current development activity shows that the "smart money" has been channelled into property, housing and leisure regeneration and that the total funds dedicated to these schemes dwarfs those being invested in port development. These are essentially privately promoted and financed although, in many cases, the Development Corporations have been the initial instigators.

Clearly the Government's political affiliation has been, and will continue to be, an important factor in determining the future of port development in the UK. Indeed it would be naive to underestimate the fundamental importance of British Political and European Community influences on attitudes to investment. However, public money has not been a particularly important factor in recent developments outside of the fishing sector, and the EC is not keen to utilise Structural Funds for port projects.

I do not want to create the impression that private initiative is good and public initiative is bad - more to indicate that, even with a change of Government being foreseeable, the provision of public funds and public initiatives within the port sector are unlikely to rank highly alongside the demands of health, education and the like.

I would suggest that we can conclude two fundamental messages about UK port development upto and beyond 2000, each of which I consider follow from the comments above :-

- privatisation of the major State/Trust ports will motivate commercial exploitation of the opportunities offered by the abandonment of the dock labour scheme, and the need to stimulate regeneration of redundant land.

- port development will be funded primarily from private sources of debt and equity (European Investment Bank finance is included in this category).

THE CONTRACTOR

I am hoping for a new era of initiative and development in the port sector and predict that the commercial environment in which that development will occur, will become increasingly more competitive. The promoters of these developments should wish to learn from and embrace the changes that have occurred in the financing and construction of other commercial, industrial and infrastructure projects.

Major contractors are coming to terms with the new business environment in which they are having to operate. New products are being offered all of which propose an increasing involvement of the contractor with the promoter and a progressively closer, and less combative, relationship between the construction disciplines. These products cover a spread of roles for the contractor ranging from his involvement as promoter/contractor through BOOT and turnkey to the more advisory and managerial responsibilities associated with construction management.

The private sector knows that contract price is only one factor in defining project viability and commercial success. Implementation time, performance, operations and maintenance costs, flexibility and risk sharing have all to be included in the project optimisation process. The contractor's involvement at the earliest possible stage of project development must positively influence the overall outcome.

The new Director General of the ICE, Roger Dobson, in an interview reported in the New Civil Engineer on 14th June this year outlined his concerns over the efficiency of our traditional construction methodology :-

> "...... it would do no harm if more civils works were run with a firm eye on schedule, rather than indulging an absurd obsession with minimizing price and then fighting over claims, "Look what lane rental has achieved" he says.
>
> Similarly he doubts whether the present bidding system is the right way to go forward. His time at Bechtel and his period with NEDO looking at private finance has convinced him that "the slave of the bottom line" is not necessarily the best way to get a competitive project. "Do we really believe that the ICE Fifth is the best set of contract conditions to suit the industry in the 1990's with the demands that are now being placed on it, particularly to meet schedule?"

Bechtel have been uniquely successful in marketing the concept of working with employers to develop and implement projects. Both the construction industry and the port promoter ignore that success at their peril. Roger Dobson's concern over meeting schedules is significant. I would emphasise that the overall implementation time comprises both pre-construction and construction schedules.

For any port owner it is clear that the development of a viable and attractive business strategy will be a key factor to his success. However, specific strategies are not generally unique, so speed of development should be a significant factor in strategic planning. Adoption of an integrated project approach offers the opportunity to minimise the pre and post construction periods by eliminating the traditional sequential approach to feasibility, design and specification, statutory approvals, financing, tendering and construction thereby allowing the naturally iterative nature of these activities to occur in parallel.

The most significant change in the construction industry, of recent years, has been the promotion of major infrastructure projects such as the Channel Tunnel, Thames and Severn Crossings, Thames and Lakeland Power Stations, by contractors or consortia incorporating contractors. All these projects are coming to fruition with almost unrivalled speed and already demonstrating the benefits of the concepts I propose. The tunnel and power station projects are offering the contractors attractive investment opportunities. The investment returns will benefit from their early and continued participation in development and construction. The two river crosings are both forms of build, own, operate and transfer (BOOT) projects from which the contractors/promoters will not earn a significant equity return.

The Planning and Public Affairs Director of Shell UK, John Wybrow, addressed a conference on UK Electricity, "New Players, New Rules" in October 1989. In the accompanying paper he wrote :

> "To coin a phrase from Peters and Waterman, we also like to "stick to our knitting". This is not to say that Shell is unwiliing to adapt and seize new opportunities; simply that we would rather play to our strengths to find ways of participating in new situations where our assets and our capabilities add value. To this end, we look to form durable commercial relationships with other participants which are conducive to the creation of synergy - the addition of mutual value".

The "In Search of Excellence" quotation has become a little hackneyed - the danger is to underestimate its validity. I would embellish Wybrow's comment by suggesting that "sticking to the knitting" is usually a sensible strategic objective for any company, however, the "pattern" needs constantly bringing up to date. The "knitting" in this context, should be the design and construction of efficient, commercially and financially attractive schemes. We are now re-discovering some "patterns" which can better optimise the outcome. These "patterns" will also assist the port owners and operators to stick to their own "knitting".

I believe the future development of UK ports will be best accomodated by adopting the integrated team approach to promotion. This will recognise the individual talents that all parties have, and enable the enhanced benefits that the combination of those skills offers, to be realised. Two plus two may not equal five but they can at least make four. Arguably, recent history shows they have only made three.

The relatively small size of the majority of UK port owners dictates that most potentially large projects will require sizeable proportions of debt finance. Generally the promoter will wish the finance to be secured against the future cash flows of the project. The funding banks will carefully assess the project risks, as they will be unable to take comfort from charges on corporate assets or investor guarantees. The banks focus on two primary areas :-

- the time and cost performance of the construction contract

- the certainty of the project's ability to generate the cash income necessary to service the debt.

Early involvement of a major contractor will help to ensure these concerns are adequately addressed at all stages of project development. Many contractors have close contacts with commercial and merchant banks, management consultants and lawyers and often can identify advisors and financiers appropriate to the scheme and to the participants. The promoter, with its design and construction participants, will negotiate the contract performance and price guarantees appropriate both to the requirements of the debt and equity financiers and to the risks perceived by the contractors. To underwrite the operational income the promotion team will have calculated detailed cash flow scenarios and sensitivities based on demand studies, long term contracts, and joint assessment of capital, operation and maintenance costs.

I do not suggest naively that all the problems associated with promoting new port projects will disappear if we all work together. However, neither do I apologise for criticising the traditional approach or for stressing, at length, that the new private port promoters will view opportunities in a more commercial manner - a way that will require promoters, contractors, engineers and financiers to adopt new forms of association. The contractors' role will vary according to the needs of the promoter - but it should, in all cases, be closer to and more integrated with the other participants.

Discussion on Papers 13–15

D. PALMER, Tees and Hartlepool Port Authority

In the scenario described by Mr Stean whereby turnkey (design and construct) contracts are let, how can the client be assured that he is getting the most economic option (following exhaustive investigations and evaluation of all options available), and a competitive bid (which does not incorporate unrealistically high risk elements) all within a reasonable period of tendering time? It seems to me that consultants play a valuable role at a relatively modest cost in doing all the preliminary investigations and design selection to identify the most economic solution and thus enable the contractor to make a reasonable assessment of the risks in a competitive situation and within a short period of time.

J. WRAY, Associated British Ports

I agree with Mr Stean's view that we should move to single point contracts covering a multiplicity of conditions. There are two points I would like to make and ask Mr Stean to elaborate. The first is that in my experience problems have arisen when the main contractor has been called upon to contract multi-disciplinary sub-contractors.

The second is that the client could have difficulty in ensuring that he obtains what he wants with a performance contract. The difficulty is in determining the terms and the performance specifications.

C. S. BELL, Shephard Hill Ltd

One of the primary requirements for the client according to Mr Stean's list was fitness for purpose. It has been my experience that designers are only able to obtain insurance for skill, care and diligence and will not accept fitness for purpose contracts. Could Mr Stean outline his own views and experiences.

A. J. VAUGHAN, Shoreham Port Authority

One aspect of European harmonization in 1992 that will

affect the majority of delegates is the new procurement regulation for the excluded sectors. To what extent does Mr Stean believe that promotion of port developments by contracts will conflict with these regulations?

H. MUIR, Dover Harbour Board
Could Mr Hansford clarify the statistics he gives estimating that 13 million passengers will be using the Channel Tunnel trains two years after opening. Could he also clarify the capacity allocated to rail freight, which is given as 35 paths for 30 major trains each way every day representing 14% of freight across the Channel.

P. S. LUCAS, Mersey Docks and Harbour Company
There has been some discussion about the difficulty of controlling multi-disciplinary projects but from my own limited experience a great deal can be achieved by strong management involvement from both the client and contractor/consultant. In my view clients need to approach such situations with a greater degree of courage.

Mr Stean has talked about design and construction contracts but I should like to ask whether he has given any thought to carrying this through to operation and maintenance.

I would also like to put the record straight that the Port of Liverpool is very much in the private sector and despite the interest which the Government still holds we are very conscious of the importance of our shareholders.

A. STIRLING, Posford Duvivier
I strongly disagree with the implications in Mr Stean's paper that consulting organizations are narrow and that projects are late, over budget and inefficient. For port projects, Mr Stirling put forward that competent port organizations and competent consultants can introduce competition and achieve projects to time and budget. I am concerned that Mr Stean's two-stage approach would delay the job and not incorporate competition to obtain the lowest cost. I believe that for a major container terminal project, for example, design and tender periods could be in the order of 20-25 weeks with project completion on time and to budget.

P. LACEY, Ove Arup and Partners
I would like to add to Alistair Stirling's complaint regarding Mr. Stean's comments on consulting engineers.

It is true that methods of designing and constructing projects have changed as quantity surveyors, contractors now with quite credible design arms and the new project management contractors all persuade clients that using their services indeed saves money.

The balance between 'over engineered' and 'under engineered' is a vexed question which deserves a platform in its own right. Much depends on the client and his understanding of the construction industry.

Ove Arup and Partners on the other hand, has made a good reputation working and designing for major contractors. Designs have been tailor-made to suit the contractors plant, programme requirements and cost. In this process, the art of design has been refined and I do not believe 'over engineering' has occurred. However, nor do I believe that Mr. Stean's comment overly criticizes the consultants but has provided a statement of the way the construction industry has changed.

A. D. M. BELLIS, Consultant

Looking at ports in the future, perhaps newly designed ones, and bearing in mind Mr Hansford's complaint that access facilities in ports are provided virtually free to road users, but charges are made for rail access, should port owners not examine the relative cost of providing road and/or rail facilities? They could later install what is the most economic or charge the users fairly for their means of access.

C. SILVESTER, Associated British Ports

I agree with Mr Hansford that all ports would prefer to be able to offer their customers a rail facility as well as road and, in my own case, canal facilities.

My problem is that over the past 100 years my port has been able to offer a rail facility, but with the restrictions noted in Mr Hansford's paper (i.e. a viable rail distance of 250/300 miles) in the future rail transport to Goole may only be considered if coming from John O'Groats or Lands End. I am not alone in the problems encountered. Could Mr Hansford comment on this observation.

W. G. STEAN, Paper 15

In reply to D. Palmer, I am not proposing that all aspects of project development should be taken over by the contractor or that the adoption of the turnkey format is the only satisfactory method of obtaining improved development performance. However, the contractor's eventual role is clearly vital to the success of any project. It would seem logical to include a selected contractor within the development team at the earliest possible stage. In fact, I would contend, it is not really feasible to make an exhaustive evaluation of opinions without a contractor's participation in the assessment of buildability, schedule and cost.

Neither am I trying to preclude competition which is, anyway, now required by the European Commission. Competition can be built into the selection process at virtually any stage, not only when designs and quantities have been virtually completed. Furthermore the degree of competition required for major contract or sub-contract packages is dependent on the particular forms of contract adopted.

I agree with Mr Palmer's comments on the valuable role of the consultant and would expect that consultants will continue to undertake the preliminary investigations. In proposing an earlier and less combative role for the contractor I am not suggesting any reduction of the consultant's workload or responsibilities.

Similarly, the assessment and evaluation of construction risks can best be undertaken by the contractor. However the risks can be taken wholly by the promoter or the contractor, or shared between the two, depending primarily on the risk adversity of the promoter and his financiers. Early involvement of the contractor must surely assist the promoter to assess better the risk/reward structure of the alternatives, in the shortest possible period of time.

I am pleased that my comments on single point contract responsibility are endorsed by the largest port owner and operator in Britain. I understand Mr Wray's comment on multi-discipline sub-contracts and consider the reason for the main contractor's unfamiliarity has stemmed from the industry's historical application of multi-point contract responsibility. Contractors in general have developed relatively specialist operations. Even those contractors which have a broad spread of capabilities within their operating divisions had not been prompted to improve internal communications and practices to generate close co-operation on multi-disciplinary projects.

The changing market-place has now prompted many major contractors to develop these capabilities and I would advise Mr Wray, to select carefully the organizations with whom he will negotiate.

This comment also applies to his question on the selection of performance criteria. If he selects carefully the organizations with whom he wishes to develop a specific project I believe the promoter, consultant and contractor team should be best able to determine the optimum balance of capital and operating costs, operational performance, contract schedule and contract risk structure.

Mr Bell's question is particularly salient and should have been addressed in my Paper. The most a consultant may agree to cover, outside his PII, is an increased liability for design related problems commensurate with his expected consultancy income on a particular project.

Our experience on other types of project has been that the largest performance risks relate to the performance of mechanical and electrical plant rather than the civil/marine design content. Plant manufacturers expect to shoulder the risks of their own responsibilities associated with their own performance although they frequently baulk at covering the full consequential penalties associated with their failure. The experienced main contractor is capable of assessing the overall and residual risks associated with performance based contracts including the residual design and plant risks is a function of balance sheet strength and contract risk/reward structure. Negotiation with the promoter enables the risks to be apportioned in the most financially efficient manner.

I believe Mr Vaughan is correct in suggesting that the new EC procurement regulations for the so-called excluded sectors will require that port related development must be competitively procured. My Paper does not in any way suggest that the way forward should be non-competitive, indeed we wholly endorse the converse general objective.

I think it is important to point out that the Directive does not require competition to be based on the traditional British tendered approach. It therefore does not imply a backward step. Indeed, it specifically allows contracts to be negotiated.

I contend that the required competition should occur as early in the development procedure as possible and that the appointment of participants should recognize other important factors in addition to the offered prices.

I welcome Mr Lucas' comments on the control of projects and agree completely with his contention that all parties should take a more confident view of their joint abilities successfully to implement multi-disciplinary projects.

Our own and other construction related groups have been developing a capability in the management and operation of plant and capital facilities. In our own case our major share in the management of the Devonport Royal Dock Yard is the largest single venture in which we have an involvement.

More generally we have pursued a number of privately financed developments at home and overseas in which we have allied with established specialist operators. We consider that this joint venture approach to the operation and maintenance of projects is likely to continue, particularly for those sectors in which we do not have a strong internal capability.

In reply to Mr Stirling, it was not my intention to criticize contractors. My intention was to suggest that the structure of construction in Britain has been primarily dictated by public sector clients to the detriment of the consultancy profession and the contracting industry. Neither of these was to blame for the inefficiencies that generally resulted.

In the future I believe there will be a continuing shift towards an integrated task force approach to project development which will better combine the strengths of the promoter, consultant and contractor. The form of that alliance will continue to be dictated primarily by the promoter. It will recognize his own ability, or inability, to control project development activities and his wish to optimize all facets of the process.

In some instances this will result in successful promotion through the adoption of traditional relationships. In other instances more integrated contracts will be preferred.

I do not think there is much evidence to support Mr Stirling's contention that the non-traditional approach results in a longer project implementation schedule. Indeed, the evidence of the Channel Tunnel and the Channel Rail Link (which was aborted due to non construction related issues point firmly to the contrary conclusion.

16. New ports for old

C. J. EVANS, MA (Cantab), FEng, FICE, FIStructE, FCIARB, Wallace Evans Ltd

SYNOPSIS. Many docks in the UK have closed or been converted to other uses in recent years. It may be sensible to continue this trend, by closing further ports and converting them to other uses and either concentrating trade at fewer ports or building new ports to meet future needs. An example of where a new port could be beneficial is seaward of Severn Barrage, if the Barrage is built. This is discussed in detail.

NEW PORTS FOR OLD

1. The process of replacing old ports with new ones is not new. It has been going on for hundreds of years, as patterns of trade and centres of population have changed, ports no longer meeting the needs of the country or regions have been allowed to die, and new ports built to provide improved facilities in new locations.

2. There are many recent examples of this both in the UK and overseas. In London, the docks stretching from Stepney to Woolwich, which were clearly dying as trade left to go to new docks at Tilbury and Felixstowe, have been cleared and the land and water areas have been used by London Docklands Development Corporation to regenerate the area for commercial, industrial, residential and recreational use. There are many other examples of docks being closed and used for other purpose, mainly for waterside and leisure developments, Salford, Swansea and Penarth being typical examples.

3. There are also many examples overseas, particularly in developing countries where ports were originally developed on the waterfront of the city. With changes in trade patterns, these ports found insufficient land available and new ports were frequently then built some miles from the city with large land areas. The old port area often has then been developed as a waterfront amenity, revitalizing the downtown area of the city.

4. The reasons for the decision to construct new ports for old, include inter-alia:

(a) increase in size of vessels

(b) containerization and other improved methods of cargo handling requiring faster turn-around of vessels and more land area for berths;

(c) value of land in port use becoming greater for other uses;

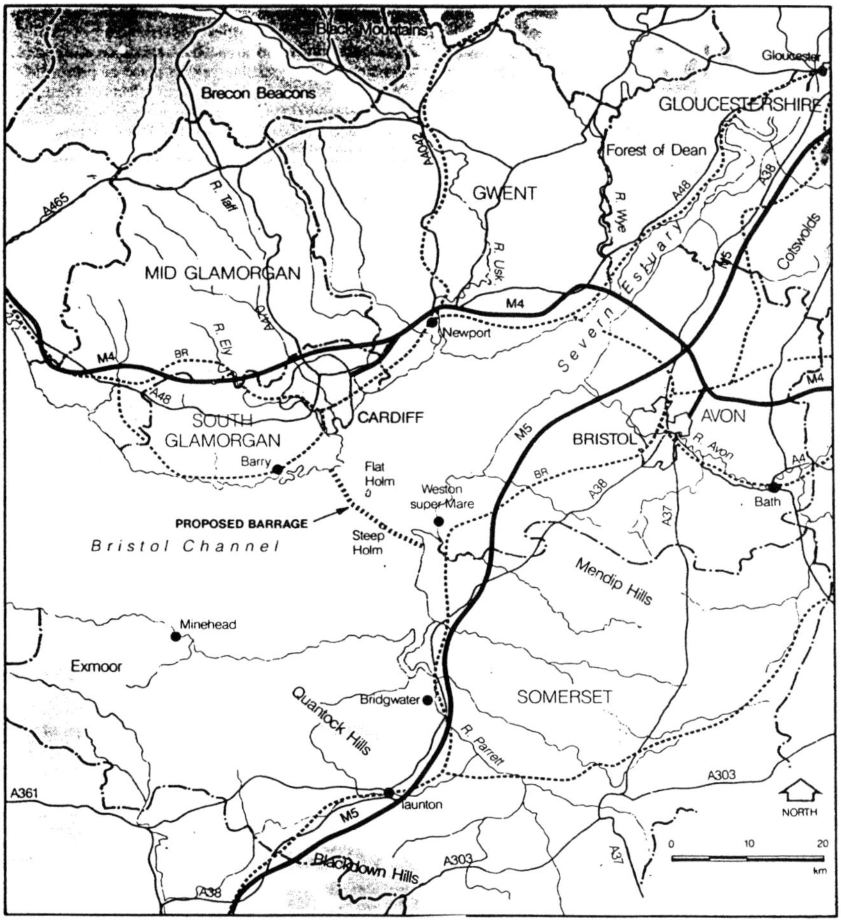

FIG. 1 **THE SEVERN ESTUARY REGION**

(d) improved technology, enabling ports to be constructed in locations not previously considered suitable, at lower costs;
(e) the need for improved transport systems;
(f) the limited access periods and delays to shipping in ports with impounded docks and lock entrances

5. Many of the above considerations are discussed in other papers at this Conference. However, the last reason is one of the most significant and there is no doubt that in the future, impounded docks and lock entrances will become obsolete, except for small ports, yacht marinas and the like. The disadvantage of limited access times, the delay in locking in and out, the high cost of locking operations are so great compared to a port which has 24 hour/day access that vessels will not use them if alternatives are available.

6. Apart from the examples mentioned earlier, there are many others where changes of this type are taking place. In Hull, Ro-Ro berths in the River Humber are replacing the impounded docks. In the Thames Estuary further developments are continuing to replace impounded docks.

7. This is one major potential site for a "new port for old", which will deserve serious consideration in the future if the Severn Barrage is built, that is immediately adjacent to and on the seaward side of the Barrage. (Fig.1).

8. The Severn Barrage scheme as proposed at present includes two locks, each 50m by 360m capable of taking 70,000 DWT (Panamax) vessels, plus 2 small boat locks (15m by 90m). Breakwaters are provided to shelter shipping entering the locks and the road across the barrage has to be elevated at the locks, to allow the passage of vessels. (Fig.2).

9. I believe that it would be a far better economic solution, to omit the main locks from the barrage thus saving perhaps £600 million. This would of course mean that commercial vessels could no longer use the ports of Cardiff, Newport and Bristol. (Fig.3). These are, however, all ports with locks and it could well be that they will be closed or uneconomic to operate by the time the Barrage is built. In Cardiff the port area still in use is adjacent to the land being regenerated by Cardiff Bay Development Corporation, which includes former port land area and contains one former dock as an amenity area, one former dock as a yacht marina (Penarth) with one existing dock scheduled to become a marina under the Development Corporation's plans for re-development.

10. At Bristol, Portbury dock was constructed more recently than the other (circa 1960) but, it is understood, has not yet operated on a profitable basis. It should therefore be possible for a reasonable figure to be agreed as compensation for loss of use, leaving the owner with a facility that can be converted to other uses, together with a much reduced or nil interest charge.

11. A possible layout for a new deep sea port adjacent to and on the seaward side of the barrage is shown in Fig.4. The main advantages of such a scheme are:

a) cost saving
b) availability of berthing 24 hours/day with no locking required
c) elimination of the high road bridge over the locks would enable

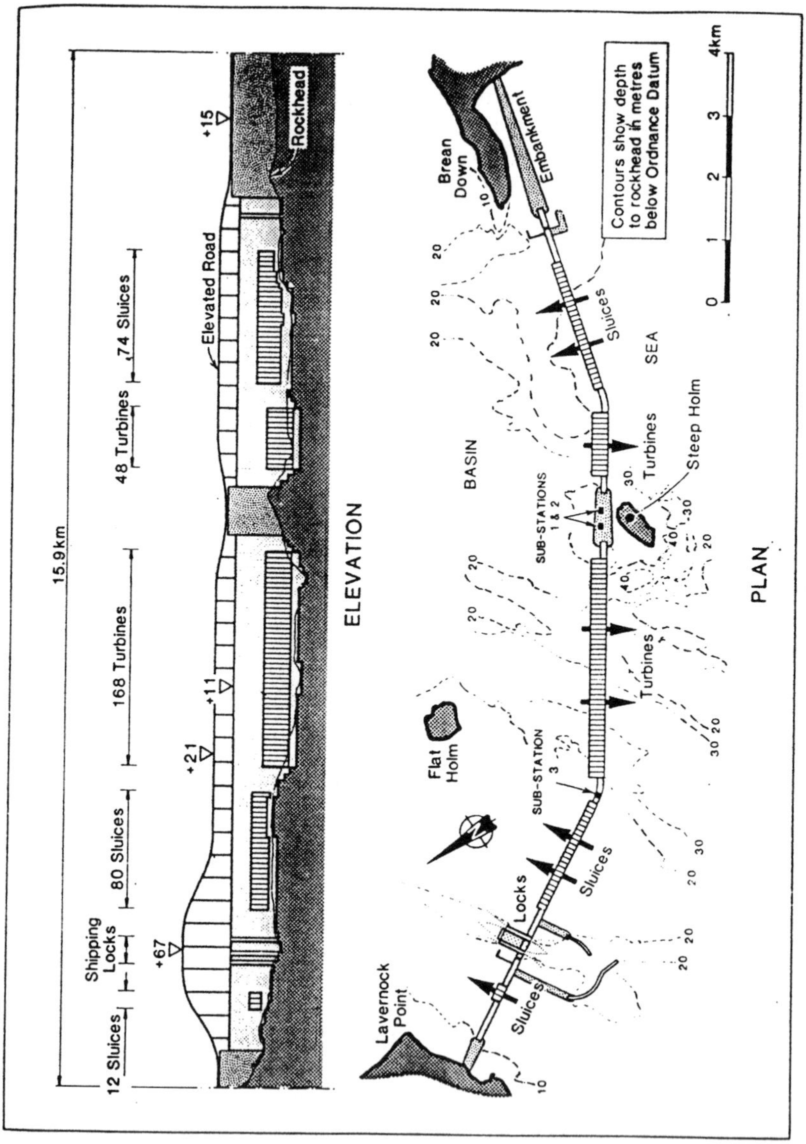

FIG. 2 BARRAGE LAYOUT

motorway standard roads and railway links to be provided from the port to both England and Wales

d) the new port could be constructed to meet the requirements of the 21st Century

e) saving in maintenance dredging costs at existing ports up-channel of the barrage

a) Cost Savings These are shown in detail below. Cost savings would arise largely from the omission of the two major locks; the breakwater would still be necessary to provide an acceptable wave climate in the entrance channel and for ships berthed. There would also be cost savings in not requiring a high level bridge over the locks to allow large vessels to pass under the bridge.

b) 24 hours/day Berthing There is a channel with a depth of water at approximately 20 metres bel ow O.D. in the location proposed for the locks, and which could be used for the new port. This would provide access and berthing for the largest vessels likely to use the port at all states of the tide. It is appreciated that the tidal range in the port would be of the order of 10 metres, and a conventional fixed berth would be undesirable. However, there is no reason why floating berths could not be provided with container cranes or other appropriate cargo handling equipment on the floating berth area, and the ramps from the floating berths to the fixed land area within the port at the appropriate elevation above sea level.

c) Transport Without the need for a high road bridge over the locks it would be possible to build a dual-two or dual-three lane motorway across the barrage, as well as a high speed rail link. Apart from the advantages of connecting the port to the national motorway system and the high speed rail lines in both England and Wales, thus providing easy movement of cargo throughout the whole country and to Europe via the Channel Tunnel, such a link would also benefit the national road and rail system. The land connections of the barrage are reasonably close to the M4 on the Welsh side and the M5 on the English side. A motorway standard connection between the M4 and M5 would provide a shorter link between South Wales and the West Country and South of England than both the existing Severn Bridge and the second Severn Crossing and would undoubtedly divert some traffic from these crossings, also relieving traffic congestion on the M4 around Newport. The mileage between say Bridgend on the M4 and Taunton on the M5 would be 54 miles across the barrage compared to 105 miles via the existing Severn Bridge. The reduction in mileage between South Cardiff and South Bristol via the Barrage compared to the Severn Bridge would be about 10 miles, which although less than that above, is significant in view of the higher traffic volume between Cardiff and Bristol.

Similarly, a rail link between the main Paddington - Swansea line and the Bristol to Exeter line would provide a useful rail link as an alternative to the Severn Tunnel and could provide improved rail access from Wales to the Channel Tunnel.

d) The requirements of ports for the 21st Century are discussed in other papers at this Conference. Building a completely new port to replace

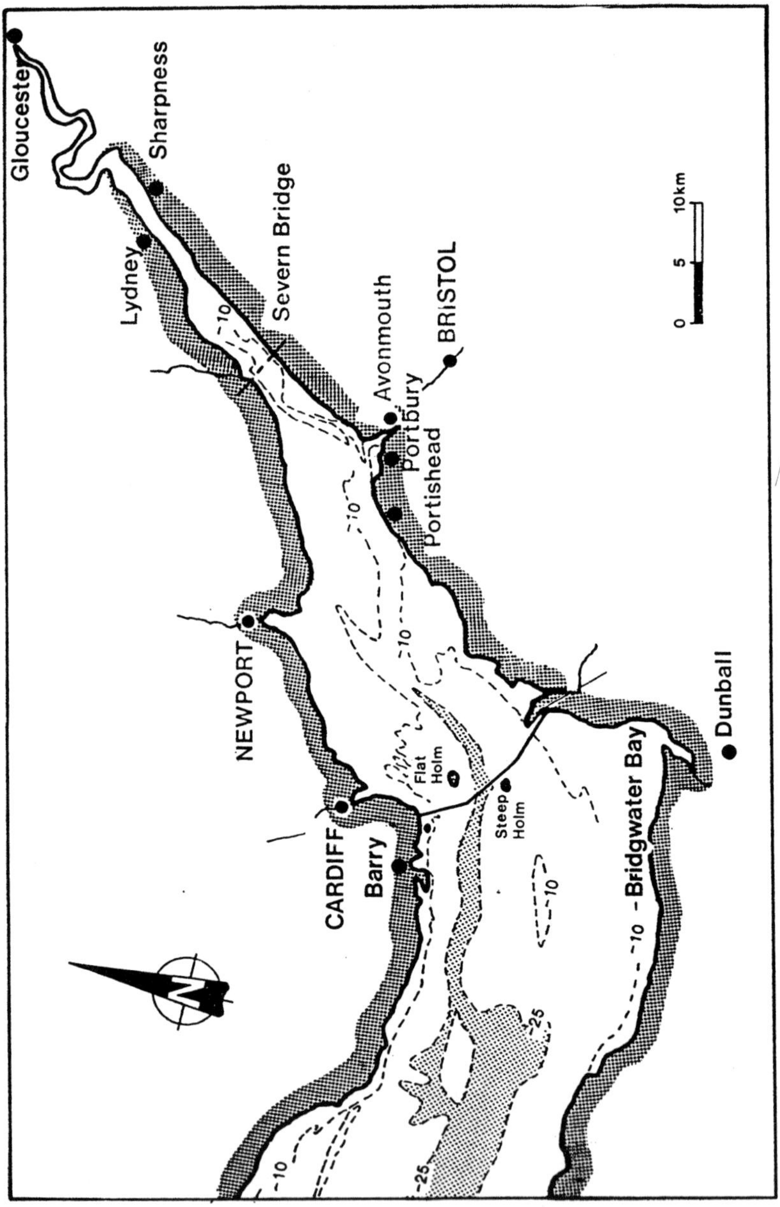

FIG. DOCKS AND PORTS IN THE SEVERN ESTUARY

several old ports which between them currently handle about 11 million tons/year provides an opportunity of utilizing the latest technology in automated cargo handling for all types of cargo including containers, general cargo, bulk cargoes, and specialised cargoes such as cars. It could include for example a completely automated unloading/loading and warehousing system using Spiralveyor and Palletveyor Cranes as in use at Houston, Texas and planned in other ports and other system such as side loading, as well as the latest types of container handling and Ro-Ro systems. Apart from becoming a major port, for UK imports and exports, it could also become a major transhipment port.

e) Although comparatively small in the context of a completely new port, the annual cost of maintenance dredging at the existing ports above the Barrage, is significant, and would be eliminated if it were no longer necessary to maintain dredged navigation channels to the existing docks.

12. New ports for old does not necessarily mean that a new port has to be sited at a new location. There are instances where a specialized port with a particular cargo pattern may become obsolete because the cargo no longer exists.

13. An example of this exists at Sagunto in Spain, where the port was originally built to handle imports and exports for the adjacent steel industry. Following the closure of the steel plant some years ago, the port became virtually derelict. Plans are in preparation to rebuild the port as an integrated Automated Terminal with a completely automated cargo handling and storage system to handle all fruit and vegetable and non-containerised cargo from the Canary Islands and with exports to the Canary islands on return journeys.

14. The loading and unloading of vessels is likely to be Palletveyor and Spiralveyor, with direct access to temperature controlled transit sheds, where sorting and movement of all cargo will be by computer controlled stations and will enable pre-ordered truck-load deliveries to be available at truck loading points for instant loading when the truck arrives. Similar automated rail trucking facilities will also be provided.

15. This is an example of a high technology cargo handling system being used to change an obsolete port into a new modern port to meet changing market conditions.

16. Another transport sector where "new ports for old" is becoming of increasing importance is that of Cruise Ship Traffic. The growth of Cruise Ship passengers throughout the world has been enormous during the last few years, and it is forecast will continue at a high rate in the future. In the past cruise ships have called at cargo ports, and in many cases still do, requiring passengers to pass through a cargo handling area. This is unsatisfactory for both passengers and cargo operations, and the trend now is for new facilities to be provided specifically for cruise ships. This has become even more important as cruise ships have grown in size, the present generation now being up to 900 ft in length and carrying between 2,000 and 3,000 passengers.

17. The requirements for cruise ships are very different from those for cargo

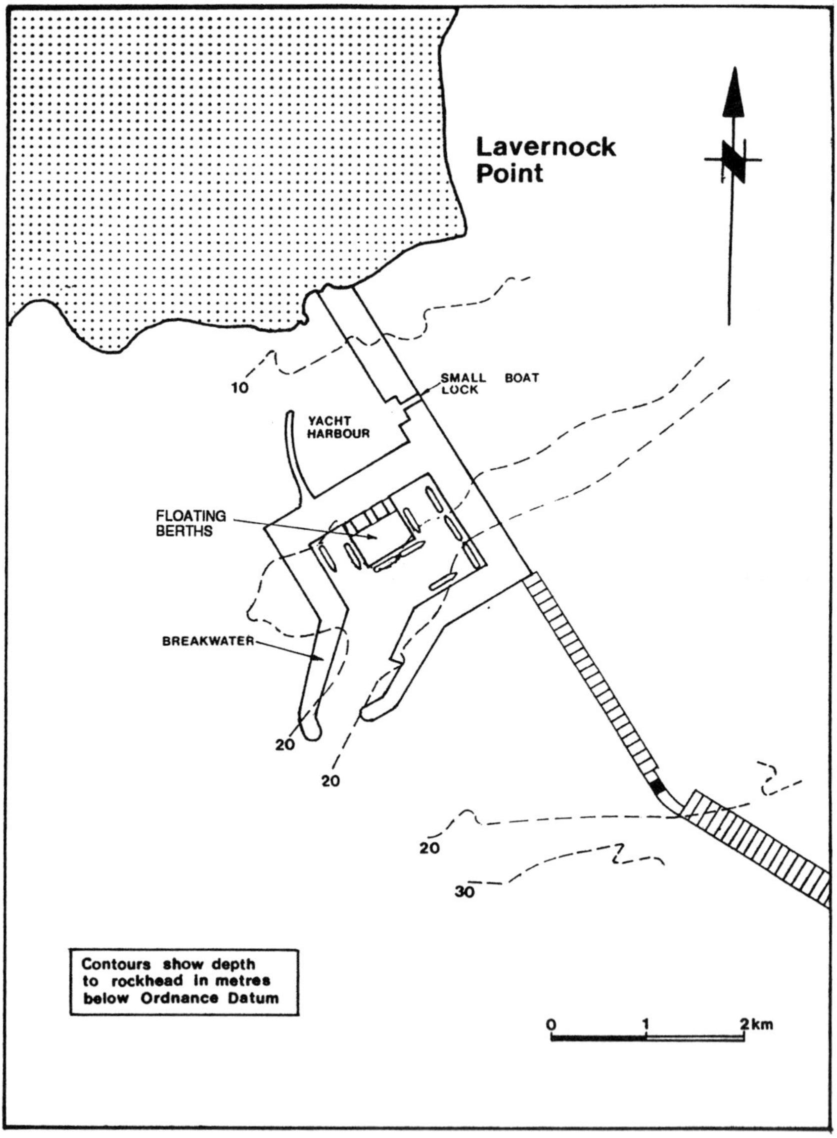

FIG. 4 SEVERN BARRAGE PORT

vessels and are much more akin to those for an oil terminal. All that is required is a number of breasting dolphins in sufficient depth of water for the vessel to berth, a platform for passengers to embark/disembark and a walkway to the shore. The requirements on shore are a passenger terminal building, and sufficient parking area for the taxies and coaches to take the passengers on the shore excursion, normally arranged in advance.

18. Although the UK is not a major area for in-coming cruise ship passengers, a small number of cruise ship liners do call at a number of UK ports, and this market could surely be increased if "new ports" specifically for cruise ships were built with appropriate facilities for transport and shore excursions at locations which tourists might wish to visit.

19. One such location could well be the Severn Barrage port which apart from being a major tourist attraction itself could provide shore excursions to Stratford-on-Avon, the West Country and Wales.

20. In conclusion, I would suggest that there is a strong argument for examining on a national basis the economics of whether it is better to maintain existing ports in use or to build "new ports for old" making use of the old ports for other uses and providing new ports to meet future needs.

ACKNOWLEDGEMENTS:
I would like to thank the Severn Barrage Tidal Group for permission to reproduce details of the proposed Severn Barrage.

17. Built-in obsolescence in ports

A. H. C. STIRLING, MA, FICE, MConsE, Posford Duvivier Consulting Engineers

This paper considers obsolescence in ports and steps to avoid it. The changes in British ports over the last 100-150 years are stated. These changes have resulted in ports being seen as having built-in obsolescence. Various factors influencing obsolescence such as seaborne cargo, shipping, cargo mode, the Channel Tunnel and port economics are discussed. Steps to be taken by ports to mitigate against obsolescence are then recommended.

Introduction

1. There have been substantial changes in British ports over the last 100-150 years. They were located up estuaries or rivers in sheltered positions near centres of population which grew around the port. Subsequently they have moved down river (but still requiring shelter) and the older upriver port facilities have been put to entirely different uses or in some cases remodelled and upgraded.

2. Ports designed and built in the late 19th and early 20th centuries were characterised by:

- impounded docks and many berths
- access restricted to high water
- narrow aprons with transit sheds adjacent to the quay
- manual operations and a large labour force
- ship's derricks and 3 ton rail mounted quay cranes
- rail access to quaysides and sheds

The vessels were small, cargo was manhandled piece small, land transportation was generally local or by rail.

3. Today's ports tend to have:

. deeper draughts alongside with access at all times for larger and more specialised ships

. open terminals or wide aprons with sheds at the rear

. sophisticated and efficient cargo handling equipment geared to handling bulk, specialist or unitised cargoes at purpose built terminals

. few dockworkers and high throughputs

4. As a result of these significant changes old ports are described as obsolete and as a sequitur the newer ports are described as having built-in obsolescence. I propose to discuss these statements and disprove the latter.

Factors

5. In this section I consider the factors that influence obsolescence such as shipping, cargo mode and volumes of seaborne cargoes in the future.

Seaborne cargo

6. Manufacturing and processing will continue to move around the world to regions where either labour is cheap or to be adjacent to raw materials. Thus we have seen manufacturing moving from Britain to Europe to South East Asia and to the Far East. Also we see the decline of international bulk crude oil shipments as refineries are built in the oil producing countries - this has resulted in the Esso refinery in Milford Haven being dismantled and sold abroad. Thus there will be a need for the transportation of manufactured items from low wage to high wage regions, and for value added production in the supply countries to be transported to the consumers. Certain bulk cargoes such as coal will continue but the countries of origin will change - e.g. greater export production from China. This pattern may be distorted due to the 'green' pressures as, say, the Japanese wish to limit pollution in their own country and establish manufacturing plants elsewhere with the consequent transportation of their output.

7. As populations increase and consumer demand rises, the volume of overall seaborne cargo will rise but as indicated above the trading routes may change. Figure 1 shows worldwide seaborne general cargo trade since 1975. It has risen at over 3% per annum with a steep rise in the last few years. Figure 2 shows world population growth.

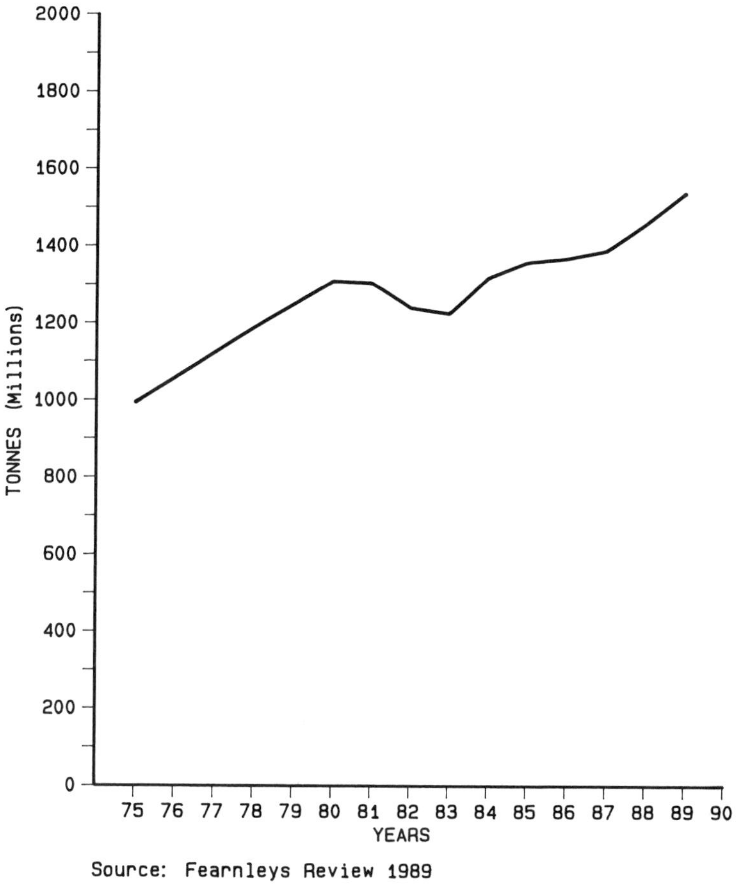

Fig. 1 World Seaborne Trade - General Cargo (excludes bulk)

Shipping

8. The total world fleet fell from 1982 to 1987, remained steady in 1987, and showed a very slight upturn of 1.75% by mid-1989. A comparison of the world fleet 1989-1979 is given in Table 1. It shows that tanker tonnage decreased, drybulks increased as did general cargo/container ships but to a lesser extent. Other vessels which includes Ro Ro vessels, passenger ships as well as fishing vessels, tugs etc. showed a 13 mill. tonne increase.

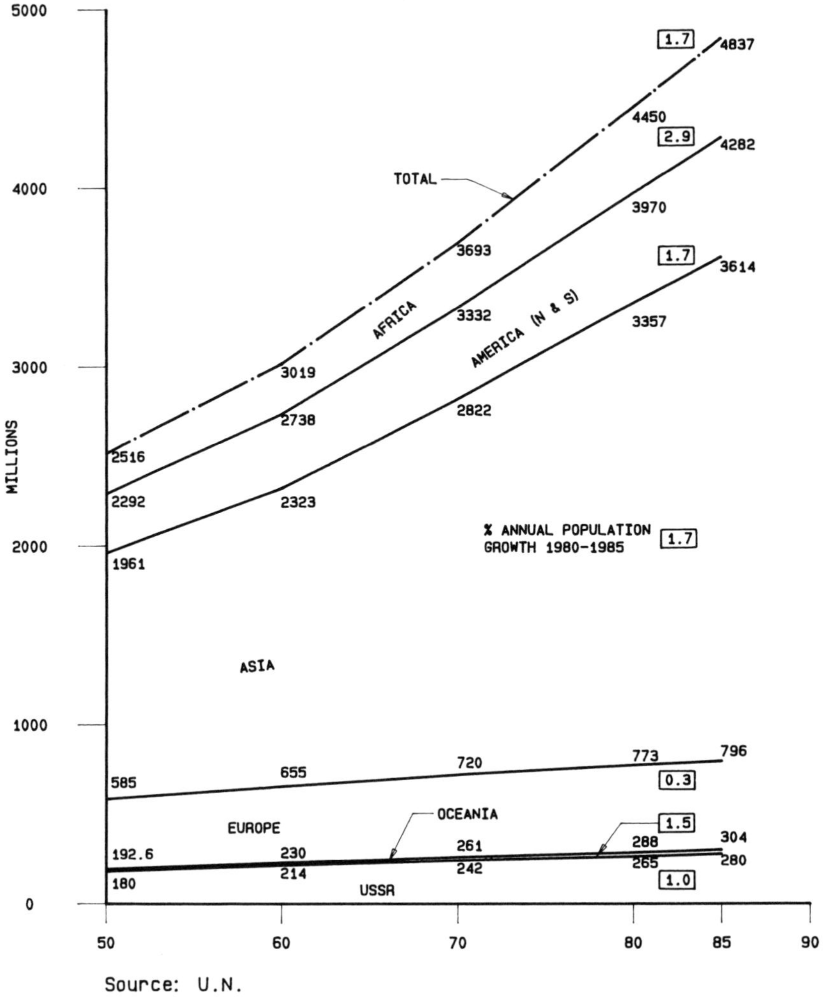

Fig. 2 World Population

Table 1. World Fleet

Vessel Type	1979 mill. tonnes	1979 %	1989 mill. tonnes	1989 %
Tankers	174.2	42.2	129.6	31.6
Drybulk	108.2	26.2	129.2	31.5
General Cargo/ Container	95.4	23.1	102.6	25
Others	35.2	8.5	48.6	11.9
	410.0	100	413.0	100

Source: Lloyds Register

9. Vessel size is a key factor in the obsolescence of ports. Ships will change. **Bulk** vessels appear to have reached an upper size limit and have even reduced somewhat. The number of VLCC/ULCCs has diminished since the 1970s in favour of the 150-250,000 tonne range but new tanker orders in 1989 reflect renewed interest in larger tankers. It is the high inventory costs that appear to be limiting the increase in the size of bulk vessels. **Container ships,** now that they have burst through the Panamax barrier, will I believe become even larger - particularly beamier, even 20 boxes wide and perhaps a little deeper in draught. The need to minimise time in port for these high cost container vessels may well result in side discharge systems rather than top lift or in faster crane speeds. The conflict between an increasing number of boxes to be exchanged at a port and the need to minimise the time in port may result in even more radical changes to container vessels such as modular vessels which leave and pick up a module at each port. **Ro Ro vessels** on short sea routes will become larger which will have a knock on effect of increasing the size of deep sea Ro Ro vessels. But there will be a practical limitation in Ro Ros due to the shore parking areas needed and the port indigestion caused by large cargoes. **Specialised paper and timber product and fruit vessels** will also increase in size but inventory costs may limit the size increase.

10. In some of our major port groupings there are depth limitations or high maintenance dredging costs in the access channels which may limit vessel draughts.

Coastal shipping

11. I see an upturn in UK's coastal shipping due to the increasingly overcrowded and congested British transportation system. The Government has failed to invest sufficiently in our road and rail infrastructure and indeed has no central transportation planning policy. I therefore suggest that coastal Ro Ro and other services may become established to relieve our inland road and rail by the end of the 1990s. I foresee these coastal Ro Ro vessels carrying Ro Ro trailers, sto ro containers and having a facility to accept swap bodies. I see central hub ports such as Felixstowe, Southampton, Hull and Tilbury with some services penetrating inland up the Trent, the Manchester Ship Canal, as well as traditional coastal port destinations on all our coasts.

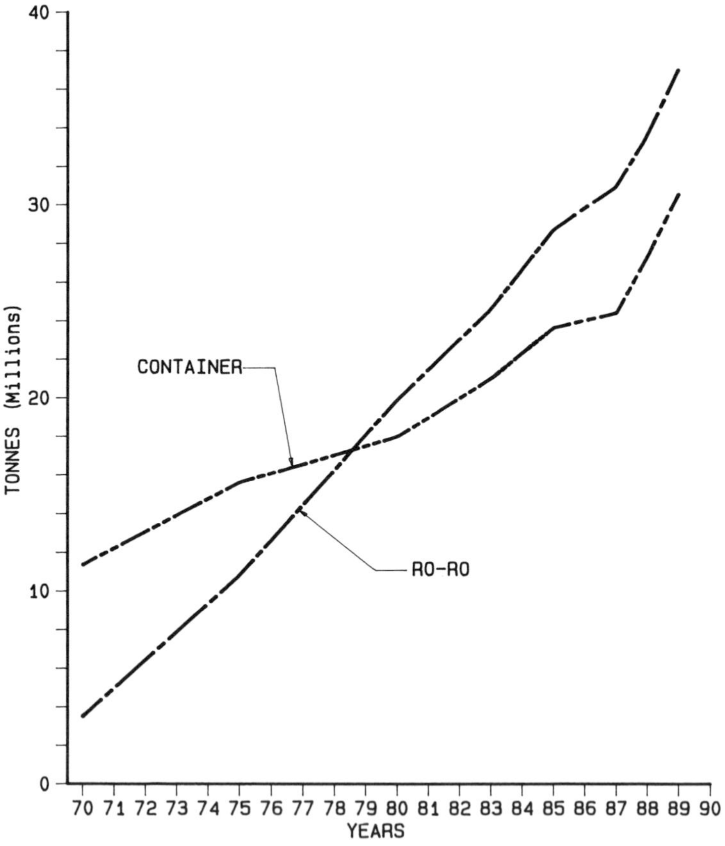

Source: Port Statistics 1988 (BPF and Dept. of Tpt.)

Fig. 3 UK Foreign and coastwise traffic
Ro Ro and Container

Cargo Mode

12. The trend to **unitisation** will continue. The spread of containerisation throughout the world will be accompanied by changes in box dimensions. Longer (45, 48 and even 52 feet), higher (9'6") and heavier boxes will become common due to the economic pressures to maximise loads in relation to transport regulations (led from America). I believe containers (albeit of different dimensions) will still be the favoured general cargo mode well into the 21st century. Within Europe swap bodies will become the norm for many cargoes and UK Ro Ro terminals will handle them increasingly. Despite the Channel Tunnel Ro Ro trade to Britain will increase and Figure 3 shows the recent increases in Ro Ro and containerised trade.

13. There may be an increase in certain solid **bulk trades** (e.g. aggregates from Scotland to England) but many will be self unloading vessels. As oil and petroleum cargoes change with decreasing North Sea production, the facilities will be used to handle imported liquids and gases. With the privatisation of power generation, a series of new coal fired stations based on cheaper imported coal are planned for the 90s with their own coal berths. I see coalfired stations declining in favour of nuclear stations which may well predominate by the middle of the 21st century.

Channel Tunnel

14. Forecasts of cross channel traffic between Great Britain and western continental Europe are much in vogue at present. I set out below the Euro Tunnel forecast (sent to shareholders on 4 June 1990).

Table 2. Cross Channel Freight Traffic

Freight	millions of gross tonnes				
	1976 Actual	1988 Actual	1993 Forecast	2003 Forecast	2013 Forecast
Unitised	14.5	35.9	46.6	75.8	111.8
Other	23.0	33.9	42.6	62.4	84.9
Total	37.5	69.5	89.2	138.1	196.7
Forecast of freight traffic via Channel Tunnel			16.2	26.8	38.0
Percent of forecast totals			18.2%	19.4%	19.3%

15. These figures confirm that rising and substantial tonnages of cross channel freight will travel by Ro Ro ferries into the 21st century.

16. I believe that one or two more twin tube drive through and/or rail tunnels to Europe are likely to be built in the 21st century.

Economic factors

17. At present economic pressures of the stock market dictate a short term view on investments and the need for high profits. This is already being reflected in the attitudes of port managers in UK. It will become more predominant as the privatisation of ports is accomplished by the late 90s. Such short term views are perhaps inappropriate for ports but as the influence of the European Community reaches Britain after 1992 a somewhat longer term view (as taken by German and French banks) should prevail into the early 2000s. This I believe to be correct for port projects.

18. A more specific economic pressure will be the need to reduce manning levels, increase investment and introduce automation throughout the ports and related transport operations. Thus by 2025 I expect that ports will be highly automated with very few men on the terminals.

Conclusion

19. In the above I have endeavoured to consider the factors which will influence ports over the next 25-50 years, in order to consider the matter of obsolescence in ports. In summary I see:

- economic factors will impose automation and reduce manning levels at ports
- private investment in UK ports will increase
- a continuing rise in seaborne cargoes
- vessel sizes will increase with the exception of large bulk carriers
- in UK coastal shipping will increase
- unitisation, particularly containers, Ro Ro and swap bodies will increase substantially
- the UK port industry will grow and change

Steps to mitigate obsolescence:

20. The port industry must consider the steps to be taken now to avoid obsolescence in our ports in the next century.

Older dock areas

21. The perceived situation is that the older docks are now obsolete and must be taken out of port use to be used for offices, recreation, housing, transportation corridors and the like. In some cases this is so but there are many cases where this is inappropriate and I counsel caution to those who wish to rid themselves of our port assets. As Felixstowe has developed one might have expected Ipswich docks to fall into disuse, be acquired by property developers and become hypermarkets. In fact Ipswich has become a major and expanding centre for transhipment cargo on short sea routes and could well acquire new trade from coastal Ro Ro. An important factor is that the Orwell Bridge was built with sufficient air draaught to ensure it is not a restriction to shipping in the future and will not be the cause of obsolescence. There are other examples of similar upriver old port facilities being used for feeder services, aggregate terminals and the like. I see this trend continuing and even increasing in the next century. Thus we should keep available space for shipping related activities at our old port sites where there is sufficient area and in locations that are advantageous in the transportation train. There are some ports (e.g. Shoreham) where a very large land asset can be partially realised in order to fund more port investment to modernise and expand the port activities on its remaining land.

Extending the life of port structures

22. As port engineers know the design life of port structures causes much heated argument between designers and users. The World Bank norm is 60-80 years for quays. The port structures built by our forebears in the last half of the nineteenth century are in many cases still in use but in others have become obsolete (not worn out). With the economic pressures mentioned earlier we have to devise port designs that satisfy the short term view of today's investors but have the capability to be upgraded (e.g. deepened) and to extend the useful life (strengthening corroding steel piles) as cash flow or changes in vessels/cargo occur. In my firm we have deepened our own designs and have strengthened corroding tubular piling - in both cases to good effect and within the economics of the situation. But port engineers have now to take into account the need to be able to modify their port structures in a positive way at the design stage and this is now happening. Certain traditional economic (at the time) designs have to be reconsidered. Figure 4 shows a

typical UK port engineer's block wall quay for which we were asked to consider methods of deepening. The difficulties are self evident on the figure and might have been avoided if the need for future deepening had been taken into account at the original design stage.

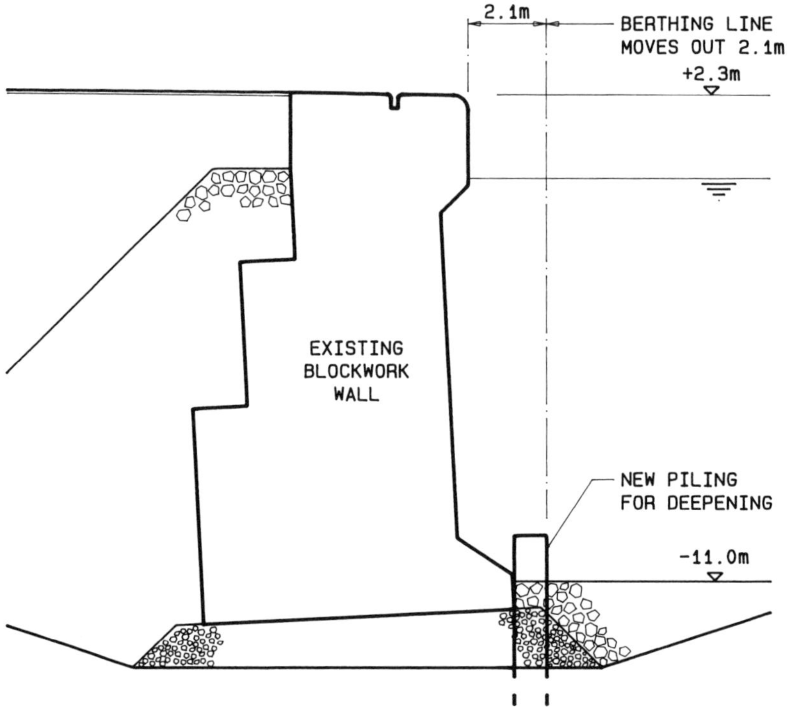

Fig. 4 Deepening of existing berth

Port planning

23. Obsolescence has come about in part due to overall port planning factors - principally lack of space and lack of flexibility (but in some cases lack of draught). These factors are now better understood by port planners and should not cause obsolescence in the future provided adequate space is reserved especially for future expansion. In the past some port areas have become obsolete due to the city growing around it and preventing port expansion and the inland distribution of cargo. Thus in addition to reserving sufficient space and providing flexibility, port planners must reserve adequate inland transport corridors. The Port of Felixstowe has lobbied for and obtained new highways to and into the port with some capacity for future growth.

Additionally in 1987 a new railway spur from the adjacent BR main line was built into the port to take the burgeoning container trains. The planning and development of the port hinterland provided for these corridors, without which the port would have been stifled but not necessarily become obsolete.

24. A particular cause of obsolescence has been the lack of adequate working areas behind the berths. The need for large open (and sometimes covered) storage areas for unitised cargoes has become more clearly understood in the last two decades. With the advent of automation there will be a need for even larger working areas. At present in my firm we are generally allowing land areas of 18 hectares per 300m of deepwater container or multi purpose berth but for the next decade we are allowing 25 hectares per 300m deepwater berth (in the late 60s we allowed only 8-10 hectares). Ro Ro terminals to handle 4-6 freight ferries a day (350,000 trailers p.a.) and with provision for a rail swap body terminal require some 25 hectares. Some additional port related industrial land is required nearby for distribution, warehousing, transport yards and the like.

Ro Ro Terminals

25. Our firm's experience of Ro Ro terminals is that they have had to be significantly remodelled within 10-15 years in order to cope with new vessel types, heavier loadings, better control technology, etc., and Dover Harbour Board have similar experience. Without the capability to economically remodel Ro Ro terminals could rapidly become obsolete.

Transhipment of UK trade

26. The emergence of mainland European ports as hubs for deep sea services with the consequent increase in transhipment of deep sea trade to/from UK is viewed with concern. There are many reasons (see Ref.1) but the trend is upwards. Continental ports have the advantage of their large hinterland and markets with good land transport communications and significant port subsidies. If the latter changed and the economic competitiveness of UK and mainland European ports becomes more equal (the so called level playing field!) then the rate of deep sea calls to UK could be maintained and the increase in transhipment slowed. Many consider that such steps will not be taken by Governments and that UK transhipment will increase and deep sea trade decrease over the next 20-30 years. We need to guard against this, since shallow transhipment berths may become obsolete more rapidly than deepwater berths and land areas may be inadequate.

THE FUTURE

General Conclusions

27. Older UK ports are described as "obsolescent and run down" and their narrow aprons with multi storey transit sheds would confirm this but the actual marine structures are generally in reasonable condition. Sixty years is the minimum design life for quay walls set out in British Standard (BS6349 Pt.1) and has been generally accepted in the industry. The first UK container terminals built in the late 60s have in some cases been deepened (e.g. Landguard Terminal at Felixstowe) but have incorporated flexible port planning features and are likely to continue in port use certainly beyond 2050 (i.e. 90 years). More recent terminals at Felixstowe built in the mid 80s have much greater open back up areas, better road and rail access and are likely to continue in port use well beyond 2050. These terminals were designed for a life 80 years and recent measurement of the steel pile corrosion rate was less than the design allowance. Thus the modern port structures can still be designed to have a life of over 80 years.

28. There is much greater awareness nowadays of the need to incorporate flexibility into port planning and port design in order to cope with future changes and thus avoid obsolescence. Many of our clients have involved my firm in the preparation of port master plans. These plans consider marketing, traffic, port facilities, inland transport links, infrastructure, hinterland area planning, financial and organisation aspects and environmental measures in conjunction with county councils, local planners and other parties. In my experience such a master plan is an essential framework for sensible port development but is a powerful tool in planning to avoid obsolescence. Such master planning can (and should) take into account the factors and mitigating steps mentioned above.

29. Finally I believe that port management, engineers and operators, must think about and take positive steps to deal with obsolescence in ports. Some port managements are doing this, some are just reacting to situations as they arise, but the necessary resources and skill are available to avoid obsolescence and I am confident that UK ports will take advantage of such skills and prosper greatly.

References

Ref.1 Transhipment of UK Trade, Ports Federation and Dept. of Transport 1989.

18. A green port: an engineer's view

A. C. BURDALL and H. J. WILLIAMSON, Sir William Halcrow and Partners

SYNOPSIS

Ports are one example of where man's activities and environmental issues are sometimes in direct conflict. This paper addresses the question "Is it possible to have an efficient and environmentally friendly port?", and suggests that a 'green port' is one that achieves a balance between environmental costs and economic benefit. Consideration is given as to environmental influences both of and on ports and contradictory conclusions drawn on a 'green port'. Inevitably port planning, design and operation of the future port must and will change to accommodate these concerns.

INTRODUCTION

1. Man is becoming increasingly aware of the impact that his activities are having on the environment but also of the impact that the environment will have on his activities.

2. Because of this awareness, there is a growing need to involve environmental considerations in decisions concerning future developments and operations. But, also a greater understanding of the processes and issues concerned is necessary for effective decision making as not all changes to the environment are caused by man. Despite concern, the public perception of environmental issues is sometimes based on misunderstandings of the possible environment impacts and the full extent of environmental concerns are not addressed objectively. These misunderstandings and biased speculation are borne from difficulty in obtaining the evidence supporting environmental change and equal difficulty in its scientific justification.

3. Ports are one such example where the basic needs of the man-made system and these environmental concerns are sometimes in direct conflict.

4. The environment influences ports in two ways: there is an impact of environmental changes on ports and ports have an impact on the environment. Consideration of both of these influences must be included in the overall balance of environmental costs and economic benefits used to form a view on the 'green port'.

5. In putting forward an opinion on the concept of a 'green port' and whether it can be both efficient and environmentally friendly, the Authors have drawn on their background and experience. Hence,it is an 'engineer's view' rather than that of a

port operator or environmentalist and must, of necessity be both subjective and personal.

"WHAT IS A GREEN PORT?"

6. It is difficult to describe what is meant by a 'green port'. The very presence of a port could be said to be unnatural but when do man's activities stop being natural and become unnatural?

7. The environment is unavoidably changed by a port's activities and its construction. Coast defence works influence the coastal processes; dredging, with associated spoil disposal, impacts on the marine environment; geological, chemical and physical processes may cause undesirable effects (for example metals such as iron leaching out of surrounding rock or water stagnation due to poor local circulation); reclamation schemes, required for port development, may lead to changed habitats for bird, fish and animal species and changed fauna and flora; effluent and dust discharges associated with port operations influence water quality and atmosphere; port developments in otherwise undeveloped coastal areas have a visual impact on the environment; sewage, water, emissions and pollution emanating from human populations and industry around ports impact on the overall port environment. These and many other factors lead to the conclusion there can be no simple practical definition of a 'green port' which can cover all environmental situations.

8. It may be argued, as an extreme, that since none of these factors are desirable, no development or operation incurring any of these or other environmental costs should be allowed. However, such an argument ignores the essential economic benefits accruing from port development. Equally the environmental costs must consider the total environment and not just local effects. Without maritime transport links, economic activity and growth would be severely restricted or result in the creation of alternative transport links which themselves incur greater environmental costs. A switch of traffic, for example, from sea to air transport requires greater fossil fuel usage with corresponding greater CO_2 emissions and global environmental impact. Hence, consideration of the debate as to the 'green port' must be expanded to include greater environmental issues than just those local to the particular port or development.

9. Because of their very location in river estuaries, or on sheltered coastlines, and because of their overall infrastructure and historical development, many ports have to cope not only with their own present environmental problems but also with inherited ones. This inheritance can be historical or from the actions of others within the waterway system on which the port is located. Hong Kong is at present, planning major studies to derive a policy for disposal of dredged spoil resulting from both capital and maintenance dredging operations. Because of both previous local industrial development and discharges upstream in the Pearl River, the dredged sediments are, at least in part, contaminated with heavy metals making traditional disposal unacceptable.

10. Any port development today requires (or should require) an Environmental Impact Assessment (EIA). This assessment will define the environmental influences of any proposed change of operation which can, as a separate exercise, be set against the economic benefits. Reconciling and balancing two such opposing interests is a matter of judgement but one which nonetheless can be used to form a view on the acceptability of a project.

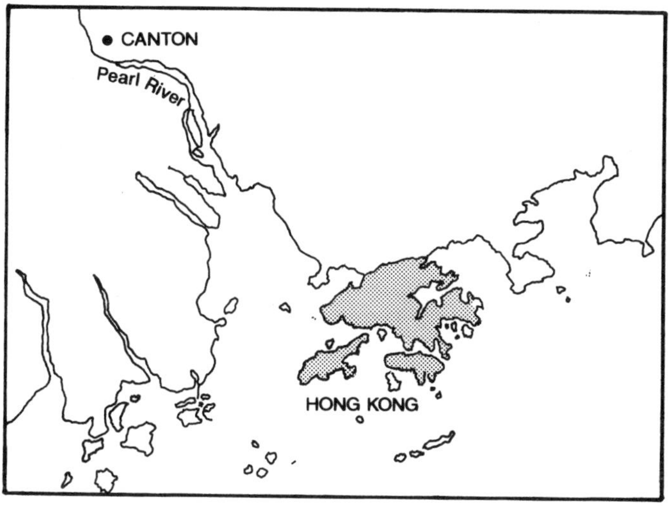

Figure 1: Hong Kong key plan

11. From these various threads, therefore, it is suggested that a 'green port' is one that achieves an acceptable balance of environmental impact and commercial operation. The constitution of an acceptable balance must be a subjective judgement based on environmental costs and economic benefits with the proviso that no irreversible environmental change is acceptable.

NATURE OF PORT DEVELOPMENT

12. The initial growth of a port and surrounding hinterland arises from local or national demand. The on-going progress or decline of a port is dependent on economic and political change but the requirements of ports and the facilities that they offer have varied over time and ports have had to keep in time with current needs. As this process of development and change takes place, so environmental conditions and constraints on future alternative development are left behind.

13. A classic pattern of port development, repeated in many places around the world, is where the original port has moved in stages downstream to accommodate changes in shipping problems and trade. An example of this process is port development on the River Tees. The original Roman port was located as far upstream as possible at the confluence of the River Tees and Levens at Yarm; to accommodate larger vessels in the period leading up to the industrial revolution main port activities moved downstream to Stockton-on-Tees; Victorian impounded docks were established downstream at Middlesbrough; the post-war development led to river wharfs downstream of Middlesbrough and the establishment of Teesport; North Sea oil, the advent of VLCC's and large bulk carriers led to the centre moving to the estuary mouth at Seal Lands and Redcar; studies have been carried out for open sea berths in Tees Bay and also for extending the Gare Sands Breakwater to provide additional port capacity. This process of movement and development has left behind a legacy of environmental constraints which must be addressed in any future development.

14. The types of cargo and handling methods have also changed. The advent of containerisation has, for example, generated a new breed of container ports with their own, capital intensive, handling methods and ship turnaround requirements. The trend towards large bulk carriers for both liquid and solid cargoes, has led to the development of specialised bulk terminals with intensive high speed handling equipment.

15. All of these various port developments with their associated economic benefits have environmental implications.

IMPACT OF ENVIRONMENTAL CHANGE ON PORTS

Overview

16. There are underlying environmental changes both naturally occurring and due to man's activities that are having and will continue to have an effect on ports. Global warming leading to rising sea levels and climate change; CO_2 emissions from shipping and other transport; changes in marine life including algae growth; and changed trading and traffic patterns due to environmental influences are all examples of such changes. Also, there can be perceived environmental factors which, whilst not having a proper scientific foundation, can have a detrimental constraint on legitimate port developments and operations.

17. Some factors may be detrimental (or even disastrous) to particular ports and maritime traffic; others may be beneficial, leading to increased throughput.

Global Warming

18. The earth is undergoing a period of global warming. It is generally accepted that there has been a global mean temperature rise of 0.5 °C over the past 100 years but with considerable variation around the trend. Within geological time, there have been other periods of both global warming and cooling but, unlike previous changes, the present trend is ascribed by the majority of scientific opinion to the

increase of greenhouse gases resulting from man's activities.

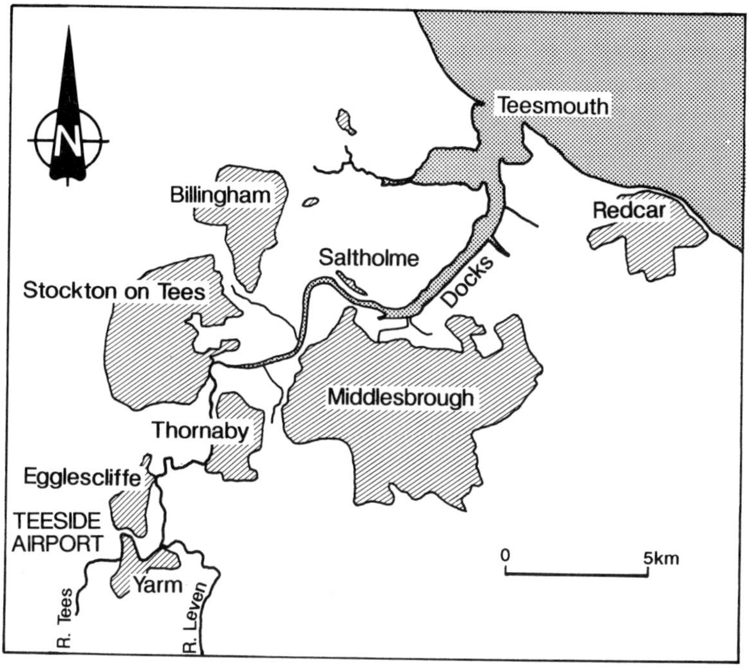

Figure 2: Development map of River Tees

19. Global warming will impact directly on ports by a rise in sea level and, in higher latitudes, an increase in frequency of occurrence and severity of storms.

20. Estimates vary enormously on the amount of sea level rise that may take place over the next 50 or 100 years. Rises of between 500 and 3500 mm by the year 2100 have been suggested by Dugdale (1989) but these are probably over estimates. A reasonable hypothesis may be 4 mm per annum, which in engineering terms means that the direct effects of sea level rise will be insignificant with regard to port planning, ship handling and cargo handling.

21. As indicated in Figure 3, a rise of 1 metre theoretically could indicate large areas in the east and south of Britain with ports such as Immingham, Grimsby and

Kings Lynne strongly under threat. These areas, however, are already at or below sea level protected by 6 or 7 lines of coast defences. Global warming effects will lead to raising of these defences but where flood defence barrages are used disruptions to shipping may arise.

22. Increase in the frequency and severity of storms, resulting from global warming, will lead to changes in the coastal regime. Wave heights will increase due to greater storm winds and increased water depths leading to reduced bottom effect. Tidal currents and levels will change due to changes in tidal wave propagation. Storm surges, however, caused by wind stress and barometric pressure changes will be most affected by greater storms.

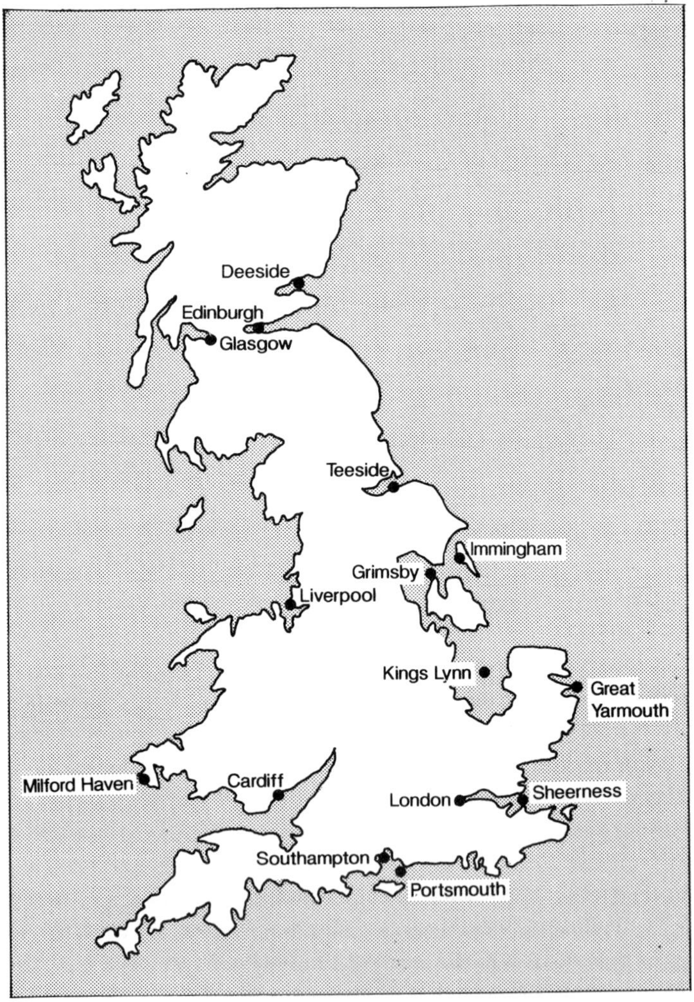

Figure 3: Revised UK Coastline with 1 metre sea level rise

CO_2 Emissions

23. Release of so called 'greenhouse gases' by man's activities is a factor in determining the global warming. As indicated by Figure 4, the major component of such gases is CO_2 accounting for some 50% of the total.

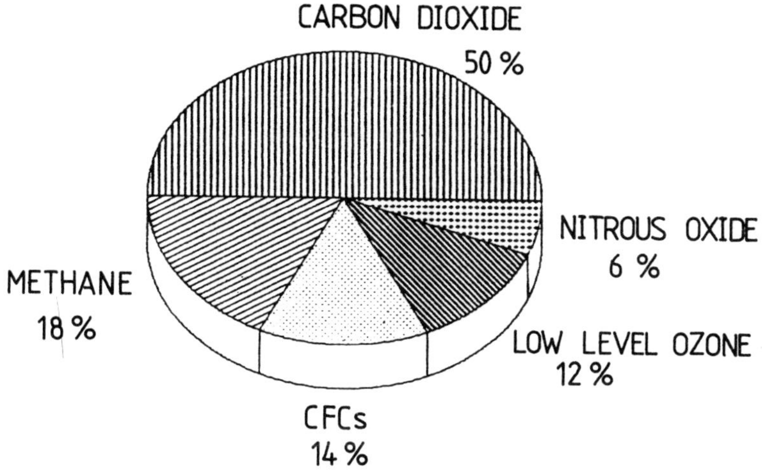

Figure 4: Make-up of greenhouse gases (Source: Dugdale 1989)

24. Future economic growth with associated energy consumption makes reduction of this proportion difficult. The social and political pressure, however, for reduction in 'greenhouse gas' emissions must lead to pressure to find more energy efficient ways of providing the necessary transport services. In terms of unit fuel cost per tonne-mile, sea transport is the most efficient transport mode and consideration, therefore, of global environmental factors should lead to increased maritime traffic at the expense of land and air transport.

Marine Life

25. Algal growth and entrophication are ecological processes occurring in port waters whose nature and extent is dependent on climate as well as nutrient load and water quality. Their effects include an increase in ship fouling with increased drag, a need for regular inspection and maintenance of marine structures and different stresses due to wave and current loading than those for which they were designed.

26. Pollutants from rivers, land run-off and discharges often cause waters to be nutrient rich and this overstimulates the growth of algae in port waters. To prevent catastrophic anoxic situations occurring, harvesting of algae, with its attendant problems of disposal, becomes necessary. Figure 5 indicates harvesting of ulva carried out at Tunis North Lake as part of a scheme to achieve an acceptable water quality. Similar problems have been experienced in Venice and, surprisingly, tidal barrage and other schemes are being promoted within the UK which will create similar conditions.

27. Other ecological processes may affect the growth of marine life in ports. Estuaries and coasts are regions where many organisms breed and where environmental stress can lead to changes in populations and a reduction in species diversity. But marine ecology is naturally dynamic and constantly evolving, imposing restraints on port activities.

Figure 5: Harvesting of ulva

Traffic and Trading Patterns

28. Ports adapt and evolve to suit the traffic they must handle. Where outside environmental pressures cause a change in trade, the port must respond.

29. This general concept is illustrated by the present debate taking place within the United Kingdom concerning electricity generation and fuel supplies. Both SO_2 and CO_2 emissions must be reduced from coal burning power stations. FGD (flue gas desulphurisation) can reduce the former but has no effect on the latter. Due to site space restrictions FGD cannot be fitted to many power stations, requires millions of tonnes of limestone (with consequential impact on the countryside due to quarrying), results in the need to dispose of millions of tonnes of gypsum produced as a bi-product and is expensive. An alternative is to import low sulphur, higher calorific and cheaper world coal which would reduce both SO_2 and CO_2. However, this will demand bulk handling facilities with a capacity of up to 30 million tonnes per annum in the UK ports.

ENVIRONMENTAL IMPACT OF PORTS

Overview

30 By their nature and very existence, ports must have some impact on the environment, resulting from their construction and operation. An Environmental Impact Assessment (EIA) is required to assess these influences and their extent. For a typical port these would include: changes in the coastal regime; effects of ship operations; dust, noise, smell and other emissions resulting from port operations; and disposal of dredged spoil. Each of these factors will have an, impact not only on the physical environment but also on the social and economic environment of the local population. Whilst not normally included in an assessment, except perhaps where a conflict exists (as in many ports) between commercial and recreational interests, these social and economic influences are a necessary part of evaluating a particular port.

31. The present discussion is limited to considering a general response of the port industry to these legitimate environmental issues as part of the argument on the feasibility of a 'green port'.

Coastal Regime

32. The coastal regime and local physical environment and its associated waves, tides and currents are affected by the existence of a port. Breakwaters and any other protection works inevitably interrupt any established pattern of sediment drift. Dredging and reclamation works change circulation patterns but also can cover existing mudflats or banks. Such changes can lead to environmental difficulties where bird or marine life habitats are threatened.

Ship Operations

33. Ship operations lead to discharges into the marine environment either accidentally or intentionally. Such discharges are direct examples of environmental issues in which the economic and environmental concerns are directly opposing and a solution which satisfies commercial port operations and the marine environment are difficult to resolve.

34. The bottom port environment and benthic community are affected by the continuous movement of shipping. Some ports, such as Southampton, exhibit communities of species which have been brought from overseas on ships hulls.

35. Fouling of ships hulls is a problem in the marine environment and encrustation by the algae enteromorpha is extensive. This leads to reduced hydrodynamic efficiency and obvious increased fuel consumption and time costs. Anti-fouling paints, based mainly on tri-organotin compounds, have been used but this biocide has been found to concentrate within some food chains, particularly in shellfish. This type of compound has been banned for certain classes of shipping.

36. Other discharges from ships encompass discharge of sewage holding tanks, oil spills resulting from shipping accidents or tank cleaning operations and discharge of ballast water. There are terminals around the world, some commissioned within the last 20 years, where facilities do not exist to receive such discharges onshore with proper treatment but such examples are becoming rare. Treatment of oily ballast water, for example, should be to a standard of better than 20 ppm with no visible oil.

37. Oil spills, either at the berth during handling or whilst at sea provide particular concern. The planning of any terminal must include for pollution control measures based on booms, skimmers and dispersants plus maybe physical protection for vulnerable facilities or areas. Studies, for example, are presently being carried out to design protection works for the Umm al Nar de-salination plant, Abu Dhabi to prevent accidental ingress of oil spillage from the adjacent tanker terminal.

Port Operations

38. Ports affect water and atmospheric quality because of dust, noise, smell and other emissions both directly from the cargo handling operations and the port related industrial activity. These problems are inherent with the running of a modern port. Whilst many of the problems, in the popular perception, are regarded as difficult to deal with they are not impossible to reduce or eliminate.

39. There will be a visual impact caused by the presence of a port and the local outlook and residential desirability often suffers. But this can be minimised by careful planning of new ports and, where appropriate, measures could be taken to improve existing ports.

40. Dust is a particular emission associated with bulk handling terminals. Over the past few years there has been considerable improvement, at the Teesbulk Handling Terminal, Teesport, UK in the methods of bulk loading and unloading of potash to reduce dust emissions. Installation of a dedusting exhaust fan, as

indicated in Figure 6, and other measures has alleviated emissions, although some minor problems are still encountered concerned with strong winds sucking dust from open holds.

Dredged Spoil

41. Both capital and maintenance dredge form an integral part of many port operations giving consequential environmental problems associated with disposal of the dredged spoil. For many ports this represents the single most important environmental issue.

42. Traditionally routine maintenance dredge spoil has been dumped at sea with a small proportion, regarded as suitable for reclamation, being pumped ashore. In many parts of the world, dumping at sea is prohibited or at least severely restrict. Experience with various geotechnical treatments is allowing ever finer sediments to be successfully used for reclamation where space exists and there is a requirement for land area. However, in many older ports the seabed sediments are contaminated particularly with heavy metals making both pumping ashore as direct reclamation and dumping at sea unacceptable. Maybe even, the act of dredging such sediments puts heavy metals into suspension in the waterway, either via the dredge water or by direct action of the dredge head. Treatment of sediments is possible to remove heavy metals but, on the scale potentially required even for a modest dredging campaign, scarcely feasible. The only realistic alternative may be to pump contaminated sediments into sealed reclamations which, in due course, can be used for development.

Figure 6: Effects of de-dusting fan on bulk potash loading (Source: Teesbulk 1990)

43. Ports with a significant dredging commitment are inevitably going to have to set aside significant areas for disposal of dredged spoil.

IS A "GREEN PORT" POSSIBLE?

44. The question therefore arises "Is a green port possible?"

45. The answer depends on what is considered by the term 'green port' and how environmentally friendly a port must be to be considered 'green'. In the broadest terms it is suggested that, although there can be no simple definition, a 'green port' is one that achieves an acceptable balance of environmental costs and economic benefits.

46. Clearly, if this balance is judged to be the point at which ports have no effect on the natural environment, then it is clearly impossible to have a 'green port'. However, if it is accepted to be at a point which incorporates measures to mitigate adverse environmental change such that the overall environmental effects do not destroy the natural ecological balance regionally or globally and, at the same time, achieves the requirements for successful port operation, the 'green port' is both viable and readily achievable. The final judgement is purely subjective as the opinion of what is 'green' and 'natural' varied considerably and is presently a matter of great debate.

47. Consideration of environmental issues as they effect ports lead the Authors to the conclusion that ports will have to respond to the present debate concerning environmental issues but that with mitigation measures an acceptable balance can be achieved. However, there is a direct conflict between achieving an acceptable environment and maximising port efficiency and some present operational practices cannot be tolerated if an acceptable balance is to be achieved.

48. New ports can be designed to minimise environmental impact if environmental factors are considered from an early stage and sufficient economic return is generated for the inevitable extra costs.

THE FUTURE PORT

49. Environmental considerations must be involved in decisions which affect future ports. Careful investigations will become necessary with, perhaps, ever increasing constraints on development and these pressures will add to the economic pressure to maximise port efficiency and investment. There may be moves towards more compact port facilities requiring less land with a reduction in the geographical extent of environmental impact. Improved port planning and methods or cargo handling will benefit the port environment. Larger, more fuel efficient, vessels will require deeper water but be less susceptible to wave action thus encouraging the development of offshore terminals.

50. Overall planning of the future port and attendant industrial area may have to be concentrated so that precious land and coastal areas can be reserved for natural undeveloped areas. The issue of water and dredged spoil disposal must be seriously investigated if the future port is to be environmentally acceptable.

51. The future port, above all else, will be subject to planning and environmental scrutiny. A possible future extension of the Port of Sheerness at Lappel Bank (Figure 6) has been and is being subjected to such scrutiny with extensive model testing solely for environmental considerations has been carried out.

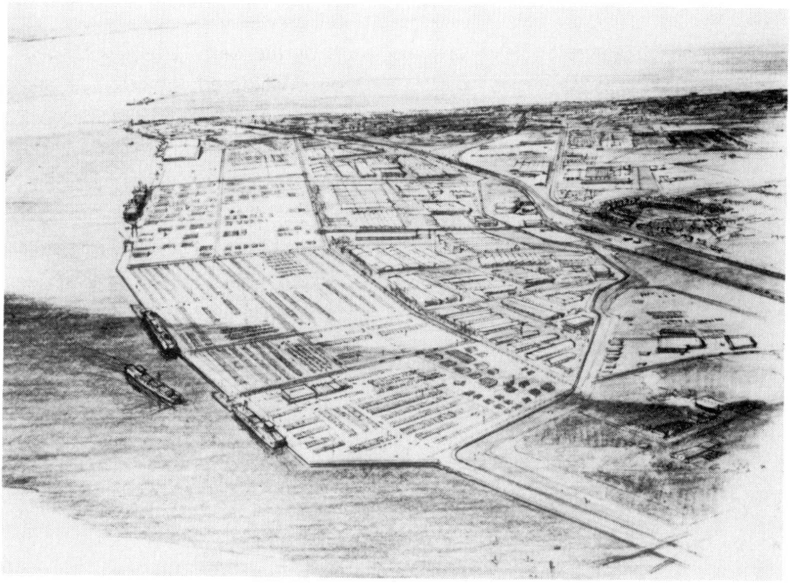

Figure 7: Lappel Bank Development

CONCLUSIONS

52. The engineer's view of a 'green port' is one which satisfies both the environmental acceptability and commercial port requirements. Present concern over the environment means that these issues must be seriously considered during port planning and development and some sacrifices, of port costs and efficiency must be made if an acceptable balance between environmental and commercial considerations is to be achieved. The future port will require much thought if an acceptable 'green port' is ever likely to be achieved.

19. A new approach to port engineering

A. D. M. BELLIS, Consultant

SYNOPSIS

For too long port construction and operation in the UK has, with a few notable exceptions, developed on the back of age old, long tried but generally conservative methods and styles. For instance: ships are still moored to berths with systems of ropes similar to those that probably applied to Jason of the Argonauts' ship, quay levels are nearly always about 2 m above maximum water level whilst ship cargo decks and hatches tower many metres above, port hydrographic surveys are still carried out by fully manned, expensive motor launches.

It is appreciated that port design is very much dictated by ship design (which for too long was too traditional for words) and cargo size and shape. This is a hen and egg situation and ports could take a lead by offering facilities that could handle ships and cargo of any conceivable kind.

To meet these objectives calls for imagination, something that in the port scene was forthcoming in the last war but not since. Some of the old ideas must be debunked, consideration given to revolutionary but commonsense ones. Minds must be freed from tradition.

Flexibility is obviously a key factor in future port design with the ability to accommodate any reasonable shape of vessel and type of cargo and any related movement or storage of that cargo throughout the port area.

Changeability is also a key word. Sections of ports should be mobile so that facilities can be remodelled to meet changing demands. Buildings should be portable and avoid being obstructive. More use should be made of today's very heavy lift floating equipment for construction or repositioning in large modules. Floating breakwaters should be developed further.

Finally obsolescence must be more closely considered as ports of the future cannot be saddled with structures and equipment built to last 50-100 years when they may not be needed for the next 20.

THE FUTURE

BACKGROUND

1. Traditionally the civil engineer provides the port and harbour infrastructure. This is defined as that part which extends from (and includes) the quay and working areas downwards and all harbour protection works. He then shares with his mechanical and electrical colleagues the tasks of providing plant, equipment, electrical distribution, above ground structures and buildings. The infrastructure referred to encompasses everything of an artifically contrived nature in the development of a port or harbour which in the main includes breakwaters, navigation channels, training walls, wharves, quays, jetties, locks and docks.

2. It is perhaps an unfortunate sine qua non in most engineering work that a construction or piece of equipment must be as safe and fit for its purpose on the last day of its operational use as it was on the day of commissioning. This, coupled with the need to provide facilities that will withstand the ravages of years of use, and abuse, by ships cargoes and the elements, has led to the building of infrastructures that will in many cases last indefinitely. In very few situations has it been possible or even considered acceptable to engineer built-in obsolescence.

3. Most of the major ports in the UK and many overseas were at their peak of development in the Victorian era and just afterwards and all the strength and durability, and some over design fortunately, that was so much the hallmark of that time has been reflected in port construction. Since the end of the basic port building spree by, say, the first World War only a handful of traditional closed docks have been built. Elsewhere, when tidal conditions and natural water depths permitted, the most significant port developments for general cargo handling have been based upon linear open deep water berths. The model for this type of facility was perhaps Southampton with a later example being Harwich and much later, Felixstowe.

4. As a result of these constraints within construction most port authorities have found themselves with vast, solid infrastructures not always suitable or adaptable to the rapidly changing pattern of shipping and cargo. It must not be assumed however that no foresight went into 19th and early 20th century design. Many port engineers were farsighted or wise enough that, with encouragement, they were able to build for the future as they saw it. Because of this we have the great open quays at Southampton, the exceptionally wide locks for their day at Immingham, Newport and Tilbury docks. These dimensions have allowed those ports to prosper and, to a large extent, meet the challenge of rapidly expanding ship sizes. Many of the other ports and docks with limited dimensions are now closed.

SHIPPING CATEGORIES

5. The introductory remarks have largely applied to general cargo shipping and to a lesser extent to liners and oil and bulk carriers. These categories with a few specialist exceptions formed the bulk of shipping using overseas and UK port and harbours in the past. Since the second World War and particularly since about 1960 changes in shipping use, in vessel sizes, turnround time and greater inter-port and international competition have thrown different emphasis on ship types. There are now, in broad terms, the following ranges of vessels using European and international ports. These, with their successors, will have to be catered for in any new port construction.

1. Oil carriers.

2. Bulk carriers.

3. General cargo vessel in several varieties

    (a) Traditional break bulk
    (b) Container carrier - lift on, lift off
    (c) Roll on, roll off vessels
    (d) Short sea vessels and coasters.

4. Ferries. Some for passengers only but an increasing number of passengers, cars, self drive freight vehicles and unit loads.

5. Leisure craft.

The last category, leisure craft, requires the facilities of marinas and the paper is not intended to cover this special subject. Suffice to say that a number of features in the construction and operation of marinas, though on a small scale, are quite novel in the maritime engineering field. Sector gates for locks, boat hoists and lifts, spud pontoon landing stages are some of these features, larger versions of which could well be adopted in major port construction.

6. The principal categories of vessels covered in 1 to 4 vary in size from those of a few hundred tonnes dwt to as much as 0.5M dwt. Most ports and harbours however are constructed to deal with ships in the middle of this range and it is for them that problems of construction and maintenance are directed.

CONSEQUENCE OF CHANGE

7. In the last 25 years the increase in ship size and the decrease in turn round time have, with the exception of some short haul ferry traffic which always turned round with speed, exceeded all the changes that occurred in the previous 125 years. Valiant efforts have been made to modify existing facilities to meet these accelerating changes, especially

where cash or land was not available for new structures, and thanks frequently to the physical soundness of much port infrastructure engineers have been able to adapt them to meet new demands. Larger vessels have usually meant deeper draughts but due to the development of bigger, more powerful and efficient dredgers, new navigation channels, berths and approaches have been created and maintained to match demand in very many locations. Regrettably in too many instances some traditional ports have not been able to adapt and much trade has been lost. There is also of course a limit to the modifications that can be made to older, traditional structures.

VERSATILITY AND FLEXIBILITY

8. This limitation on the ability to modernise a port mainly because of its lack of flexibility has meant the end of many ports or at best a limit to their expansion. Even though the upward trends in ship sizes must be nearing a plateau there are still changes occurring and it is of paramount importance in all new civil engineering developments in ports and harbours to provide adaptability and flexibility perhaps even more than innovation.

9. Engineers must build into their designs not obsolescence, which is all too often called for and is all too often impracticable, but versatility. Very frequently they will be pressed to design something very specific for a new shipping service. It is often difficult or impossible to resist providing a tailor-made berth but how often does one see this service collapse or leave the berth or port well before its financial or physical life has expired. What is then left may be quite unsuitable for another service. Structures which can be adapted for more general use are what is required with a greater freedom of use incorporated in the designs.

10. Unfortunately the port industry, in keeping with so many other things associated with maritime activities and their long history, can be very conservative and departures from the norm may be difficult. There is also less opportunity to-day for port construction which is not for established or agreed customer demand. This leaves less scope for speculative building and little encouragement or training in novelty and versatility.

11. Yet as far back as the second World War, now some 45 years ago, the Mulberry Harbour was conceived. It was a port and harbour that could be taken anywhere, up-anchored and removed to another site if necessary, its configuration changed and it had an ability to deal with both military and civilian vessels. Many port engineers worked on that project as designers or contractors and yet the number of its features or principles that have been used in subsequent port and harbour developments have been woefully few.

12. It is true that many floatable concrete caissons of varying forms have been used as the basis of later quays, dock

works and breakwaters and the pontoons and link spans were key features or early ro-ro terminals but all too often new port work followed the solid, immovable pattern of pre-war(s). The mobility, flexibility and versatility which was the theme of Mulberry has not been perpetuated in any noticeable measure.

13. Some new designs using diaphragm walling and other so called economic features have followed but still producing very permanent and unalterable structures. Perhaps the greater use of sheet piling for wall construction goes a little way along the road to a readily adaptable design.

14. Port civil engineers and consultants should be encouraged to free their minds from tradition, look well into the future and think both unconventionally and flexibly.

15. Developments that can perhaps help this thinking have occurred in the North Sea off-shore oil industry where there was no long tradition of structures or systems to follow and many unknowns had to be faced in structural design. These unknowns were not future ship sizes and shapes and cargo trends but the unknowns of deep water, rough seas and uncertain locations. What did the industry do? They built portable and mobile structures, some as big as ocean going ships, complete with mechanical handling equipment and operators accommodation. When use of a unit in one place was exhausted it was moved to another. Admittedly the money available in the off-shore industry is of a different order to that in ports but the approach can be the same, if on a different scale.

CONSTRUCTION EQUIPMENT FOR INFRASTRUCTURE

16. Very much as a result of these North Sea developments coupled with new bulk terminals being built worldwide, there are many items of maritime equipment of exceptional characteristics and capacities available to today's engineers. There are floating cranes that will lift several thousand tonnes in one go, submersible ships and pontoons that can carry and launch complete structure, jack-up barges that can be used for temporary construction platforms for port works and high capacity dredgers that work efficiently in soil, sand and rock. There is much sophisticated diving equipment and expertise available also.

17. Some of this equipment has been used for port construction and in particular the modern generation of dredgers has enabled quays and jetties to be established in deep and often open water with financially viable construction and maintenance of approach channels and dredged areas. The use of items of plant has normally been at the choice of the contractor. Seldom has the promoting port engineer conceived a design which could use this high capacity equipment to its full potential. However it does give the opportunity to envisage a port in large prefabricated sections capable of subsequent removal or modification if the usage changes. Some of the equipment can even be embodied in the permanent port works. A version of a jack-up barge could well be used in a

ro-ro terminal in tidal waters as the adjustable intermediate link between ship and shore. It would be infinitely variable and mobile.

BREAKWATERS

18. Breakwaters on the mammoth scale necessary to create new harbours for the safe berthing and working of VLCCs etc. are a very specialist subject requiring a chapter on its own. There have been some spectacular failures in this field and some interesting reading on the designs and constructions can be found in the proceedings of recent conferences at the Institution of Civil Engineers.

19. On a more modest scale however, there have been many recent attempts to introduce floating breakwaters to protect exposed berths. In theory these have the advantages of flexibility and economy of cost. Materials used have included scrap vehicle tyres, floating concrete units or pontoons all linked together and moored to the sea bed by piles or anchors. None appear to have been very successful which demonstrates that wave energy can only be absorbed by something massive or immovable.

20. Perhaps there is another lesson to be learned here from 'Mulberry' where ships were scuttled in line to form an instant breakwater. Although not environmentally too pleasing perhaps such a system could be acceptable in certain locations. There appears to be no shortages of cheap redundant shipping and once grounded and the hulls opened up the 'shipwrecks' become virtually immovable.

FENDERING AND MOORING

21. Whilst on the one hand there must be as many systems of fendering to quays and jetties as there are consultants and port engineers, on the other hand the methods of mooring vessels to fixed structures or at anchorages have hardly changed since the ark. For the former function the key in the future must be simplicity and ease of maintenance. There are far too many over-complicated fender systems and these, by definition, bear the brunt of ships berthing, they can become a port engineer's nightmare.

22. In the case of the latter, moorings, we are stuck with perhaps an over-crude system. Whether it is a small fishing vessel or a supertanker the same equipment, namely ropes, bollards and winches, differing only in size and strength and used in the same general configuration of head and stern ropes, springs, etc., is universally used. All this is cumbersome and labour intensive and must be particularly unwelcome in the range of vessels with which most ports are concerned. In the last fifty years or more about the only advances made have been in constant tension winches, quick release bollards and polypropylene ropes.

23. It must be time to look for big changes with perhaps a reversal of the degrees of complexity in fendering and a progression to more sophisticated systems of mooring particularly with larger vessels.

MOORINGS

24. It is easy to known traditional rope mooring systems but they are cumbersome and by no means without their shortcomings and failures. The movement of ships in exposed berths due to rough water from both short and long period waves, tidal ranges and the ships own periodicity does present problems for which only conventional harnesses of mooring ropes have so far proved effective. There appears however to be room for a mooring system which reduces the number of ties between ship and 'shore'.

25. An obvious simplification would be to provide the berth with, ideally, two booms fully pivoted at the ends attached to the quay and the others fitted with a universal and flexible coupling to the ship. Booms of this style have been used successfully in the off-shore industry and the single anchoring of large vessels to tower loading facilities. This is an equivalent but more rigid version of the single buoy mooring (SBM) which is in itself a possible system for the future handling of those commodities, other than oil, which can be reduced to granular or slurry mixes suitable for pumping. There seems as yet no overriding reasons why similar boom moorings cannot be designed for use at traditional parallel fixed terminals. Physical model tests of ships moored to berths in a variety of environmental conditions can now be carried out in laboratories with very reliable loadings calculated in any system of mooring.

26. Another possible solution to the problem which is very radical and perhaps too simple to be practicable is to hold a ship at a berth by magnetism. A ship is a large steel object and there seems no more obvious way to hold it in place than by a series of powerful electro-magnets fitted to the berth. There would be no fixed ropes to part, no heavy equipment to handle and in theory it would be a system that could cope with any direction of movement of the ship. Critics will say that even if it is physically possible to hold a ship this way its polarity will be drastically altered and with it the host of electrical and electronic devices that are now indispensable at sea. Ships were protected against magnetic mines during the last war by de-gaussing and 'wiping'. Surely some converse of that system could be used to protect ships' equipment from electro-magnetic mooring? It would at last seem advisable for some model or small scale testing of the system to be carried out and the proposal fully investigated.

DRY DOCKS

27. The day of day or graving docks being provided in UK ports seems to be over. With a few exceptions those constructed within port systems are either too small for today's requirements or too dilapidated or uneconomic to retain. Much development in ship lifts (synchrolifts) has taken place and systems can now be provided for 'docking' vessels of Panamax or greater size. The infrastructure to accommodate these lifts is considerably less than for a

conventional dry dock and these devices should be given close consideration when a demand arises.

SUPERSTRUCTURE

28. After having provided the basic infrastructure for a port the civil engineer will be required to surface it where necessary, lay out roads and in some cases railways and tracks for cranes, conveyors and other equipment. Water supply, drainage and general services are also necessary but these do not give much scope for innovation however vital they are. Then there is the provision of buildings, the major ones ranging from operations offices and administration blocks to sheds, warehouses, silos and storage accommodation for cargo and cargo related activities.

29. Of all these features those that give scope for innovation and flexibility are probably surfacing, including roads, and buildings for cargo storage or handling.

SURFACING AND ACCESS

30. In the case of quays for general cargo and unitised loads, surfacing will be continuous and road access to the working areas, to the port appliances and to the ships themselves should not be a physical problem. Care must however be taken to provide safe access for port workers and other pedestrians, especially non-port employees such as ships crews, ship repair and provisioning staff. This is vital in highly mechanised berths.

31. For jetties and terminals for handling oils and bulks it is very important to ensure that access to and along such jetties is adequate for all purposes. It must be strong enough for fire appliances, supply lorries and necessary maintenance equipment such as mobile cranes and spares for the cargo handling equipment. Too often clients and designers have been over-economical in 'non-production' areas and this is a mistake.

32. In respect of cargo handling areas, the keynote must be to keep them as unobstructed as possible. The trend in unitising cargo and handling it by ro-ro and lo-lo methods calls for completely open quays and back up areas. Sheds, offices, small cabins etc. must be kept well clear of the operational areas. With the increasing use of portable VHF radios by operating and stevedoring staff it is nowadays unnecessary to have control offices near the scene of the action. These large uncluttered spaces give the flexibility needed to meet changing patterns of cargo operations and new, predominantly mobile, equipment.

33. Generally when surfacing or paving is mentioned in the context of flexibility it is the construction and characteristic of the paving itself that is referred to. 'Flexible' paving is either an asphalt or bituminous macadam surface, prefabricated relayable concrete slabs, or blockwork. The last mentioned is very fashionable at the present time though it is ironic to recall that earlier and original versions of this construction, namely stone setts and wooden

blocks, were ripped up by the mile in the 1950s and 1960s as being unsuitable for port working. It is claimed that block paving and concrete slabs can be readily and relatively cheaply relevelled and if necessary replaced if they suffer settlement from cargo and vehicle loadings. This may in part be true, and relevelling will certainly be necessary with such flexible designs, but none of this can be accomplished without disruption to the services using the area. There is still much to be said for an uncomplicated surface of thick reinforced concrete, on a properly laid and compacted formation, designed to withstand the heaviest foreseeable loads. The lack of maintenance and its associated interruption will be (or should be) much appreciated by the operators and in the long run this construction will be cheaper than other systems. If at any time a concrete surface has to be altered or removed to permit a change of use then there is adequate equipment available for breaking, drilling or cutting it without unbearable expense or inconvenience.

BUILDINGS

34. With very few exceptions no building of a permanent nature should be established in a cargo working area. Exceptions may have to be made for substations and small structures housing ro-ro link span and bridge controls and, say, conveying equipment.

35. If covered transit or cargo assembly sheds are required within a quay crane's reach of a berth, and this is becoming less and less so, then very serious consideration should be given to the use of inflatable buildings or light framed and clad storage sheds. All of these can be readily moved away from the berth area and to other locations when a change of use occurs. Consideration could even be given to rigid sheds on wheels, perhaps in sections, which could be towed to and from location. With not too much ingenuity these could be made as secure as any traditional warehouses and transit sheds both to meet anti-theft and customs requirements.

36. Further away from ship working areas other buildings such as passenger terminals, agents offices, administration blocks and maintenance depots should, where possible, be designed for ease of modification (internal and external) and extension to meet changes in demands. It is often very difficult before new services and facilities are introduced, particularly for passenger and vehicle processing and some types of cargo handling and storage, to establish the ultimate requirements demanded by all the parties concerned. This will include stevedores, agents and forwarders, Customs and Immigration, all too many of whose representatives are not good judges of space and movement and untrained in interpreting drawings and plans. They are often only able fully to appreciate a new facility after it has been constructed. Then come the surprised reactions and the pressing demand for modification more space, etc. etc.!

RESEARCH

37. Although covered fully in another chapter, references have been made to the use of hydraulic and related maritime research under laboratory conditions. Physical modelling is a tool available to the civil engineer and run by the scientific professions, as also are mathematical models. There is a tendency however to put new schemes to the 'laboratory or computer test' which in some instances is a fashion rather more than an essential requirement. The need for modelling a scheme should be very closely examined before a client commits himself to the expense and the time involved. Such research may already have been done elsewhere and can be ferreted out and made fresh use of. The field work necessary to mount a model proposal may in itself be enough to give the engineer the basic information he needs. Experience, observation and common sense must be used in judging the best way forward.

MAINTENANCE

38. Maintaining port and harbour facilities is an unavoidable feature of operating an undertaking. Adequate financial and labour provision must be made for this activity as must the opportunity for carrying out the work. It is difficult enough effecting repairs underwater or in tidal conditions and the least the maintenance engineer can expect is some workable period of possession.

39. Where elements of a facility are subject to day to day damage viz. fendering units, it is desirable for these to be readily removable, with a replacement unit at hand, and repaired off site. The disruption and danger of in situ repairs can then be lessened.

40. It is however up to those responsible for handling ships and for working them to see that no thoughtless damage is inflicted on structures and plant. A good discipline for ship manoeuvring and berthing is required and, where port facilities cannot themselves be fendered, the use of suitable ships' or berthing staff's fenders must be insisted upon.

41. Nothing will give good service unless operated with care and maintained with skill. Funds for doing both must be available. A port and its equipment need no less careful driving and regular maintenance than a motor car.

SYNOPSIS. For too long port construction and operation in the UK has, with a few notable exceptions, developed on the back of age old, long tried but generally conservative methods and styles. For instance: ships are still moored to berths with systems of ropes similar to those that probably applied to Jason of the Argonauts' ship, quay levels are nearly always about 2 m above maximum water level whilst ship cargo decks and hatches tower many metres above, port hydrographic surveys are still carried out by fully manned, expensive motor launches.

It is appreciated that port design is very much dictated by ship design (which for too long was too traditional for words) and cargo size and shape. This is a hen and egg situation and ports could take a lead by offering facilities that could handle ships and cargo of any conceivable kind.

To meet these objectives calls for imagination, something that in the port scene was forthcoming in the last war but not since. Some of the old ideas must be debunked, consideration given to revolutionary but commonsense ones. Minds must be freed from tradition.

Flexibility is obviously a key factor in future port design with the ability to accommodate any reasonable shape of vessel and type of cargo and any related movement or storage of that cargo throughout the port area.

Changeability is also a key word. Sections of ports should be mobile so that facilities can be remodelled to meet changing demands. Buildings should be portable and avoid being obstructive. More use should be made of today's very heavy lift floating equipment for construction or repositioning in large modules. Floating breakwaters should be developed further.

Finally obsolescence must be more closely considered as ports of the future cannot be saddled with structures and equipment built to last 50-100 years when they may not be needed for the next 20.

This paper was first published in the Harbour Masters' Handbook. It is reproduced by kind permission of the Nautical Institute.

Discussion on Papers 16–19

A. C. EDMONDSON, Harbour and General Works Ltd
With reference to the point raised by Mr Burdall concerning treatment of contaminated dredged spoil. My company has developed portable thermal treatment plants for land based operations but, since dredging costs are already currently at £3.0(plus)/m^3 treatment would cost approximately a further £30/m^3 making the operation not feasible. The treatment of soil containing heavy metals is not possible in large/medium dredging contracts.

J. BARKER, Posford Duvivier
I agree that a return to NPC control is not desirable but am concerned that some form of planning control is necessary to stop irreplaceable port hinterland being developed for financially attractive but non-port related use. There have been examples in this country in the past ten years where developers have persuaded councils to grant them planning permission for non-port related activities on land that clearly should have been preserved. It would then have provided space, and the potential for jobs, for increased seaborne trade which has now in fact materialized and is being inhibited due to lack of space.

As UK Ltd we need to take care - especially at this time of privatization that we don't give away our birthright.

D. PALMER, Tees and Harlepool Port Authority
In his Paper, Mr Stirling suggests that port authorities and planners should reserve, in an economy which has historically expanded and which he predicts will continue to expand into the next century, sufficient land for future port expansion. How does Mr Stirling propose to square the difficulties in protecting that land against development for other purposes as a result of commercial pressures on port authorities, many of whom are being privatized and will need to respond to shareholders pressures? How would

he also protect it against the possibility of derelict land becoming a site of special scientific interest and becoming impossible to develop having laid fallow for a score of years or more.

D. COOPER, ABP Research and Consultancy Ltd
Mr Bellis has implied in his Paper that many hydraulic model structures are undertaken more as a fashion than an essential requirement. I am not sure that I agree. For many of our clients hydraulic model studies represent a worthwhile investment in terms of peace of mind in arriving at a successful design. More than this, in some instances they represent the only way ahead in satisfying petitioners against Parliamentary bills that their fears are unfounded or will be satisfactorily accommodated in the design. They also have an important public relations role.

R. N. APPLETON, Poole Harbour Commissioners
Does Mr Burdall consider that while at Poole we attempt to provide the balance between commercial, recreational and conservation interests, there should be firmer guidelines to the conservation bodies on the value of conserving locally rare but internationally common species? e.g. a species existing out of its natural environment.

B. TATHAM, Livesey Henderson/Binnie and Partners
A number of contributors have given the impression that they believe environmental awareness to be a passing battiness - it is not. There is a feeling throughout the country that we must look after the environment better and this view has been taken up by all the main political parties. Engineers must plan their role in looking after their part of the environment.

W. G. STEAN, Balfour Beatty
Many Authors have touched on the question of the adoption and development of a national policy for transport.

What are the Authors' views on the subject? How would it sit alongside the inevitable privatizations within the ports industry?

E. LOEWY, Sir William Halcrow and Partners Ltd
Could the Authors comment on the use of electromagnetism not only for ship mooring but also, by reverse polarity, for ship berthing.

A. H. C. STIRLING Paper 17
In reply to Mr D. Palmer, ports are in the business of receiving vessels, handling cargoes and other port related activities. Port management must ensure that

the port continues into the future, very often by drawing up a master plan which is regularly updated. Such a master plan must make provision for the future, albeit based upon forecasts of various sorts and must reserve sufficient land for future port expansion. Thus port management can logically resist pressure from developers et al. Also it is possible to lease spare land, initially with a view to using it for port purposes at a future date - it does not have to remain unused and such a course may prevent derelict sites from becoming SSIs. This latter can be a problem which perhaps only local port management flair can prevent.

As Mr B. Tatham notes environmental awareness is not a passing battiness, it is something that port engineers and port managements have to grasp and be very positive about. No longer can we develop, build or operate without mitigating undesirable environmental consequences.

In reply to Mr W. G. Stean I am an unrepentant supporter of a national transport policy. It seems to me that in these days of scarce resources and Britain's increasing transport problems a national transport policy is essential and needed urgently. Unless Britain establishes a national transport policy I believe we will be rapidly overtaken by our EC neighbours with consequent economic penalties. I do not see that a national transport policy is fundamentally incompatible with the privatization of ports but I appreciate there will be problems to be overcome in particular cases.

A.C. BURDALL, Paper 18

As R. N. Appleton notes in his question, the level of conservation achieved is a matter of balance; in the case of Poole, a balance between preserving particular species which may locally be under threat and commercial and recreational port uses. I cannot comment on the particular circumstances relating to Poole but could perhaps offer a comment on the more general points.

Guidelines are required. However, a national environmental agency legislating for the entire country would perhaps not be appropriate. Guidelines should at present be applied and it may be preferable to remain with the present situation. There are guidelines developed as part of the planning process for new developments or projects and guidelines defined for each individual port as part of an internal environmental policy statement.

For the conservation of particular species the Nature Conservancy Council are responsible for the establishment and protection of sites of special scientific interest.

Other conservation bodies become involved in particular projects or situations. The extent to which firm guidelines can be established (and by whom) on the value of conserving particular species must be debatable and may even be counter-productive.

As Mr Tatham notes, as engineers, we have a particular responsibility for environmental issues. In promoting, planning and designing projects, we are in a unique position to make an informed judgement on the balance of environmental costs and economic benefits. Throughout these processes we must remember that 'we do not inherit the earth from our ancestors - but borrow it from our children'.

A. D. M. BELLIS Paper 19

In reply to Mr D. Cooper, I am not knocking the use of models but merely asking scheme promoters to put them into perspective. Mr Cooper is well aware of my own involvement in hydraulic modelling over many years and I respect the work that he does. It is however often adequate to obtain much of the required information from the existing physical situation (the prototype) and this should not be overlooked just for the sake of having a model. Such a thing can be quite an expensive public relations tool.

I am delighted that Mr Loewy has also for a long time considered that electromagnetic mooring is a concept worth examining. The idea of using the phenomenon for ship berthing, with the repulsive effect, is also a very good one and I hope someone will seriously investigate both uses.